W9-AMT-194

Beyond Economic Liberalization in Africa:

Structural Adjustment and the Alternatives

edited by

Kidane Mengisteab

and

B. Ikubolajeh Logan

Beyond Economic Liberalization in Africa was first published by
Zed Books Ltd, 7 Cynthia Street, London N1 9JF, UK, and
165 First Avenue, Atlantic Highlands, New Jersey 07716, USA,
and in southern Africa (Angola, Botswana, Lesotho, Malawi,
Mozambique, Namibia, South Africa, Swaziland, Zambia, Zimbabwe)
by Southern Africa Political Economy Series (SAPES),
50-53 van Riebeeck House, 14 Loop Street, Cape Town, South Africa,
in 1995.

Cover designed by Andrew Corbett.
Cover photograph by Jacky Chapman/Format.
Printed and bound in the United Kingdom
by Biddles Ltd, Guildford and King's Lynn.

A catalogue record for this book is
available from the British Library.

US CIP data is available from
the Library of Congress.

ISBN 1 85649 293 1 Cased
ISBN 1 85649 294 X Limp

Southern Africa
ISBN 0 9584007 4 1 Limp

Contents

Contributors

Adebayo Adedeji is the Executive Director of the African Centre for Development and Strategic Studies and former Executive Secretary of the Economic Commission for Africa.

Cyril Daddieh is Associate Professor of Political Science at Salisbury State University.

Hartmut Krugmann is the Principal Regional Program Officer for Environmental Policy at the International Development Research Centre in Canada and Kenya.

Howard P. Lehman is an Associate Professor of Political Science at the University of Utah.

B. Ikubolajeh Logan is Associate Professor of Geography at the University of Georgia.

Mahmood Mamdani is Professor at Makerere University in Kampala, Uganda.

Kidane Mengisteab is Associate Professor of Political Economy in the Department of Political Science/Geography at Old Dominion University.

Berhanu Mengistu is Associate Professor and department Chair of Public Administration and Urban Studies in the College of Business and Public Administration at Old Dominion University.

J.C. Munene teaches at the Department of Psychology at Makerere University in Kampala, Uganda.

Abdoulaye S.M. Saine teaches in the departments of Political Science and Comparative American Cultures at Washington State University.

1

Introduction

B. Ikubolajeh Logan
Kidane Mengisteab

Structural adjustment programmes (SAPs) have now been in operation for over a decade in many sub-Saharan countries. Yet their appropriateness for overcoming Africa's economic crisis remains as controversial as when they were first introduced. The IMF and the World Bank, the principal sponsors and implementers of economic adjustment in Africa, argue that the strategies have already produced considerable positive results. The World Bank, for example, claims that the economies of adjusting sub-Saharan countries grew at the rate of 4 per cent during 1988–90 compared to 2.2 per cent for non-adjusting countries.[1] The IMF also claims that countries such as Ghana, one of the early adopters of SAPs in sub-Saharan Africa, and even war-ravaged Mozambique, have already recorded significant economic rehabilitation as a result of adjustment programmes.[2] Other proponents of SAPs compare Ghana's favourable export growth rate of 94 per cent (1984–90) with an average of only 21 per cent for sub-Saharan Africa during the same period.[3]

The positive commentaries on the impacts of SAPs are questioned by many sceptics, including the Economic Commission for Africa (ECA), which provides the most vocal challenge to IMF and World Bank claims. The ECA argues that there has been little difference in the economic performance of strong and weak reform countries.[4] Supporting the ECA position are data which show, for example, that the ratio of domestic savings to GDP in adjusting economies was 4.9 per cent during 1988–90 compared to 8.8 per cent in non-adjusting economies. There is also some evidence that adjusting countries have underperformed their non-adjusting counterparts in the critical areas of income growth and social welfare development.[5]

Both sides of the adjustment debate use macro-economic indicators such as growth rates of GNP and exports, current account balance, domestic savings and inflation rates to make their case. While such indicators are important, they present a limited perspective of, and insufficient insights into, the cause and effect linkages surrounding adjustment. This book, therefore, attempts to address some broader political economy concerns that have not yet received sufficient attention in the adjustment literature. Such issues include political and economic democratization, the transformation of the subsistence sector, and internal and regional integration.

This introductory chapter has two objectives. The first is to set the stage for the discussions and analyses in subsequent chapters; the second is to introduce the reader to the content and orientation of those chapters.

The essence of structural adjustment programmes

Since the mid-1970s, sub-Saharan African countries have suffered from a litany of woes which have included slow economic growth, food shortages, frequent famines, high rates of unemployment, widespread poverty, declining export earnings, burgeoning debts, and a growing marginalization from the global economy. While many developing countries have faced similar economic problems, the crisis is generally more serious in Africa for a variety of reasons, including the issues of democracy and peasant transformation. As a substantive case in point, thirty-two of the world's poorest forty-seven countries are in sub-Saharan Africa.[6] The difficult economic realities faced by these countries have made social, political, and economic reforms imperative. However, there is little consensus over the most appropriate reform strategy that must be adopted. Part of this dilemma may be attributed to the inability of scholars and policy makers alike to isolate and explain the reasons for Africa's economic dislocation and disarticulation.

Proponents of SAPs ascribe a significant part of the region's problems to the magnitude of state intervention in the economy through mechanisms such as the direct ownership of assets, and the control of prices, exchange rates, and imports.[7] The relatively large size of the public sector in sub-Saharan Africa has been associated, in turn, with inefficiencies in the allocation of resources.[8] State intervention in the workings of the market is also viewed as being detrimental to the performance of agricultural producers and exporters in particular, and to the ability of African economies to adapt to changing international conditions in general.[9] Government intervention is also seen to promote the interests of self-serving state functionaries, while simultaneously impairing the growth of the larger economy. Producer price controls, for instance, generally benefit the bureaucracy and the more powerful urban consumers at the expense of rural producers.[10]

It is likely that African economies are generally more interventionist than other (non-socialist) LDCs.[11] However, the interventionist explanation of the African crisis is rather reductionist. African countries differ from other LDCs not only in the magnitude of state intervention but also in the fact that the structures of their economies weaken their position within the global division of labour (this issue is addressed in more detail in later chapters). Furthermore, as Hamilton points out,[12] intervention in the Third World is not always a hinderance to the development of the private sector as often claimed. For instance, South Korea's rather rapid economic growth has been carefully planned by a strong government,[13] and state intervention and patronage may be used as a means of maintaining political stability, as in Côte d'Ivoire.

SAPs prescribe essentially three groups of reforms to counter the problems of state intervention-led economic dislocation: 1) deflationary measures such as the removal of subsidies and reduction of public expenditures; 2) institutional changes that consist of privatization and decontrol of prices, interest rates, imports, and foreign exchange; and 3) expenditure-switching measures, which include devaluation and export promotion.[14] These three groups of reforms are obvious attempts to make significant reduction in the role of the state in economic activity, to replace it by market forces, as well as to integrate African economies more thoroughly within the international market system.

This broad approach to adjustment, however, has serious limitations. First, it does not differentiate between different types of state intervention in Africa. Thus the same policies are being recommended for radically different states, such as the self-serving regime of Mobutu in Zaire and the reform-oriented government of Mugabe in Zimbabwe. Second, SAPs fail to address sub-Saharan Africa's position and role in the international economic system. It is doubtful whether African economies can be integrated fully within the global economy when they are internally disintegrated and when SAPs do not, and cannot, address issues of international trade. Finally, while claiming to address structural reform in the domestic economy, SAPs fail to accommodate the dynamics of the peasant sector. Due to these problems, SAPs continue to face opposition among many scholars as well as policy makers despite the widespread recognition of the crisis of statist socio-economic systems in Africa.

Africa's economic structures

The dominant position of the subsistence sector within sub-Saharan African economies is one of the most important differences between that region's economic structures and those of other LDCs. In no other LDC region does the subsistence sector account for as much as 70–80 per cent of population.[15] Since the subsistence sector has very weak links with the market economy, this characteristic has very important implications for the performance of African economies, as well as for their ability to absorb international market shocks.

It must be emphasized that the subsistent peasantry is by no means totally insulated from the broader market system. The former is a source of cheap labour, sells limited quantities of food, and buys farm inputs and some basic consumer goods such as clothing, oil and sugar from the latter. Yet the subsistent peasantry is structurally removed from the market by the use-value orientation of its production. According to Ghai and Smith, only 12 per cent of peasant output is marketed.[16]

The fragmentation between the subsistence and modern exchange sectors in Africa (commonly referred to as dualistic development) deprives the economies of the internal dynamics necessary for growth. This occurs through two types of distortion. First, the modern sector is deprived of domestic markets and other linkages with the large peasant sector; it therefore operates essentially as an overseas enclave. Africa's private enterprises, especially the bigger and more modern ones, largely bypass domestic social needs (the needs of the peasantry) and rely on the international market for their survival and expansion. Second, resource allocation is largely dissociated from the needs of the large peasant population. As a consequence, the peasantry is seldom able to raise its productivity and to participate effectively in the market by translating its needs into demand.

A further manifestation of uneven (dualistic) development is that the non-export food sector is often neglected in favour of exports. For example, the ratios of the average amount of fertilizers used (Kg/ha) in the cash-crop sector to those used in the food sector in 1979–81 were 313:1 in Mauritius, 63:1 in Mozambique, 56:1 in Mali, 53:1 in Senegal, and 32:1 in the Sudan.[17] Government rhetoric concerning food production notwithstanding, there is little evidence of any actual policy aimed at strengthening the food sector so that it can compete against the cash-crop sector in attracting investment.[18]

The deprived status of the peasantry could certainly be attributed to colonial policy and the failures of the post-colonial state. However, it is unlikely that the problem can be corrected simply by superimposing the market over such conditions. Unlike more diversified economies in Asia or Latin America, social need and market-guided allocation of resources in much of Africa do not necessarily correspond with each other because the market operates under distorted conditions. The ability of the market to coordinate resource allocation with social needs improves with diversification of the economy and with reforms that create access to resources for disenfranchised segments of society. At this stage of African development, however, the ability of the market, by itself, to orchestrate these various economic and social means to some equitable end is quite limited.

The history of state allocative strategies also gives cause for pause and concern. State intervention in the allocation of resources has often advanced the interests of the élite and their political supporters, and of state functionaries.[19] Despite state control of the allocation of credits in most African states, for instance, no more than 5 per cent of African farmers are said to have access to institutional credit.[20] The failure of the state to correct these problems has been largely due to lack of political will, resulting from the absence of representative government in policy making.

Africa's position in the international economic system

Another problem that is related to the structural distortions of African economies is their weak position in the international economic system. In general, African countries inherited the least diversified economies from the colonial era and they still rely, more so than any other region, on non-oil primary commodities for their export earnings.[21] In 1986, for instance, exports of non-primary commodities from twenty-seven sub-Saharan African countries averaged only 13.8 per cent of total exports, compared to 43.3 per cent from thirteen Asian and Pacific countries (excluding Japan, Taiwan, Singapore, Hong Kong and the two Koreas) and 25.1 per cent from twenty Latin American and Caribbean countries.[22]

Due to their narrow technological, managerial and production base, African countries also rely more than other regions on foreign technology and capital. The worsening terms of international trade have exacerbated

Africa's problems by reducing its ability to initiate and maintain export-led development.[23] Plunging terms of trade are further exacerbated by product substitution for some key exports and also through commodity oversupply, as a large number of countries simultaneously embark on export promotion drives which focus on products that generally have low income and price elasticities.

The gravity of Africa's economic crisis is thus partly attributable to deep-rooted internal and external structural problems. African economies are the most disintegrated internally and regionally. The neglect of domestic social needs, the resultant excessive dependency on international markets, and the reliance on a few primary exports for capital accumulation have made them more vulnerable than other regions to adverse fluctuations in the global economy. They are also the most marginalized in the global economy.

Unfortunately, structural adjustment has directed attention only at internal difficulties while ignoring those related to the international market arena, but it seems to be obvious that the one cannot be corrected without the other. For domestic adjustment to succeed, African products must have fair access to markets for their exports. It is also unrealistic to perceive adjustment as a purely domestic strategy when it touches so forcibly on exchange rates, imports and exports. Finally, even within the domestic economy, adjustment has failed to move beyond the market enclaves to accommodate and contemplate on the activities of the peasantry. Adjustment, therefore, does not tackle some of Africa's deep-seated economic difficulties.

Relevance of democratization

If our analysis is correct, redressing the marginalization of the peasantry and correcting the disconsonance embedded in dualistic development are preconditions for establishing a properly functioning market system in Africa, and for ameliorating the weak position of African economies within the global economic system. These preconditions will only be met if the subsistence sector is offered access to critical resources, and becomes transformed into a surplus-producing exchange economy. The economic democratization implicit in this process is unlikely to take place without genuine political democratization, which would provide the peasantry with a voice in decision making. Economic and political democracy are essential twin points of departure for tackling Africa's economic crisis.

There is an emerging debate as to whether SAPs and democratization should be implemented simultaneously or in sequence, and if the latter, in what order. Some scholars have argued that there is a trade-off between the two, and that attempts to implement them simultaneously may cause both to fail.[24] Others have argued that the implementation of SAPs is best achieved when political leaders have fewer political constraints.[25]

The relationship between democratization and economic reform is one area of emphasis of this book. Several of the chapters argue that genuine democratization is the best means of achieving a properly functioning market system. This argument seems to be supported by the current popular pressures for democratization that many African governments are facing.

Relevance of integration

Another area to which the book draws attention is the relationship between SAPs and regional integration in Africa. There is a general consensus among scholars and policy makers that the integration of African economies (collective reliance) is crucial for their sustained development. On the basis of this consensus, a number of market integration schemes such as those of ECOWAS, PTA and SADCC have been attempted. There is also a vision on the part of the OAU that the entire continent will be integrated into a common market by the year 2025.[26]

Unfortunately, to date, the performance of African integration schemes has been disappointing, and trade among African states remains scarcely more than 5 per cent of their total trade. The marginalization of the peasantry, and the consequent excessive reliance of Africa's modern economic sector on the international market, are partly responsible for the failure of regional integration on the continent. It is imperative that regional integration, democracy, and domestic economic adjustment all become conceived of as components of the same strategy.

This book

The contributions may be divided into two general categories. Chapters 2 to 6 provide empirical and conceptual accounts of the failure of liberalization (especially privatization and devaluation) in Africa. These chapters attempt to come to terms with some of the reasons why African countries should move with caution toward the market liberalization model. The next group of contributions build on this foundation by elaborating on the factors that have mitigated against the successful implementation of adjustment. These chapters highlight critical concerns and considerations that should guide policy as Africa stands poised to enter the twenty-first century. The essential question they ask is, where do we go beyond structural adjustment? Chapters 7 to 10 focus on the issue of democracy and mass participation as a response to this question. The final group of contributions (Chapters 11 to 13) looks at the potential for regional integration and a new industrial agenda for further delineating Africa's participation in the evolving 'new international economic order' that is being created by the dissolution of the USSR and Eastern Europe, the strengthening of the EC, and incipient economic cooperation between the US, Canada, and Mexico (NAFTA).

Chapter 2, by Mahmood Mamdani, contemplates three issues dealing with rural development in Africa: agricultural stagnation, environmental degradation and population explosion. All three have been at the core of economic development in Africa. Agricultural growth has been at the heart of most post-independence development agendas, and it remains a major target of structural adjustment. Market liberalization, population growth and environmental degradation are tied together in the population-poverty nexus in which Africa's poverty is seen to be a direct outcome of population growth.

Mamdani's discussion evaluates the failure of past policies to grapple with Africa's economic difficulties. He advocates an insightful assessment of African conditions in policy formulation and implementation. Part of this insight is the recognition that Africa's 'oneness' is not 'sameness'; Africa is a unity that is neither monolithic nor homogenous. Policy formulation should, therefore, draw out generality from specificity that deal with 'the nature of the socio-historical context, the societal and global forces that shape each outcome and bind them together in a wider totality'. Using this conceptual springboard, Mamdani reflects on agricultural stagnation, environmental degradation and the population explosion and uses three case studies for general explanations.

In Chapter 3, Cyril Daddieh builds upon the general conceptual thrust established in Chapter 2, but focuses on the specific case of privatized education in Africa. Using Ghana as an example, the author notes that privatized education must be approached with caution because of divergences between theoretical expectations and Africa's empirical reality. He concludes that it is highly problematic to assume that the benefits of a free-functioning market will be sufficient to obscure the deleterious potential outcomes of privatized education. Privatization is seen to be more likely to entrench, rather than improve on, the present low rates of literacy in Africa.

Ikubolajeh Logan, in Chapter 4, elaborates upon the actual and potential difficulties of privatized social services by examining the case of health care. Like Daddieh in Chapter 3, Logan regards social welfare development as a national security issue that should not be left entirely to the market. He moves beyond the strictly empirical concerns of Chapter 3 to examine the theoretical attributes of a private, a merit and a public good, concluding that health care should qualify under the latter two categories. In addition, he examines the structural constraints on the operation of the market in Africa, focusing especially on economic dualism. He argues that populations in the traditional and informal sectors are likely to be further disenfranchised under a market-led health care system. Finally, he comments on the apolitical and asocial nature of market liberalization, noting, like other contributors, that these strategies possess an inherent potential for social unrest because of the absence of democratic and market-support institutions in Africa.

Chapter 5, by J.C. Munene, provides an innovative exploration of the psychological dimensions of structural adjustment. His is at once a theoretical exploration and a social commentary/critique. Several studies look at the impacts of adjustment on society, but seldom has there appeared such an incisive analysis of the impacts of adjustment on flesh-and-blood people, as opposed to abstract numbers. Munene investigates how adjustment has forced employers to break their 'psychological contracts' with their employees. In response, employees no longer feel obligated to use their 'discretionary time' to enhance both the volume and quality of output. Rather, they 'steal' actual time from their employers and use this to supplement their discretionary time to gain supplementary income. The consequent undermining of collective morale and psychological integrity is seen to be one of the most insidious outcomes of adjustment.

By examining the responses of African countries to currency devaluation, Kidane Mengisteab (Chapter 6) ventures out of the domestic arena to examine the interplay of international and domestic factors in structural adjustment. He examines two theoretical perspectives regarding devaluation: that it reduces external imbalances through the expansion and diversification of exports; and that it is an inappropriate strategy to generate export-led growth and equilibrate balance of payments. The major contribution of this chapter is that its empirical assessment of the responses of African economies to devaluation makes it possible to reach more definitive conclusions about the relative effects of the state and the market in fixing exchange rates. While agreeing that state-fixed exchange rates are problematic for the development process, the author stresses that as an alternative, market-led exchange rates also have attendant difficulties: first, the low demand and price elasticities of primary commodities reduce the potential positive impacts of devaluation on balance of payments; second, devaluation, by itself, cannot result in export diversification without concomitant economic and political changes in both the domestic and international economies.

Hartmut Krugmann's contribution (Chapter 7) brings together several strands in the debate over SAPs. He couches his arguments within the rubric of sustainable development and, as a result, touches upon a complex mixture of issues including mass participation, the globalization of the world economy, environmental management, contraction of agricultural production and the new international economic order. He examines the ability of SAPs to correct the problems emanating from, or ameliorate the conditions created by, these various issues individually or in tandem. It is clear that Krugmann's assessment of SAPs is pessimistic. He expects SAPs, as they are presently designed and implemented, to exacerbate worsening socio-economic conditions in Africa.

The next three chapters build on the previous ones by exploring the political implications of market liberalization in Africa. These chapters focus specifically on the issues of access to resources, democracy and mass participation in decision making.

Chapter 8, by Kidane Mengisteab, revisits in a forcible way one of the central themes of the book: whether the market is more efficient than the state at allocating resources to every segment of society. Instead of advancing a case for either institution, the chapter outlines a theoretical argument for a formalized (rather than haphazard) state–market partnership. Mengisteab's defence of such a partnership is based on a three-tiered argument: (i) the African state, as represented by state-owned enterprises (SOEs), has been self-serving and inefficient at meeting the needs of large segments of the African population; (ii) although the market may be efficient at maximizing returns from scarce resources, its optimal conditions may not always be consistent with the realities of the African political economy; and (iii) despite the shortcomings of the state, neither a workable market system, nor sustainable development are likely to be obtained without considerable state participation.

In Chapter 9 Abdoulaye Saine argues for a more pivotal role for democratization principles in Africa's development agenda. Yet his is an advocacy that is cautious enough to ask a number of incisive questions: what type of democracy, for whom, in whose interests, through what means, and to what ends? The main focus of Saine's contribution is to explain a three-pronged linkage between the democracy movement in Africa, Africa's political economy crisis, and the influence of World Bank economic reform. An important question that arises from the discussion is which of these problematics begets which? As the discussion unfolds, it is clear that Saine perceives mass participation to be a necessary condition for economic progress. However, the orientation of the current democracy movement is viewed with suspicion for a number of reasons: it is too closely aligned with World Bank conditionalities rather than being 'home-grown', and it represents the interests of the same class of society that has been ruling Africa since the 1960s. The democracy movement, therefore, might be orchestrated by dictatorial 'wolves' dressed in the 'sheep's clothing' of sloganeering democracy.

The main objective of Chapter 10, by Howard Lehman, is 'to explain the paradox of the simultaneous existence of both strong and weak components in the African State'. The strong state is defined here as one in which decision making is not controlled by social interests, and the weak state as one that is consumed by social interests. Lehman does not believe that African states fall along a strong–weak state continuum, since state–societal interests are juxtaposed; sometimes complementing each other, at other times in conflict with each other. The reasons for this have their roots in the historical tradition of the region, together with the current internal and external dynamics of decision making in Africa. The examples of Kenya and Zimbabwe are used to deliberate and elaborate upon these theses, further emphasizing the fact that a monolithic approach to Africa's problems is essentially a failed approach.

Chapter 11 takes a future-oriented perspective that is underlain by a normative/prescriptive deliberation. Adebayo Adedeji's contribution offers a panoramic view of the future path for development, calling for a shift from 'stabilization and adjustment' to 'adjustment with transformation'. This approach, documented in the African Alternative Framework to Structural Adjustment for Socio-economic Recovery and Transformation (AAF-SAP), is broad and flexible, allowing each African country to draw upon its unique economic and political circumstance to shape economic restructuring. This plan of action harks back to Mamdani's admonition in Chapter 2 that policy should not confuse Africa's oneness with sameness. For the AAF-SAP to be successful, several other transformations must occur in the international and domestic arenas: there should be support for the programme by the international community, especially the US and the EC; and this support should be reflected in more equitable commodity prices and terms of trade and financial assistance. An improved international climate will strengthen the ability of governments to initiate and implement policy changes in economic development and grass-roots participation.

The following two chapters address the relationship between adjustment and regional cooperation/integration. In Chapter 12, Cyril Daddieh deals with the relationship between adjustment and regional integration in West Africa. Adjustment programmes are seen to perpetuate negative economic tendencies – for example, a heavy reliance on a few export commodities. Simultaneously, adjustment is seen also to mitigate against elements which favour sustainable development – for instance, regional integration. Instead of fostering regional integration, Daddieh believes that adjustment reinforces competition among several countries. The impact of adjustment on regional integration are examined by looking at the experience of ECOWAS during the past decade.

The theme of regional integration shifts to focus on the PTA in Chapter 13. Berhanu Mengistu proposes that PTA members can offset their debt obligations and foreign exchange squeeze by engaging in counter-trade. Analysis of production and export patterns for PTA countries over a number of years proves that each country possesses a different level of comparative advantage which could be exploited to create the bases for intra-regional exchange through counter-trade. The decreased need for hard currency that this arrangement could create is seen to be one approach for tackling the debt trap and the region's balance of payment difficulties.

Notes

1. World Bank, *World Bank Annual Report* (Washington, DC: World Bank, 1991).
2. International Monetary Fund (IMF), *IMF Survey* 20, no. 23 (16 December 1991).
3. Ishan Kapur, Michael T. Hadjimichael, Paul Hilbers, Jerald Schiff and Philippe Szymczak, 'Ghana Adjustment and Growth, 1983–91', IMF Occasional Paper no. 86, 1991.
4. Economic Commission for Africa (ECA), *African Alternative Framework to Structural Adjustment Programmes for Socio-Economic Recovery and Transformation* (Addis Ababa: E/ECA/CM.15/6/Rev 3, 1989).
5. *Africa Recovery* 5, no. 4 (December 1991): 21.

6. Ernest Harsch, 'More African States Are "Lease Developed": Botswana Set to Graduate from the Group', *Africa Recovery* 6, no. 1 (April 1992): 11.

7. World Bank, *Accelerated Development in Sub-Saharan Africa* (Washington, DC: World Bank, 1981).

8. Bruce Bartlett, 'The State and the Market in Sub-Saharan Africa', *The World Economy* 12, no. 3 (September 1989): 293–314; Elliot Berg and Mary M. Shirley, *Divestiture in Developing Countries*, World Bank Discussion Paper no. 11 (Washington, DC: World Bank, 1987); R. John Nellis, *Public Enterprises in Sub-Saharan Africa*, World Bank Discussion Paper no. 1 (Washington, DC: World Bank, 1986); Richard Vengroff and Ali Farah, 'State Intervention and Agricultural Development in Africa: A Cross-National Study', *Journal of Modern African Studies* 23, no. 1 (1985): 75–85; Daniel Landau, 'Government and Economic Growth in the Less Developed Countries', in *Report of the President's Task Force on International Private Enterprise: Selected Papers* (Washington, DC: US Government Printing Office, 1984), 17–41.

9. Bela Balassa, 'The State and the Market in Sub-Saharan Africa', *The World Economy* 12, no. 3 (September 1989): 293–314; Keith Marseden and Therese Belot, *Private Enterprise in Africa: Creating a Better Environment*, World Bank Discussion Paper no. 17 (Washington, DC: World Bank, 1987).

10. Robert H. Bates, *Markets and States in Tropical Africa* (Berkeley: University of California Press, 1981), 11–44.

11. World Bank, *Africa's Adjustment and Growth in the 1980s* (Washington, DC: World Bank, March 1989); Bartlett, 'The State and the Market in Sub-Saharan Africa'; Larry Diamond, 'Class Formation in the Swollen African State', *Journal of Modern African Studies* 25, no. 4 (1987): 567–96.

12. Clive Hamilton, 'The Irrelevance of Economic Liberalization in the Third World', *World Development* 17, no. 10 (1989): 1523–30.

13. Amartya Sen, 'Development Which Way Now?', in Charles K. Wilber (ed.), *The Political Economy of Development and Underdevelopment*, 4th edn (New York: Random House, 1988), 37–58.

14. The Social Dimension of Adjustment was launched in 1987 to protect the poor from the hardships of adjustment. The 1989 World Bank report (World Bank, *Sub-Saharan Africa: From Crisis to Sustainable Growth* [Washington, DC: World Bank, 1989]) also recognizes the importance of creating access to basic resources for the deprived segment of the population to enhancing development. However, the implementation of such programmes remains external to SAPs.

15. Whether the resilience of the subsistence sector is due to the recalcitrance of the peasantry or a product of the marginalization of the peasantry made possible by the peripheral capitalist system has generated widespread debate. For details see Alexander Schejtman, 'The Peasant Economy: Internal Logic, Accumulation and Persistence', in Charles K. Wilber (ed.), *The Political Economy of Development and Underdevelopment* (New York: Random House, 1988), 364–92; N. Kasfir, 'Are African Peasants Self-Sufficient?',

Development and Change 17, no. 2 (1986); and Mahmood Mamdani, 'A Great Leap Backward', *East African Social Science Review* 1, no. 4 (1985). Despite the disagreements on its causes, the weak links between the subsistence sector and the modern market system is not seriously disputed.

16. D. Ghai and L. Smith, *Agricultural Prices, Policy and Equity in Sub-Saharan Africa* (Boulder, CO: Lynne Rienner, 1987).

17. FAO, *Atlas of African Agriculture* (Rome: FAO, 1986).

18. Osita Ogbu, 'Farmers' Response to Structural Adjustment Programs in Sub-Saharan Africa: The Need for Democratic Reforms', in Lual Deng, Markus Kostner, and Crawford Young (eds), *Democratization and Structural Adjustment in Africa in the 1990s* (Madison: African Studies Program, University of Wisconsin, 1991), 69–74; Osita Ogbu and M. Gbetibuou, 'Agricultural Supply Response in Sub-Saharan Africa: A Critical Review of the Literature', *African Development Review* 2, no. 2 (1990): 83–97; U. Lele, *Agricultural Growth, Domestic Policies, the External Environment, and the Assistance to Africa: Lessons of a Quarter Century* (New York: World Bank, Media Study, 1988).

19. Bates, *Markets and States in Tropical Africa*.

20. Claudio Gonzalez-Vega, 'Cheap Agricultural Credit: Redistribution in Reverse', in Dale W. Adams, Douglas H. Graham, and J.D. Von Pischke (eds), *Undermining Rural Development with Cheap Credit* (Boulder, CO: Westview Press, 1984), 120.

21. Thandika Mkandawire, 'The Road to Crisis, Adjustment and De-Industrialization: The African Case', *African Development* 13, no. 1 (1988): 11–12.

22. World Bank, *Sub-Saharan Africa: From Crisis to Sustainable Growth*.

23. Among such factors are the relative small size of African markets, which prevents economies of scale; limitations of liner routes; and interfirm ties that make it possible for subsidiaries to be overcharged by parent companies for their imports in order to transfer profits and capital out of Africa. Alexander J. Yeats, 'Do African Countries Pay More for Imports?', *Finance and Development* 27, no. 2 (June 1990): 38–40.

24. For example, Donald K. Emmerson, 'Capitalism, Democracy, and the World Bank: What Is to Be Done?', in Lual Deng, Markus Kostner and Crawford Young (eds), *Democratization and Structural Adjustment in Africa in the 1990s* (Madison: African Studies Program, University of Wisconsin, 1991), 9–12.

25. Stephen Haggard, in Emmerson, 'Capitalism, Democracy, and the World Bank'; Crawford Young, 'Democratization and Structural Adjustment: A Political Overview', in Deng, Kostner and Young, *Democratization and Structural Adjustment in Africa in the 1990s*, 13–20.

26. *Africa Recovery* 5, no. 2–3 (September 1991).

PART 1

Structural Adjustment Programmes:
Part of the Problem

2

Democratization and Marketization

Mahmood Mamdani

Introduction

Africa is a unity, but is not homogeneous. Oneness should not be confused with sameness. Rural Africa comprises capitalist farms alongside labour reserves, landlords alongside tenants, and peasants with no direct social overlord apart from state functionaries. I shall focus on peasants – cultivators and pastoralists.

My approach will be to confront the bird's-eye view conceptualization of the problem with a frog's-eye view. The eye of the bird is essentially deductive, that of the frog inductive. I shall proceed by discussing three examples. I make no claim for the statistical representativeness of my examples, but I do make a claim for their theoretical relevance. My examples are not typical, not even of the societies in which they are embedded. But then, it is my view that the very idea of a typical example is a socio-biological myth. What I seek to understand is not the specific and the unique in each example, but the nature of the socio-historical context, the societal and global forces, that shape each outcome and bind them together in a wider totality. In short, my endeavour shall be to extract the general from the particular.

Case study 1: Northern Uganda

From 1981 to 1984, when Uganda had its first structural adjustment programme, I was doing research in a number of villages. In a village in Northern Uganda, I learned a few facts:

1.   Peasants are a differentiated group: rich, middling and poor. I could not explain this disparity by the amount of land each group owned, for poor peasant households owned roughly the same land as did middle peasant households. But poor households could only cultivate on average 40 per cent of the land they owned, whereas the figure for middle peasant households was slightly over 70 per cent. When I probed into reasons for this, I learned a second fact.

2.   The poor, roughly 83 per cent of the village population, faced a double constraint. They had fewer, more worn-out implements of labour; as a result, only a portion of family labour could be translated into productive labour. But even this could not be expended entirely on the family farm, for the family was required to make compulsory contributions whenever the village chief called for them. These took the form of compulsory labour (from clearing local roads to weeding the chief's garden), and forced payments (grain when a higher chief visits, a cock when a district officer visits, more should the President visit). Carefully, I counted the number of hours a rural poor household loses as a result of forced contributions, and it came to 15 per cent of an average family's labouring time. For the middle peasants, roughly 12 per cent of the village population, it came to around 10 per cent of family labour time; and for rich peasants, only 3 per cent of the village population, it was of nominal significance. When I returned to Kampala, and pondered over the situation of different peasant strata, I learned a third fact.

3.   The dilemma of the poor peasant was not the same as that of the rich peasantry. For rich peasants, the primary problem was prices of agricultural crops in the market; for the poor peasantry, the problem was a regime of compulsions right down to the local level. I realized that while liberalization gave better prices to rich peasants in the market, it reduced the budgets of local administrations and intensified the regime of compulsions that squeezed the rural poor. In the context of that village, liberalization and democratization were opposites. Liberalization address-ed the problem of 3 per cent of peasants, democratization those of the rest.

4.   As the 'demand management' of the structural adjustment programme moved into gear, I learned a fourth lesson. In my first-year political economy class at the university, I had always taught my students that there are no pre-existing markets simply waiting to be freed; markets have to be created. I taught them of limited markets in England before the fifteenth century, markets where only the nobility and merchants came together to exchange luxury goods; and of the Great Peasant revolt which

removed the regime of forced labour and gave peasants direct access to markets because it increased their incomes. Markets multiplied as they came to include transactions in mass consumption goods. I taught them that the greatest force in expanding markets, particularly for mass consumption goods, is the democratic struggle.

But then we witnessed, from 1981 to 1984, and then from 1987 to now, two structural adjustment programmes that began by reducing popular demand and by destroying domestic markets for popular consumption goods. I learned that there must be a difference between the perspective of an accountant and that of a development economist: the former can even balance the budget in the midst of the Ethiopian famine by reducing demand – perhaps at the cost of another million lives!

Case study 2: Karamoja

My second example concerns the question of ecology. I direct a research centre in Kampala; one of its projects focuses on pastoralism in Karamoja. Part of the research addresses the question of ecological degradation. It is no exaggeration to say that our encounter with the people of Karamoja and their environment has radically changed our conception of the ecological problem. Let me recount what we have learned in a step-by-step manner.

1.   Over four decades, from the 1920s to the 1960s, the Karimojong lost nearly 20 per cent of their grazing land as a result of the redrawing of boundaries and the creation of game parks for tourism.

2.   The result has been twofold. One, to alter drastically grazing practices. The customary practice was to divide grazing lands into those fallow and those for use, to burn the fallow land before the rains. The annual burning fertilized the soil with ash and checked the harvester ant population. With 20 per cent of grazing land lost, annual burnings ceased; all the land was grazed all the time. The harvester ant population multiplied. What was a savanna grassland in 1920 had by 1990 turned into a semi-exposed mixture of grass and shrubs. On the other hand, the Karimojong were cutting down forest land to increase pastures. In short, an ecological crisis.

3.   The second result was to increase conflict between grazing communities over diminishing pastures. These conflicts were compounded by the response of the state.

4.   The response of the state, both colonial and post-colonial, was to try and balance the equation by reducing the cattle population through periodic 'destocking'. The response of the Karimojong, who saw the forcible seizure of cattle as a follow-up to the forcible seizure of land, was to resist this. The ecological crisis was combined with a political crisis.

Case study 3: Population and reproductive decisions of individual families

My third example concerns the 'population explosion'. Neo-Malthusianism became fashionable in the late 1960s, when I was a graduate student at Harvard. I too was drawn into it, and went to do research on 'the population problem' in the Punjab in India. As preparation for that research, I attended a few lectures by Professor Kuznets. He made the point that while neo-Malthusians juggle statistics and draw conclusions at the macro level, birth rates are determined by reproductive decisions of individual families. He insisted, and I will never forget, that the decision by a family to have or not to have a child is essentially a judgement of its circumstances; to change that decision, you have first to change the circumstances. I combined Professor Kuznets' wisdom with library reading on the 'demographic transition'. I could find no instance of a demographic transition that was outside of the context of a social transformation.

With that preparation, I was in an excellent position to benefit from my research experience in that Punjabi village. What did I learn?

1.   I began by conducting a census of the village population. I realized that while reproductive statistics are territory-specific (for a village, a region, a country), reproductive behaviour is socially-specific. In the same village, there will be families that try to limit their numbers, and those that try to augment them.

2.   I found that, no matter how impossible its circumstances, every family had worked out some strategy for improving its position. The strategy was shaped by the family's understanding of its options in that given context, so the strategy differed mainly from one social group to another. I will give you two examples. Poor peasants had rightly concluded that they had little chance of increasing either the farm equipment or the land at their disposal; what they could increase was

family hands. They looked to large families as a possible avenue to prosperity.

Families of tailors, on the other hand, without any land or farming tradition, had arrived at a middle-class strategy. They wanted large families so that everybody would work to put the youngest through college. But for that to be possible, none could marry early. So, even though the parents had a large family to educate one son, the sons could not have as large a family since they married late!

What am I saying? Two things. One, I am not arguing that the poor peasant or the tailor strategy necessarily succeeded, or even that it succeeded for the majority. But I am saying that, given their constraints, the poor peasant or tailor response was in the main reasonable. Two, I am questioning the neo-Malthusian formulation of the problem. People are not poor because they are many; rather, they are many because they are poor.

In the African context, judgements of families are also shaped by their collective memories. It is instructive to bear in mind the main contours of Africa's demographic history. From 1600 to 1900, the centuries of European slave trade, Africa's population remained stagnant, at roughly 100 million, but that of Europe increased fourfold. In this century, we can identify at least three periods. In the first two decades, there was drastic loss of population in the face of colonial 'pacification' campaigns, epidemics and famines. With the stabilization of colonial rule, there was a dramatic upsurge in birth rates. The two are not unconnected. For the last decade, we are once again in a period of war, instability, hunger and epidemics. Once again, to change popular judgement of the circumstances, the circumstances need to be changed.

Lessons to be drawn

I am sure that the architects of structural adjustment will argue that even if having large families is reasonable from the point of view of a poor peasant, or cutting down forests from the point of view of a pastoralist, this intuitive rationality is counter-productive. The cumulative effect of large families and deforestation can only be negative. Who can disagree? But my point is different. How you conceptualize a problem sets the parameters within which you can formulate a solution. If you define popular behaviour as the problem, as opposed to circumstances that evoke that behaviour, then your solution is bound to run against popular resistance.

Neither the World Bank nor the IMF has a monopoly on claims to counter-intuitive rationality. Counter-intuitive rationality is the fig-leaf of every anti-democratic programme. It was the swan-song of colonial powers who, when faced with nationalist opposition, argued that good government was not necessarily self-government. And it was, in turn, the rallying cry of militant nationalists, up to the various self-described Marxist regimes in Africa. Each of them had a programme for a 'revolution from above'. Each argued that in the face of Africa's development priorities, democracy was a luxury.

It is surely a supreme irony that a view which claims to be rational has to be imposed as 'conditionalities' on Africa's peoples; that every African country has to be brought to reason, tied, hand and foot, with golden chains of credit.

I have argued that where the market is a partial construct, a structural adjustment whose very starting point is to undercut popular purchasing power must end up by destroying domestic markets and reinforcing the regime of compulsions all over rural Africa.

No talk of improving governance can hide this fact. For governance, as defined by the architects of structural adjustment, has nothing to do with democracy. Its scope is efficiency of management, law and order, not democracy. For democracy to have any meaning, African governments must be accountable to African peoples, not only for the resources they receive and spend, but for the very policies they formulate and execute.

Today, the world is divided between two types of countries: those who restructure, and those who adjust. It is my humble view that the point of view of adjustment, of counter-intuitive rationality, of revolution from above, is part of the problem, not the solution.

Note

This chapter is derived from the text of remarks made as a response to a speech by Robert McNamara on 'Africa's Development Crisis', at the Wesley H. Copeland Annual Lecture organized by the Institute on African Affairs at the World Bank, Washington, DC, 3 April 1991.

3

Education Adjustment Under Severe Recessionary Pressures: The Case of Ghana

Cyril Daddieh

To survive and compete in a competitive world in the 21st century, Africa will require not only literate and numerate citizens, but also highly qualified and trained people to perform top-quality research, formulate policies, and implement programs essential to economic growth and development. Institutions of higher learning must be able to produce, at an affordable and sustainable cost, well-trained people in academic and professional disciplines applicable to diverse African work environments.[1]

Education cannot be merely dependent on economic development but is in fact an integral part of it. Training of agricultural workers, for example, is no less essential than any other steps for the improvement of agriculture. Thus education must be seen as fundamental to all policies.[2]

Over the last decade, a much greater degree of scepticism has developed as economic stagnation and civil wars have occurred widely across the region. The dynamic of expansion inherent in educational systems remains but there is less belief in its social benefits. At the same time, declining government revenues are resulting in pressures to slow down education expansion and to reduce the resources for each pupil. These trends are occurring in most countries at all levels of education.[3]

Introduction

Throughout much of sub-Saharan Africa the unrelenting recessionary pressures are compelling governments either to introduce education reforms as part of the overall effort to restructure their economies, or at the very least to place them on the national agenda for public debate. This trend toward increased national debate and reform has generally been preceded by, as well as linked to, the privatization, deregulation and liberalization measures that have been mandated by the Bretton Woods institutions and reluctantly embraced by African states struggling to keep their economies afloat and avert social catastrophe.

To understand the rationale for these reforms and their implications for African societies, we need to cast a retrospective glance at the genesis of education policy and examine several facets of the educational systems: their structure, the ills currently plaguing education, the solutions proffered by these reforms, the consequences they might engender not only for the schools, but for the state and society as well, and the struggles being waged by different groups as they respond to the new policy initiatives.

This chapter contends that while certain policy reforms in the education sector are long overdue, there are clear and current pitfalls which, if not given sufficient attention by African states, can undo the gains achieved by previous efforts. There are, for instance, certain imperatives of balanced development and national integration that should not be overlooked in the rush to adopt new educational packages. To illustrate the issues involved, I shall begin with a general discussion of African educational systems, to be followed by a more direct focus on the educational reforms currently being implemented in Ghana.

The choice of Ghana is compelling for a number of reasons: the country was the torch-bearer of African independence and continental unity in the 1960s. Under the able leadership of Dr Kwame Nkrumah, a concerted effort was made to provide education to as many children of school age as possible. Ghana operated one of the most vigorous and comprehensive educational systems in Africa, thereby becoming the trend-setter of the explosion of educational institutions. It gained worldwide acclaim for producing not only the greatest number of international civil servants of any one African country, but some of the most competent as well. It wrestled illiteracy down to a respectable 35 per cent only to watch it climb back up again in the 1980s.

Education was, indeed, the gold that glittered in the crown of the Ghanaian state in the 1960s. In the 1980s Ghana once again became the bell-wether state as far as structural adjustment and educational reform were concerned.[4] It has become an important test case as the first African country to be given a World Bank loan and administrative support from the UNDP to embark on a far-reaching Educational Sector Adjustment Programme involving structural and curricula changes and new methods of financing, known euphemistically as cost-recovery measures.[5] Finally, the country's experience, with the meteoric rise and subsequent fall in access to and quality of education, mirrors those of other African countries and therefore holds meaningful lessons for all.

Evolution of educational systems and policies in Africa

The first decade of African independence was characterized by a political mood that was decidedly optimistic. That unbridled optimism spilled over into, and was reinforced by, the proliferation of educational institutions at every level. The gains were both quantitative and qualitative and were all the more impressive given the continent's unenviable inheritance after almost a century of European colonial rule. Indeed, the various educational achievements seemed to make the struggle for political emancipation well worth the collective effort.[6]

For instance, on the eve of independence in 1960 there were only six universities and university colleges in sub-Saharan Africa. Nowhere was the dearth of educational institutions more odious than in the vast and rich territory of the Belgian Congo (now Zaire) where after almost a century of Leopoldian (or is it antipodean in this case?) rule there were only eight university graduates and one senior civil servant at independence. Not surprisingly, the first independence cabinet of Prime Minister Patrice Lumumba included a lonely university graduate who, by his own admission, was politically unseasoned. Another colonial power, Portugal, bequeathed to Mozambique the dubious distinction of enjoying a 90 per cent illiteracy rate among its population.

While Belgium and Portugal may have been the worst offenders in terms of the dereliction of their self-imposed 'civilizing mission', they were not alone in impeding their colonies' march toward greater educational progress. Britain and France were not exactly paragon facilitators of African education. Kenya, Tanzania, and Uganda, with a combined population of 23 million, turned out only ninety-nine graduates in 1961 from their universities, while Zambia, in spite of its copper wealth, had 100 university and 1,000 secondary school graduates at the time of independence.[7]

Compared to this dismal legacy, each African state now enjoys at least one institution of higher learning. A few can even boast of several. A case in point is Nigeria which, with its petro-naira and considerably larger population size, has experienced a sixfold expansion in the number of its universities, with proportional increases at primary and secondary levels, although it is still faced with an undiminished appetite for more.[8] During the first decade from 1960 to 1970, enrolments in sub-Saharan Africa grew at annual average rates of 5.4, 11.4 and 11.7 per cent for primary, secondary, and higher education respectively. In the following decade the growth rates were 7.3, 13.4 and 11.5 per cent. Between 1960 and 1980, the average enrolment ratio for primary rose from 36 to 60 per cent, for secondary from 3 to 14 per cent, and from almost zero to 1.4 per cent for higher education.[9]

These improved statistics tell part of the story of Africa's long-standing respect for education. But equally compelling as an index of the seriousness with which Africans and their governments have embraced education is the proportion of the budget that goes to this sector. Indeed, the high growth rates of enrolment have been associated with large public and private expenditures. Since independence in 1960, public expenditures on education have risen faster than both gross national product and aggregate government expenditure. For all sub-Saharan African countries combined, the share of education expenditure in gross national product rose from 3.2 per cent in 1965 to 4.1 per cent in 1980.[10] With few exceptions, education continues to soak up the lion's share (about 20 per cent) of the annual budget of most governments, with Côte d'Ivoire spending as much as 45 per cent on education in recent years (see Tables 3.1 and 3.2).

The new political kingdom and educational proliferation

To account for both the proliferation of educational institutions and the growth of budget allocation to this sector, one has to look to three interactive processes, pressures and needs. The pre-independence quest for popular approval rested on the ability of different nationalist politicians to co-opt their countrymen with promises of the good life to come. Since the chances of securing the good life were considerably enhanced by the attainment of education, the provision of new schools became the locally visible evidence that the nationalist leadership was committed to meeting the aspirations of the populace. Under these circumstances, the legitimacy of the nationalist leaders and the authority of the emergent state became intertwined with the construction boom in education. Expanded access to education came to be popularly associated with the successful attainment of Nkrumah's political kingdom. Once in office, the new leadership had really little choice but to assume responsibility for the building of schools.

TABLE 3.1

Educational enrolments and expenditures, sub-Saharan Africa

Country	Year	Total central gov't expenditure on education (%)	Distribution[a] of educational expenditure (%)			Higher enrolment ratio (%)
			P	S	H	
Botswana	1982	–[b]	56	32	12	–
Burundi	1981	19.0	44	29	27	1.00
Comoros	1980	25.4	49	34	17	1.40
Djibouti	1984	11.9	74	26	–	0.60
Ethiopia	1981	11.1	50	28	22	0.45
Kenya	1982	21.2	65	16	19	–
Lesotho	1982	16.9	40	33	27	1.30
Madagascar	1977	24.0	53	28	19	3.10
Malawi	1981	11.4	50	18	32	0.40
Mauritius	1983	4.0	52	40	8	1.00
Rwanda	1983	24.5	72	16	12	0.40
Seychelles	1979	22.4	44	43	13	–
Somalia	1981	10.5	50	44	6	1.00
Sudan	1980	–	–	–	–	–
Swaziland	1983	20.4	51	34	15	3.00
Tanzania	1980	17.7	64	14	22	0.30
Uganda	1980	16.1	29	46	25	0.60
Zaire	1981	26.4	–	–	10	2.00
Zambia	1980	11.1	52	25	23	1.50
Zimbabwe	1981	19.5	62	32	6	0.50
Benin	1979	35.0	62	30	8	1.00
Burkina	1983	21.7	43	29	28	0.03
Cameroon	1978	16.0	34	45	21	1.30
CAR	1979	20.6	–	–	–	0.70
Chad	1976	21.7	–	–	–	0.20
Congo	1978	27.7	–	–	–	4.00
Gabon	1977	8.4	–	–	–	2.80
Gambia	1977	6.5	60	32	8	–
Ghana	1976	15.5	–	–	–	–
Guinea	1979	–	31	35	34	7.00
Ivory Coast	1981	45.0	36	50	14	1.90
Liberia	1980	19.6	48	25	27	2.90
Mali	1981	21.7	54	30	16	0.90
Mauritania	1978	16.9	33	42	25	0.37
Niger	1978	16.6	52	43	5	0.20
Nigeria	1977	9.6	–	–	–	0.17
Senegal	1977	23.0	46	34	20	2.20
Sierra Leone	1977	16.6	–	–	–	0.60
Togo	1978	26.5	38	35	27	1.60

Notes: [a]Only those parts of total educational expenditure which can be directly attributed to each level of education are included; [b] – indicates no information.

Source: Keith Hinchliffe, *Higher Education in Sub-Saharan Africa* (London: Croom Helm, 1987), 163–64.

TABLE 3.2

Public expenditure on education, selected countries and years

| Region/ Country | Year | Educational expenditure as a % of | |
		GNP	Total public expenditure
Africa	1965	3.2	–
	1970	3.5	–
	1975	4.0	–
	1980	4.1	–
Ivory Coast	1970	5.4	19.3
	1979	8.6	29.8
Kenya	1970	5.0	17.6
	1979	6.1	18.0
Liberia	1970	2.5	9.5
	1980	6.1	24.3
Niger	1970	2.0	17.7
	1980	4.3	22.9
Tanzania	1970	4.5	16.0
	1979	5.8	10.7
Zambia	1970	4.7	10.9
	1980	4.6	7.6

Source: Keith Hinchliffe, *Higher Education in Sub-Saharan Africa* (London: Croom Helm, 1987), 165.

To be sure, this populist nationalist impulse was partially structured by the post-war reformist posture of many colonial governments as they tried to upstage the nationalist leaders by unveiling five-year development plans centred on social infrastructural developments. However, even if the expansion had not been essentially driven by the political context of the time, the boom might well have ensued because, as Joel Samoff et al. suggest, 'unlike clinics and hospitals, clean water supplies or even tarred roads, schools could appear quickly throughout the countryside'.[11]

Whatever the initial motivational basis for supporting the construction of schools, the nationalist leaders soon found compelling practical reasons for investing so heavily in education. Schools were needed to produce a critical mass of trained manpower, including civil servants, doctors, economists, engineers, lawyers, teachers, nurses, clerks, etc., who would step confidently into the shoes of the departing Europeans as well as provide direction, leadership and energy for the all-important task of nation building. Indeed, educational expansion became the *sine qua non* of progress or modernization. Education was regarded as a necessary complement to, if not an integral component of, national development, as the delegates to the 1961 Addis Ababa All-Africa Conference on Education held under the auspices of UNESCO unanimously agreed.[12]

Aside from the quest for qualified manpower to promote rapid economic development and strengthen state administrative capacity for policy formulation and implementation, there was an unspoken belief that the newly educated citizens would become exemplars of modernity by internalizing new ideas or modern values, and by developing genuine national sentiment, leading to national identity and unity. Education would enable the new African to transcend ethnicity and foster the transfer of ethnic and regional loyalties to the new state. In that case, education was widely viewed as a viable instrument in modern nation-building. As Keith Hinchliffe has noted in his own highly suggestive work, 'In the period of greatest optimism, in the early 1960s, education was widely regarded as capable of producing rapid economic growth, greater equality between social and ethnic groups, stronger feelings of national unity, and in general was taken to be the route to "modernization".'[13]

As it happens, the political leadership was not alone in counting on education to produce social benefits. Ordinary citizens also came to view it as the single most important route to upward social mobility for their 'sons' and their entire community. It was rightly perceived as the best route to security of employment, influence, prestige, affluence, 'big man' status, etc.[14] This shared élite–mass understanding took on added significance, particularly in those societies like Ghana

> where the leadership sought to reduce the role of race, religion, region, ethnicity and perhaps gender as criteria for selection and promotion in employment and public service. That perception of the role of schooling in determining individual life chances was reinforced by the image of meritocracy.[15]

The ameliorative power of education stimulated an insatiable popular appetite for schooling that paralleled, and may have even exceeded in some cases, the leadership's sense of obligation and capabilities. It was this combination of obligation and demand that elevated education to a basic right of citizenship and fuelled the construction explosion of the 1960s.

African leaders went beyond the construction boom however. At the Addis conference of 1961 they committed themselves to an education blueprint that included the goal of a universal, compulsory and free primary education by the year 1980. Compulsory and free education were fanciful ideas from the start, given the finite resources available.[16] Nonetheless, so intoxicating was the optimism of the decade that the leaders pressed ahead with varying degrees of compulsory primary education, undaunted by the very real possibility of running out of money. They provided heavy subsidies for room and board at secondary and tertiary levels. They awarded generous scholarships to both deserving and well-connected students for studies overseas, creating a class of 'been-to's', with all the expectations and perquisites that it implies, while compensating the less fortunate university students at home with living allowances and room-cleaning services. To listen to this 'fortunate few' reminisce leaves little doubt that these were the good old days of privileged ivory-tower existence.

To summarize briefly, three views of education have predominated in Africa: education for self-improvement, education for nation-building, and education for national development. For a while at least, all three seemed to point in the same direction, providing both the impetus and the rationale for expanding expenditures on education.

The nature and structure of African education

The first feature of African educational systems that leaps at any observer is that, structurally, they resemble a pyramid: despite the attempts to broaden the base through universal primary education, they become progressively narrow as one moves up the ladder through secondary school to the pinnacle of the system, the university. In other words, the entry levels approximate to a 'mass' system but at higher levels the system becomes more selective, hence more élitist. As was noted earlier, even primary school enrolment may still only hover around 50 per cent, although it varies widely from slightly less than 10 to over 90 per cent. At the secondary level, the narrowing becomes more pronounced, with rarely more than 4 or 5 per cent of the relevant age group actually enrolled in school (see Table 3.1). As a number of researchers have pointed out,[17] secondary schools are extremely significant because they are terminal institutions for the bulk of the relatively small number of students who enter them in the first place and they also control access to colleges and universities.

Most schools in the all-important secondary sector started out as residential or boarding schools. They were islands protected by barbed wire and concrete walls. They elicited little or no involvement from the communities in which they were located. The night-lights from their electricity generating plants or national energy grids should have illuminated the paths of their less fortunate, non-literate communities. However, rarely, if ever, did that happen. Ironically, even secondary schools located in rural areas tended to nurture the ivory-tower aloofness, seemingly impervious to the existential concerns and developmental needs of the host communities. Just as they made no real contributions to improving the existential conditions of their communities, so they also by and large failed to draw upon the vast cultural and practical resources of these communities to enrich their own educational experiences.

In the Ghanaian case, recent data show that roughly 8 and 0.8 per cent of the relevant age groups are enrolled in secondary and tertiary schools respectively. Only about 24,000 out of the approximately 130,000 pupils who take the common entrance examination for admission to secondary schools are able to find places. Roughly 5,000 of these get sixth-form places. And out of 14,000 students (5,000 sixth formers plus 9,000 additional private candidates) who take A-levels, no more than 3,000 are admitted to Ghana's three universities.[18] Enrolments in 1985 were 3,352, 3,088 and 1,568 for Legon, Kumasi and Cape Coast respectively. Total enrolments apparently had not changed since 1979.[19]

African educational systems are also characterized by substantial regional and ethnic disparities, both in terms of the availability of educational institutions and of recruitment into post-primary school. To be sure, such uneven distribution of education, and hence of differential access, among ethnic groups and regions is related to past advantage. As R.E. McKown and David J. Finlay have indicated:

> Much of the disparity in access to education can be attributed to the fact that geographic concentration of ethnic groups often coincides with localized patterns of educational development. The location, support and expansion of schools since independence have largely been concentrated in areas where at least a modicum of social and economic modernization have already taken place. Not only are local financial resources greater in such areas, but demand for education is often stronger and political pressures applied more skillfully.[20]

This helps to explain why, in spite of Nkrumah's best effort to remedy this colonial legacy, the north still lags behind the rest of the country. Such rural–urban, regional, and ethnic disparities pose a serious threat to peaceful and successful nation-building because these uneven patterns of access to education and other forms of development 'create the causes behind much of the conflict that has been defined as "tribalism".'[21]

The striking ethnic stratification characteristic of selection into secondary school is overlaid by a related systematic over-representation of students from higher socio-economic backgrounds, whether measured in terms of parental occupation or education, urban origin or a combination of these factors. In Ghana, as elsewhere in Africa, the level of parental education is usually the strongest predictor of access to a secondary school. During 1961, the selectivity indices for student categories at the secondary level ranged from 5.8 for the sons and daughters of professional and clerical groups, down to a low of 0.1 for the children of unskilled, mainly urban workers, with the offspring of farmers and fishermen in an intermediate position of 0.5. In essence, the child of a professional or clerical worker has approximately sixty times the chance of entering secondary school as the child of an unskilled worker and approximately eleven times as much chance as the child of a farmer.

The university data show that a disproportionate number of students at the University of Ghana-Legon have parents in high status occupations. In 1974 approximately 45 per cent of the students had fathers or guardians who held white-collar jobs even though less than 7 per cent of the adult population fell into this category (see Table 3.3).[22] It is equally interesting to note that the positive correlation between family socio-economic background and rates of attendance is also reproduced in differential rates of attendance between regions, with the more affluent families and wealthier southern regions of Ghana enjoying considerably greater access to secondary and tertiary education than the less affluent northern regions and families. In other words, household and regional disparities are closely correlated with enrolment differences. Tables 3.4, 3.5 and 3.6 provide vital statistics on access and enrolment rates for different regions, income groups, and gender.

Indeed, the gender gap at secondary and tertiary levels is even more pronounced. Whereas in 1961 female students comprised 38 per cent of the primary and 31 per cent of the middle school pools, they represented only 23 per cent of secondary, 6 per cent of technical (1962), and a mere 12 per cent of the university student population in 1973. And yet, ironically, it was the renowned Ghanaian educator, Dr James Kwegyir Aggrey, who underscored the multiplier developmental benefits of educating women with these memorable words: 'If you educate a man, you simply educate an individual, but if you educate a woman, you educate a family'.[23] As Daphne Topouzis laments, few have taken Aggrey's message seriously:

TABLE 3.3
Education and the poor (in percentages)

	Poorest 10%	Poorest 30%	All Ghana
Education of household head			
None	80.8	71.7	53.9
Primary	3.5	6.9	8.1
Middle	15.7	20.6	31.3
Secondary: O Level	0.0	0.0	3.0
Secondary: A Level	0.0	0.0	0.3
Teacher Training	0.0	0.5	1.8
Other tertiary	0.0	0.3	0.4
University	0.0	0.0	1.2
School attendance by household members			
Age 6–10	43.2	57.2	66.8
Age 11–15	46.0	60.5	70.8

Source: *Ghana Living Standards Survey* cited by James Cobbe, 'The Political Economy of Education Reform in Ghana', 103.

Illiteracy in Africa is four times as high among women as among men, and the higher the level of education, the lower the percentage of girls. In Côte d'Ivoire, 82 women among 707 students completed university studies in 1983. In 13 out of 18 African countries for which figures are available, expenditure per pupil in primary school decreased dramatically, up to 40 percent, between 1980 and 1984-85.[24]

Such a trend is distressing because the decline in primary school expenditures has a much greater negative impact on girls since it is at the primary school level that they are better represented.[25]

Another characteristic feature of African education is that post-primary schools are highly differentiated in terms of prestige or status which, in turn, is related to success rate in national examinations. These prestigious schools also draw a disproportionate number of their student body from higher socio-economic and certain ethnic backgrounds. And virtually all of them are located in the major urban centres.

In the case of Ghana, the following ten schools will generally feature prominently in any listing:[26] Wesley Girls' High School, Presec (Legon), Achimota School; Aburi Girls, St. Augustine's College, Adisadel

TABLE 3.4

Junior and senior secondary school data, national average/totals, 1988–89

	JSS/M	Senior secondary
Total enrolment	608,690	154,477
% enrolment female	41.3	32.7
Enrolment per school	118	631
% Repeaters	0.69	2.72
% Repeaters female/% repeaters	1.01	n.a.
Total teachers	34,584	8,528
Teachers/class	1.62	2.09
Pupils/teacher	17.6	18.1
Classes/classrooms	1.15	n.a.
% Teachers untrained	28.2	29.9
Classrooms/school	3.60	n.a.
Teacher load, periods/week	n.a.	18.9
% Science stream, forms 4 & 5	n.a.	22.4
% Arts stream, forms 4 & 5	n.a.	36.7
% Business stream, forms 4 & 5	n.a.	40.9
% Science, form 6	n.a.	35.4
% Arts, form 6	n.a.	37.8
% Business, form 6	n.a.	26.8

Notes: SS/M = Junior secondary schools and middle schools; n.a.=not applicable or not available.

Source: Ministry of Education, as cited by James Cobbe, 'The Political Economy of Education Reform in Ghana', 113.

College, Mfantsipim, Holy Child, St Peter's, and Prempeh College. Cooke argued that these schools have a common ethos, with emphasis on such things as pastoral care, discipline and diligence. The Ghanaian élites, most of whom are themselves products of these institutions, naturally, keep their eyes on the prize, to borrow a civil rights phrase. Out of the thousands of students who sit the common entrance examinations – theoretically the only means of gaining entry into secondary schools – only about 2,000 or so manage to gain a place at one

TABLE 3.5
Access to primary school by region, 1987–88

Region	Calculated radius of primary school catchment areas (km)	Private sector enrolments as % of total	Primary 1 enrolment as % of 6-year-olds	Apparent enrolment rate
Ashanti	2.20	4.5	72.3	88.4
Brong Ahafo	3.14	1.3	79.2	86.5
Central	1.76	1.4	77.9	94.6
Eastern	1.90	1.3	79.1	93.7
Greater Accra	1.25	18.9	56.2	77.5
Northern	4.92	0.0	56.5	49.5
Upper East	3.10	0.0	46.2	33.5
Upper West	4.83	0.0	52.5	49.4
Volta	2.27	0.5	73.1	88.5
Western	2.65	0.5	77.0	89.6
National	2.75	3.7	69.1	79.1

Source: Ministry of Education (Planning Budget, Monitoring and Evaluation Division), Pandit and Asiamah Report, Table VII, as cited by James Cobbe, 'The Political Economy of Education Reform in Ghana', 113.

of these schools (of course, most students do not even dream of applying to them). While these élite schools are beyond the reach of most students, there exists a second category of about fifteen schools that command a reasonable amount of respect; they take in about 3,000. 'Some 20,000 would gain a place in other institutions whose names excite little interest, with the rest being left to face a wilderness of doubt.'[27]

This distinctive status hierarchy among secondary schools becomes all the more important because the secondary schools control access to the all important universities. A related point is that access to post-primary institutions is dependent upon measured academic achievement. Entry into secondary schools and universities in Africa is by and large achieved through superior grades in national examinations. This places a premium on those educational institutions that can meet the rigours of the competition. As the competition intensifies in the face of limited

TABLE 3.6
Indicators of regional disparity in primary schools, 1988–89

Region	Enrolment per school	Classes per classroom	Class size	Pupils per teacher	% Girls	% Repeaters	% Repeaters girls/% girls	% Teachers untrained
Ashanti	195	1.06	30.6	28.5	46.2	3.6	1.05	32.9
Brong Ahafo	145	1.10	25.2	23.0	45.4	3.7	1.09	51.8
Central	184	1.05	30.6	27.7	44.7	3.1	0.98	41.9
Eastern	165	0.90	27.6	23.2	44.8	4.7	0.96	33.5
Greater Accra	320	1.29	42.3	38.1	48.9	2.7	1.10	12.0
Northern	102	1.39	19.1	18.1	32.8	3.7	1.05	59.4
Upper West	157	0.99	27.2	20.2	37.5	4.4	1.08	37.7
Volta	161	1.00	24.9	24.2	45.2	3.3	0.98	32.0
Western	170	1.05	27.7	26.5	43.9	4.9	1.11	58.3
National	171	1.06	28.0	25.5	44.5	3.8	1.03	39.7

Source: Ministry of Education, as cited by James Cobbe, 'The Political Economy of Education Reform in Ghana', 114.

employment opportunities in Ghana, as elsewhere, the educational process degenerates into a kind of frenzied search for formulae for success in examinations.

As one teacher confided in Colleen Morna: 'The bulk of students are only here to pass exams. We prepare notes and copy them on to the board, and give the students sample answers to exam questions, instead of educating them to really face life and face realities.'[28] Morna also found out that at schools like Presbyterian, where most students are from professional or middle-class backgrounds and can afford extra tuition, exam results have been consistently high. By contrast, in poorer schools like Nungua, results dipped dramatically during the worst of Ghana's recession. To counteract these nefarious educational effects of Ghana's recession, students and parents have been turning increasingly to tutorial sessions outside class, for a handsome fee, of course. At the secondary level, in particular, many teachers are supplementing their paltry salaries by teaching outside classes. This growing industry has had a corrupting influence on the educational process to the point where 'teachers deliberately leave sections of the syllabus so that students will have to seek extra classes during the vacation. Students have to pay up to $100 to get the necessary tuition for one subject'.[29] The fallout, as Morna indicates, is that students do not feel obliged to stay in school or treat their teachers with respect. The profession is being forced by the recession to prostitute itself.[30]

Not surprisingly, the various problems adumbrated above interact and reinforce each other in such a way as to inform parental judgements about educational expenditures and student attitudes and orientations. In this case, the responses may at times appear to reflect logical inconsistencies. This is to be expected, because quite often educational decisions involve motivational bases that are complex.[31] Thus, even as some families and communities cut back on their educational investments because of the perceived poor rate of return, others are continuing to make the necessary financial sacrifices. It may well be that it is families and communities (whether rural or urban) for whom the decision does not represent a devil's choice between basic needs and education who are able to continue this educational gamble. The evidence from Ghana is, again, revealing: 'unlike in Ghana's impoverished north, where many parents are questioning the value of an education because of the generally poor exam results and low remuneration for skilled jobs, those in the Accra area have continued to send their children to school'.[32] Contrast that with another respondent who explained that there is still a measure of prestige associated with education in Ghana's urban areas.

Finally, bear in mind that the pattern of recruitment into African education has neither remained static nor followed a path of unilinear progression. The Ghanaian experience is a good barometer. Access was pretty much restricted in the earliest stage (colonial pattern), became more open in the intermediate period of rapid educational growth (optimistic phase of independence), only to be followed by a more unegalitarian pattern (mature? or frustration phase of independence). In other words, by the early 1980s there was a discernible trend toward closure after a period of democratization of educational opportunity in Ghana.[33] Ironically, that trend continues and may even be worsening precisely at a time when Africa has embarked upon a process of political openness or democratization. How can Africa sustain the latter if the former trend persists?

The state in education and the state of education

The patterns of recruitment into, and the structure of, the educational systems are generally reflective of state policies and goals and the concomitant financial burdens the state is willing to assume in the pursuit of those goals. These policies, goals and financial responsibilities are, in turn, structured within a political–economic and intellectual complex that has domestic, continental as well as international dimensions.

As suggested earlier, for about two decades, African states were apparently willing to bear the financial burdens in order to broaden access and expand the pool of trained people. However, despite an official commitment to compulsory and universal primary education, the systems that most governments installed were decidedly élitist and sexist, in their recruitment patterns, locational distributions, programmatic emphases, and financial allocation decisions. They were also 'colonized' in the sense that they remained wedded to European notions of appropriate education and modes of behaviour. They focused almost exclusively on academic or classical education to the neglect of the kind of functional or vocational training that had characterized the best of the so-called traditional or 'bush schools' of yesteryear. It is precisely such an imbalance that has been found wanting and that has led to calls for educational relevance. The general consensus is that the Eurocentric curricula are not suited for Afrocentric life after the classroom.

Moreover, a much greater emphasis had been placed on higher education, as evidenced by the lion's share of the education budget going to this sector. This emphasis has come under attack from international donors not only because the university caters to the fortunate few, but also because it is perceived to produce the lowest social return on investment. The World Bank is in the forefront of the recent revisionism. In spite of the glowing tribute it pays to the vital role of higher education, as in the opening citation, the Bank essentially argues that higher education is not cost-effective and has sought to shift resources to lower levels. The social rates of return on investment in education are apparently 26 per cent for primary, 17 per cent for secondary, and 13 per cent for higher education. Given such an understanding and faced with making choices among competing claims on limited resources, the Bank has been insisting that basic education should receive funding priority. The Bank's new thinking on funding stipulates that resources going into basic education should grow faster than at any other level because 'education is intrinsic to development in the widest sense; empowering people, especially the poor, with basic cognitive skills is the surest way to render them self-reliant citizens'.[34]

Quite aside from the issues of cost and the appropriate level at which the benefits of investments can be maximized, African higher education suffers from a lack of clearly defined philosophy and vision that are uniquely African. Instead of a genuine Africa-centric education, as Professor K. Twum-Barima has lamented,

> University development proceeds in Africa according to the dictates of European philosophies and practices of higher education. Africa took no notice of the fact that it lacked the non-university research facilities provided in Europe by private industry, and the government supported applied research which has played such a role in their own development. . . . they all turned to imparting European knowledge dressed as international or universal knowledge, which had neither Asian nor African components; while university research, more often than not, was directed towards confirming the supremacy of European knowledge and its doubtful application to African situations. Do we wonder why Africa remains underdeveloped?[35]

Last, as already suggested, African states play a vital role as providers: they build schools, provide basic supplies (chalk, pencils, pens, crayons, textbooks, exercise books, erasers, etc.), subsidize room and board, pay teachers' salaries, and provide subsidized campus housing for secondary school teachers and university faculty.[36] In keeping with their role as primary providers, African states have sought to exert maximum control over the education process, ostensibly to give it direction, to coordinate implementation so that there is uniformity of purpose and standards and to ensure that the skills being acquired are compatible with national developmental goals. They have done so by placing the entire system under the control and supervision of ministries of education or equivalent central bureaucracies.

In practice, there has been more to the relationship than mere coordination and guidance. Since the state is the one that pays the piper, it feels that it has to call the education tunes. In the best of economic times, the financial and administrative responsibilities associated with state commitment to education are accepted with relative equanimity. However, in times of fiscal crisis, the relationship can become quite ticklish as officials seek vastly expanded powers of control over the governance of academic institutions and as students and some faculty resist these intrusions. This tussle invariably leads to a loss of academic freedoms, which is most acutely felt at the university level where the politicization of appointments, the arbitrary dismissal of dissident intellectuals, the ejection of students and teachers from campus housing, the expulsion of students, and the closing down of educational institutions have become rather routine. They have not only had a chilling effect on academic pursuits but are painful reminders of the continuing tensions between African states and students over national goals and priorities, programmes, funding, social returns and burden sharing.[37]

The crisis in education

In short, after a period of real growth in the quantity and quality of schools, African education is in a state of crisis. There has been a generalized erosion of the gains of the first two decades of independence. African education is now increasingly vilified by analysts and donors, parents and students alike. A long catalogue of everything wrong with African education has been compiled by a variety of analysts and organizations.[38]

The current crisis is clearly reflected in the precipitous decline in public expenditure per pupil across the board. For instance, in 1988 public expenditure per pupil was only $89 compared to $129 for all developing countries and $2,888 per pupil in the developed countries. In the Ghanaian case, government expenditure per capita on education had risen steadily from $4.2 in 1960 to $20 in 1972 only to decline to $10 in 1979 and then plummet even further to $1 in 1983 (using constant 1975 dollars). As the economic crisis has reduced the ability of the African state to sustain high levels of budgetary support for education, the quality of the schools has been eroded. Spending cuts have resulted in severe shortages of basic educational items, including textbooks, chalk, paper and pencils. Moreover, there has been a virtual breakdown of the whole infrastructure of support services – school inspections, in-service teacher training, curriculum development, and school health and food services. Equipment, furniture, and physical facilities have been allowed to deteriorate for lack of maintenance.

Teachers have been overworked and underpaid, when they have been paid at all. In the 1980s, average teacher salaries in Africa fell by 33 per cent. In Ghana, an experienced secondary school teacher earned the equivalent of $25 a month, about a third of what was needed to feed a family. 'The result is that teachers have to take second and third jobs to make ends meet, class times become flexible, and discipline is lax. At the universities, research comes to a halt and lectures are ill-prepared.'[39] Meanwhile, the pupil–teacher ratio of 34:1 is among the highest in the world, equalled only in Southern Asia; in Burundi, CAR, Chad, Congo, Malawi and Mozambique, the pupil–teacher ratio is as high as 60:1 in the primary schools; expansion has not kept pace with population growth so that the number of illiterate adults is expected to climb from 139 million in 1990 to 147 million by the year 2000.[40]

While the need for competent and motivated teachers has increased in Ghana, as elsewhere on the continent, poor and/or unpaid salaries and other unbearable service conditions have combined to create a growing deficit of teachers at all levels. The shortages have meant that so-called non-academic courses such as music and fine arts and athletic programmes are simply neglected. As the headmaster of Nungua Secondary School confessed,

> Faced with progressive belt-tightening measures, the first things that suffer are maintenance, equipment, and extra-curricular activities. When your budget is cut, the first thing you cut are subjects like music. You concentrate on exam subjects and sometimes you have to close your eyes to shortages of furniture, electrical fittings, and sports equipment.[41]

Furthermore, many of the teachers who have stayed on, especially those at the primary level, are either unqualified or are simply marking time and using whatever salaries come their way as supplemental income. Nearly half of all primary school teachers were unqualified in 1982–83, as were about a third of the middle school teachers and a fifth of the secondary school teachers. The chronic neglect of duties by teachers who have had to take up secondary occupations as a survival strategy is not peculiar to Ghana.[42] The following Nigerian rejoinder to criticism of teacher behaviour underscores the pervasiveness of the problem even as it puts it in its proper perspective.

Some, for instance, have been known to spend much time on their farms, or pursuing other business interests. However, it must be pointed out that many teachers often abandoned their duties out of necessity rather than lack of concern for pupils. They go out to farm for a living because they are frequently owed arrears of salaries running to several months.[43]

Ripe for resolution: Ghana's education sector adjustment programme

Unable to balance their budgets, faced with the prospect of ever greater numbers of educated unemployed who can provide the fuse for political fires, frustrated by the perceived limited social return to the nation from the already huge investment in education, especially as graduates vote with their feet by migrating to relatively greener pastures overseas or to other African countries, most governments are finding ways to privatize some of their obligations to education. Thus far, because of their shared experiences, I have been weaving the Ghanaian and African stories together. I now turn attention to a case study of Ghana's education adjustment effort.

When the PNDC came to power on 31 December 1981, the economy was teetering on the brink. Public finances had been seriously eroded, along with public confidence in the capacity of the state to foster the pursuit of happiness through education. As the economic situation went from bad to worse, the PNDC turned to the World Bank and the IMF for assistance to arrest the decline. The resultant Economic Recovery Programme (later Structural Adjustment Programme) was complemented in 1986 by a World Bank Educational Sector Adjustment Credit (EDSAC), supplemented by an additional $1.4 million coming from the UNDP for planning, policy analysis and evaluation of the reforms.[44] Rather than tinker with the existing system, the reforms sought to overhaul it completely. The reforms envisaged the shortening of the length of schooling, the overhaul of its basic structure, altering and expanding the curriculum, and finding new ways to finance education. They were informed by four nagging issues: accessibility, efficiency, relevance and sustainable funding.

The official view is that the reforms are absolutely essential if funding of the schools and universities is to be sustained so that the greatest number of students can continue to enjoy improved access to each of the three levels. In particular, it is expected that the changes would help raise overall literacy levels as well as boost the current 57 per cent attendance rating for Ghanaian school children. They are designed to ensure a more efficient use of available resources and stimulate a regeneration of those resources. The new education is intended to be much more attuned to Ghana's needs by emphasizing the provision of the kinds of skills and knowledge that would allow the students to adapt to their communities and make a contribution to national development. Partly for this, but more especially for financial reasons, community involvement has been made a cornerstone of the new reforms.

STRUCTURAL AND CURRICULUM CHANGES

The old Ghanaian education system consisted of six years of primary school, followed by four years of middle school, five years of secondary school, two years of 'sixth form', and then three years of university, assuming one passed the A-level examination, which was the gate-keeper to the university. Over the years a large consensus had built up around a certain number of issues: the process was too time-consuming (a twenty-year process, assuming no repetition) and very expensive. It was also discriminatory because the children of the well-heeled could frequently skip the four years of middle school by attending élite private primary schools (known revealingly as Preparatory or International Schools) which vastly improved their chances of coming through the 'common entrance examination' for secondary schools with flying colours. This also enabled them to be disproportionately represented at the élite secondary schools. As a result, the system appeared to be perpetuating inequalities from one generation to another and quite possibly exacerbating them.

The widespread recognition of the need for education reform, a need that had been partly reflected in the abortive April 1974 plan to streamline the system, provided an enabling environment for a relatively peaceful acceptance of the elementary and secondary school reforms.[45] Launched in 1986, the reforms altered the structure of the system by introducing junior and senior secondary schools. Junior secondary schools (JSS) replaced middle schools, giving all students three years of education after the six-year primary school cycle and then for those students who qualified to proceed to the next level, only a further three years at senior secondary schools (SSS).[46]

Substantial curriculum changes are also being attempted. The curriculum has been expanded and now covers thirteen subjects. They include cultural studies, Ghanaian languages, environmental studies, health, and agricultural science. The core of the curriculum consists of English, Ghanaian languages, science, maths, life skills and physical education, along with a choice of two out of five specialized programmes, including agriculture, business, technical subjects, and vocational and general education. These courses are to be taught through specially prepared Ghanaian syllabi and textbooks written by Ghanaians and published in Ghana.

Furthermore, all students are to learn the rudiments of a trade at school in the hope of preparing them for gainful employment on leaving school and thereby reducing the escalating problem of youth unemployment. The new curriculum is expected to promote national development by increasing the knowledge of all students in science and technology. The introduction of more practical subjects is 'in response to criticism that in the past this level of education has been overly academic and removed from the country's development and manpower needs'.[47]

The reforms are also touted as being much more egalitarian because they seek to provide access to the nine years' basic education for every Ghanaian child. Half the graduates of JSS are expected to gain access to SSS and a quarter of the SSS graduates are to be admitted to the universities. Meanwhile, the normal three-year undergraduate degree programme which was modelled after British universities is to be extended to four years (an American model?).

FUNDING THE NEW SYSTEM

The funding for the education adjustment programme is expected to come from four basic sources. As indicated earlier, the initial funding was provided by international donors, notably the World Bank and the UNDP, with additional food aid to provide low-cost nutritional food for students from the UN World Food Programme (WFP). Funds were made available by the international community for the rehabilitation and upgrading of existing buildings and for the provision of books and equipment needed to support the revised curriculum for secondary schools.

Second, substantial cost savings are expected to be realized from the structural changes and from improved cost accounting. At the insistence of the World Bank, which is adamantly opposed to what it perceives to be disproportionately high amounts spent on higher education by African governments, the burden of university education is being shifted from the government to the student beneficiaries and their families. In the long run, the total burden of paying for food and lodging, estimated at about $200 per student per annum, or half of per capita income, is to be shifted to parents. Critics view this policy thrust as a prelude to the real intention of the government and the Bank, which is to de-emphasize state-sponsored higher education while at the same time emphasizing non-residential secondary schools and universities. The rationale is that non-residential campuses would enable more students to be admitted and lead to more efficient use of limited resources.[48]

In the short term, part of the financing will come from a shifting of budget priorities away from the highly subsidized university system, which was receiving about 60 per cent of the education budget. Moreover, according to Nicholas Bennett, the Bank's education and planning officer for the Africa desk, Ghanaian universities spend 16 per cent of their budgets on feeding and lodging students, 40 per cent on municipal services, including the salaries of cooks and gardeners, and only 25 per cent on academic services, with the rest spent on administration.[49]

In the long term, however, both the donors and the PNDC government expect the sector as a whole to become self-financing as the reform progresses. As a result, cost-recovery measures are being instituted at all levels, especially at the tertiary level. These measures have taken the form of retrenchment of non-teaching staff; freezing teaching staff levels while student enrolments rise; a two-step elimination of residential and boarding subsidies at secondary and tertiary levels; increasing book-user fees at secondary and tertiary levels; a loan/scholarship system for indigent students; and reduction of financial embezzlement. The new educational ethos envisages a partnership between the private sector, the state, and international donors. The JSS, in particular, is viewed as a 'community school', to be partly financed by the local government and the community. Ultimately, the community is not only expected to make the JSS self-supporting by providing the necessary capital and equipment but also to help in the teaching of vocational and cultural subjects. Parents, local businesses and churches are expected to become partners in the running of the schools.

In many respects, the Ghanaian education sector adjustment programme is commendable not simply because it is trendy, but because it is imaginative, practical and catholic in its curriculum coverage. It points in the right direction, by seeking to achieve educational relevance, make the system sustainable from domestic sources and, with relevance and sustainability achieved, to attract more students into the classroom and recover the glory days of Ghanaian education. As one analyst has observed, 'It is easy to see why the JSS initiative has attracted the attention of development agencies and loosened the purse-strings of the European funders. It is an ambitious, imaginative and potentially workable plan and is based on some concrete, progressive educational premises'.[50]

OBJECTIONS TO THE REFORM PACKAGE

While the goals of educational reform and the restructuring of elementary and secondary education have generally been applauded, parts of the reform package have generated intense debate and controversy. The reform of higher education has been the most contentious. University students have been galvanized into protest action over what they perceive to be a concerted effort to devalue rather than enhance higher education. Their protests have already led to the shutting down of the universities on numerous occasions.

Campus criticism of the government's university reforms revolve around the 'cost-recovery costs', to borrow Bentsi-Enchill's felicitous phrase. The students have protested the new 'pay as you go' educational ethos of the government on the grounds that shifting the burden of boarding and lodging to parents would drive poorer students out of school. The non-residential policy would be similarly discriminatory, because the universities are concentrated in the three main cities and thus favour urban students or those with strong urban ties. It would raise the cost of higher education for residents of rural areas who would be forced to pay high prices for rent as well as contend with the vagaries of the transportation system. Furthermore, they have expressed opposition to the loan scheme because it would merely postpone the burden until they begin gainful employment even though their salaries are unlikely to be enough to feed their families, if current trends continue.

It is interesting to note that the students seem to be supported by Akilagpa Sawyerr, a serious-minded educator and former Vice-Chancellor of University of Ghana-Legon. Dr Sawyerr acknowledges that the introduction of the cost-recovery concept in education is 'an extension of the process of privatization' spreading through the national economy (hospital fees, abolition of subsidies, attacks on state enterprises, etc). He concedes that these measures may be individually defensible on economic grounds, but worries that their combined effects 'foreshadow a basic change in the way social costs are allocated' in Ghanaian society. Hence, 'it is time Ghanaians take a close look at these trends and their implications' for the political and social development of Ghana and assess their impact on social relations.[51]

At the secondary level, while the JSS and SSS reforms have generally been well received, some nettlesome issues associated with their implementation and consequences remain. Writing from her excellent vantage point as a new recruit from Britain, working, as it were, on the front lines of the education adjustment programme in Tamale, Northern

Region, in 1987, Helen Scadding made a number of very perceptive observations. She noted that the new system is likely to intensify the pressures on teaching staffs in a situation in which teachers already feel undervalued and unmotivated, with many coming to teaching as a second- or third-choice career and many aiming to 'get out'. She noted that while the recent improvements in teaching salaries will help, they are not sufficient to overcome the serious staff shortage that many schools now face. Without additional teachers, the already high pupil–teacher ratio will be even greater. The prospect of yet larger class sizes is a distinct possibility, especially if the reforms succeed in expanding access.

In Tamale, the acute staff shortage has led to a doubling and tripling of teaching loads. Moreover, teachers have been grouped into three curriculum areas: one language and arts based, one science and mathematics, and one cultural and vocational studies. As a result,

> Many English teachers now find, for example, that they are expected to teach French, social studies and a Ghanaian language, without even initial qualifications in these subjects. Inevitably with low motivation and a total lack of training, many students will suffer from either inadequate teaching or no teaching at all in these subjects . . . teachers have less time for each subject and are increasingly under pressure to cover the syllabus which has been laid out by the Ghanaian Government for every subject.[52]

These observations echo one of Dr Sawyerr's earlier cautions about the lack of a credible programme for training, on a serious, sustained basis, the kind of new teacher required for the new system. Without an adequately trained and motivated teaching cadre, the new system can be expected to reproduce the old.[53] Lack of ongoing training remains an unresolved problem. A compulsory two-week training course took place across the whole country in the summer of 1987 to outline the philosophy of JSS and discuss the syllabi. However, that proved woefully inadequate. The participating teachers worked through every subject *en masse* and there was no time to discuss specifics. As Scadding lamented:

> Despite the Government's claim to provide further in-service training, I am unaware of any being provided in the Northern district, except my own training courses and those of my colleague in mathematics. Most teachers feel they have been left to get on with it. In a country with few telephones, difficult transport, a hesitant postal service and a struggling administration, the isolation of working in a rural school can be quite extreme. Teachers can work, or not work, for whole terms without receiving a visitor, an inspector, a trainer, an advisor, a meeting, a talk or a letter. There are no resource centres, few working associations and no acknowledged forums for discussion.[54]

On the issue of relevance, Dr. Sawyerr insists that there is no 'scientific basis' to the notion that you can 'predispose' junior and senior secondary pupils to agricultural, vocational, and technical work: 'so long as selling dog chains or imported apples along the streets of Accra, or opening a kiosk anywhere, proves more lucrative and requires less capital outlay than farming or tool-making', the JSS and SSS products will drift into trading, and youth unemployment will persist.[55]

Relatedly, Scadding takes issue with the vocational studies curriculum. From the perspective of the government: 'This basic education is not to train children for specific jobs or vocations, but to give them exposure to a wide variety of ideas and skills.'[56] However, in the absence of equal opportunity 'watch-dogs' in Ghana, Scadding's fear that 'vocational studies' will mean training for 'jobs for the boys' and domestic service for the girls merits serious consideration. Her contention is that:

> Most of the new equipment for vocational studies is for metalwork and carpentry, which few, if any, girls will study . . . the danger of 'vocational' education at such a young age (about 11 years), as in Britain, is that the supposed widening of choice that education can bring to bear on a child's future life is removed through the child effectively being channelled into a particular field of employment. . . . At its worst it may handicap those who wish to pursue an academic career, confuse the less academic with a plethora of subjects, narrow the choices of girls and perhaps falsely raise the expectations of boys, training them for jobs they may well be unable to pursue.[57]

Another significant issue facing the education reform programme is how to lay the scientific and technological foundations for Ghana's future development. In this connection, the absence of specific provisions to encourage pre-university science education has been viewed with alarm. In the current situation, the universities are unable to fill all places for science and science-based courses with qualified applicants. Meanwhile, the proposed 5 per cent increase in university admission will worsen the ratio of science-to-humanities graduates. This objective reality makes a mockery of the government's own 1987 promotional brochure, 'Things you need to know about the JSS programme', which asserts that 'Today's world is a scientific and technological one, and the barest minimum education for every Ghanaian child must tune his or her mind to this fact, so that the children can understand and live competently in today's world.'[58]

If inadequate attention has been paid to effective science education under the new system despite the official rhetoric, gender stereotyping in science, mathematics, and technology education is likely to exacerbate the gender gap. The director-general of the Ghana Education Service (GES), Professor J.S. Djangmah, notes that the low percentage of women in the science-based professions is a worldwide concern. He attributes this situation to societal prejudices that have built up over a very long period of time. He observed that most of the few women in the sciences go into the biological sciences such as home and food sciences, as opposed to the physical sciences. He argues that the root of the problem is that not enough girls take STM courses. To illustrate the problem, he cites the results of the 1986 Advanced Level examinations which showed that of the 3,133 students who took physics, 315 were girls; of 3,201 who took chemistry, 340 were girls. However, of 980 students who did English literature, there were 479 girls and 501 boys.[59]

Conclusion

In this chapter I have attempted to present an overview of how far African education has come and to illustrate how severe recessionary pressures have undermined the educational systems and eroded earlier gains in Ghana, as elsewhere in Africa, and made them ripe for official and international donor resolution through various forms of privatization, euphemistically called cost-recovery measures. The lesson from the Ghanaian experience is that Africa needs to proceed with caution toward educational privatization. In this era of democratization, officials need to involve the grass roots in serious, open, public dialogue about the development priorities of their societies in order to fashion education systems that fit those priorities. In the meantime, it is worth recalling that not all the theoretical promises of privatization are likely to be translatable into practical benefits. Particularly in the area of primary and secondary education, an unabashed application of privatization could seriously affect social relations and jeopardize the chances of orderly nation-building. Africa would do well to heed the warning about privatization and the American political firmament so eloquently articulated by Robert Bailey:

> Privatization adds another policy instrument to the tools of the public manager and policymaker. If fully aware of the hidden costs, the potential for failure, and the inadequate guarantees for obtaining the efficiencies that theory indicates will accrue, policymakers can decide to privatize. For the public manager, it should not be a matter of ideology, however, but of informed judgment based on experience in public management and on policy analyses more exacting than is currently presented by advocates of

privatization. . . .Americans let the market establish the price of pork bellies, not the future of children. . . .Privatization will be applied only to things that the American people are not willing to risk; that includes every policy and program that several generations have put into place to protect themselves from the whims, uncertainties, instabilities, and unintended consequences of the marketplace.[60]

The nub of the Ghanaian debate is whether the reforms will resolve the inequities in the old system of education while making the new education relevant to national development. While the jury is still out, given the recency of the reforms, there are issues that await serious national debate, some of which have been raised above. Among that mix, the issue of access is crucial, as already suggested. In that regard, let us recall that access to SSS is not automatic. It is still governed by examination. In which case, the private or 'international' schools will still be in a better position to provide their students with the best chances of 'making it' to SSS in historically prestigious institutions which, in turn, will ensure that going to the university becomes

> almost a matter of course. They will find the friendships made at school coming in very handy in this world of 'old boy networks' (witness the charges that have been made to the effect that too many members of the present government are old Achimotans).[61]

In other words, while the reforms abolish middle schools and give everybody a nine-year JSS education, replete with vocational training, the programme fails to resolve the basic dichotomy between low- and high-status schools associated with the old order. There are still low- and high-status JSS, with most girls and rural and low-income urban boys likely to be found in the low-status JSS. Philip Foster's assessment of the situation is just as valid today as it was before the reforms.

> Thus, competition for access to the intermediate and higher educational sectors will increase, and if this analysis is correct, then it is the children of the elite of new 'middle classes' who will take advantage of the situation, not only through their possibly higher levels of academic performance, but because their parents know how to use and manipulate the educational system.[62]

At this juncture the community emphasis does not hold out much promise for overcoming the inequalities. Differential community resources are likely to translate most powerfully into differential facilities, funds, and performance. For, as Scadding has testified,[63] 'educated' Ghanaians often live in close proximity to each other, near large educational establishments, and, as in Britain, such parents fund their

children's education generously. Hence, the inequalities that already exist
in Ghana may become entrenched by the community funding of junior
secondary schools. Scadding confirms that

> it is not uncommon to visit one school that is literally a series of empty,
> dusty rooms and then enter a neighbouring school that has an equipped
> staff-room, supplies of wood and tools and wall displays. If communities are
> to play a large part in the funding of JSS, it is imperative that the
> Government ensures that some basic equity of facilities is achieved. If not,
> 'community involvement', as in Britain, may become a misnomer for the
> beginnings of an unequal privatization of education.[64]

Notes

1. World Bank, *Sub-Saharan Africa: From Crisis to Sustainable Growth*
    (Washington, DC: World Bank, 1989), 81.
2. 'Editorial: The Mirage of Education', *West Africa* 3657 (14 September
    1987): 1771.
3. Keith Hinchliffe, *Higher Education in Sub-Saharan Africa* (London: Croom
    Helm, 1987), 8.
4. See Donald Rothchild, 'Ghana and Structural Adjustment: An Overview',
    in Donald Rothchild (ed.), *Ghana: The Political Economy of Recovery*
    (Boulder, CO and London: Lynne Rienner, 1991), 3-17.
5. Nii K. Bentsi-Enchill, 'Cost-recovery Costs', *West Africa* 3621 (2 February
    1987): 192-4; Colleen Lowe Morna, 'An Exercise in Educational Reform',
    Africa Report 34, no. 6 (1989): 34-7.
6. To be sure, there are disparities, sometimes considerable at that, between the
    educational achievements of African states. These disparities are to be
    expected, given differential resource endowments, regime and leadership
    capabilities as well as the interests of the governments in power.
7. Jennifer Seymour Whitaker, *How Can Africa Survive?* (New York: Council
    on Foreign Relations, 1988), 38-40. As Whitaker points out, the colonial
    governments tried to upstage the new nationalist leaders who were promising
    to let wealth and privilege flow once the Europeans left by unveiling their
    own belated programmes to deliver elementary education, clinics, and social
    amenities more broadly.
8. 'Editorial', *West Africa* 3657 (14 September 1987): 1771; Maxwell
    Nwagboso, 'Nigeria: Education in the Doldrums', *West Africa* 3668 (30
    November 1987): 2342-43.
9. Hinchliffe, *Higher Education in Sub-Saharan Africa*, 5-6.
10. Ibid., 6.
11. Joel Samoff, John Metzler and Tahir Salie, 'Education and Development:
    Deconstructing a Myth to Construct Reality', in Ann Seidman and Frederick
    Anang (eds), *Towards a New Vision of Self-Sustainable Development*

(Trenton, NJ: Red Sea Press, 1992), 105.

12. See note 2 above.
13. Hinchliffe, *Higher Education in Sub-Saharan Africa*, 7–8.
14. Robert Price, 'Politics and Culture in Contemporary Ghana: The Big Man Small Boy Syndrome', *Journal of Modern African Studies* 1, no. 2 (Summer 1974): 173–204.
15. Samoff et al., 'Education and Development', 105.
16. Not surprisingly, it was honoured more in the breach. Sierra Leone, for example, announced the introduction of free primary education in 1987, a full seven years after all African countries were expected to have implemented universal primary education. See *West Africa* 3657 (14 September 1987): 1771. In Liberia, 'compulsory education has been on the books since 1912, but you cannot compel anyone to go to school unless you have enough schools and teachers who are given the necessary incentives. If you want quality education, we must pay proper salaries'. See James Butty, 'Liberia: Education and National Change', *West Africa* 3657 (14 September 1987): 1788.
17. Lois Weis, 'Schooling and Patterns of Access in Ghana', *Canadian Journal of African Studies* 15, no. 2 (1981): 311–22; John Bibby and Margaret Peil, 'Secondary Education in Ghana: Private Enterprise and Social Selection', *Comparative Education Review* 47, no. 3 (Summer 1974): 339–418; Philip Foster, 'Education and Social Inequality in Sub-Saharan Africa', *Journal of Modern African Studies* 18, no. 2 (June 1980): 201–36.
18. See 'What Kind of Reform', *West Africa* 3618 (12 January 1987): 68–70.
19. Hinchliffe, *Higher Education in Sub-Saharan Africa*, 170.
20. R.E. McKown and David J. Finlay, 'Ghana's Status Systems: Reflections on University and Society', *Journal of Asian and African Studies* 11 (July–October 1974): 166–79.
21. Ibid.; see also Remi Clignet, 'Ethnicity, Social Differentiation, and Secondary Schooling in West Africa', *Cahiers d'études africaines* 7, no. 26 (1967): 360–78.
22. Lois Weis, 'The Reproduction of Social Inequality: Closure in the Ghanaian University', *Journal of Developing Areas* 16, no. 1 (October 1981): 21–22.
23. Daphne Topouzis, 'The Feminization of Poverty', *Africa Report* 35, no. 3 (July–August 1990): 63.
24. Ibid., 63.
25. My own research has shown that presented with the choice most rural mothers tend to fund the education of their sons. This may be perfectly rational, given limited financial resources, household needs and employment prospects after schooling. This rational choice is also structured by the perception that education is essentially designed to land a bureaucratic job afterwards, and not too many of these jobs are available for women beyond clerical or secretarial tasks. It is not surprising that most of the few women at the university also come from relatively affluent, more urban, households. For fascinating parallels, see Ngugi wa Thion'o, *Weep Not Child* (London:

Heinemann, 1964) and Camara Laye, *The African Child* (London: Collins: 1954).

26. Thomas Cooke, 'The Nub of the Debate', *West Africa* 3657 (14 September 1987): 1792.

27. Ibid.

28. Morna, 'An Exercise in Educational Reform', 35.

29. Ibid.

30. For a devastating critique of the Nigerian case, this time at the university level, see Julius O. Ihonvbere, 'The State and Academic Freedom in Africa: How African Academics Subvert Academic', paper presented at the Annual Meeting of the African Studies Association, St. Louis, Missouri, November 1991.

31. Richard Marvin, '"Economic Baba": Is This a Satisfactory Explanation of Why African Parents Value Schooling?', *Journal of Modern African Studies* 13, no. 3 (September 1975): 429–45.

32. Morna, 'An Exercise in Educational Reform', 35.

33. Weis, 'Schooling and Patterns of Access in Ghana', 311–22; 'The Reproduction of Social Inequality'. It is interesting to note that ethnic and social selectivity does not necessarily decline as the educational system expands. Equality of ethnic opportunity does not necessarily translate into equality of outcome, as evidenced by data from Ghana and Côte d'Ivoire. Selectivity by socio-economic background was more pronounced in Ghana than in Côte d'Ivoire, even though Ghana provided far greater opportunities for secondary schooling. For more on this, see Clignet, 'Ethnicity, Social Differentiation, and Secondary Schooling', 360–78; Philip Foster, 'Ethnicity and the Schools in Ghana', *Comparative Education Review* 6, no. 2 (October 1962): 127–35; Jahoda Gustav, 'The Social Background of a West African Student Population: I', *British Journal of Sociology* 5, no. 4 (December 1954): 355–65; and McKown and Finlay, 'Ghana's Status Systems', 166–79.

34. World Bank, *Sub-Saharan Africa*, 77.

35. K. Twum-Barima, 'The University Dilemma', *West Africa* 3657 (14 September 1987): 1785. While this emphasis may have been warranted during the formative years of independence when Africa needed to produce people to fill new bureaucratic positions, by the early 1980s a bloated bureaucracy had become part of the development nightmare. The schools had become machines for churning out bureaucrats, who are largely consumption-oriented, not to say parasitic, instead of training students who could act as effective agents of production.

36. Even with these subventions, the actual and hidden costs of supporting a child through secondary school in particular are not inconsequential and can put a severe strain on limited household budgets. This, along with various opportunity costs, explains the differential rates of school attendance by households in Ghana as elsewhere in Africa.

37. Cyril K. Daddieh, 'The Management of Educational Crises in Côte d'Ivoire', *Journal of Modern African Studies* 26, no. 4 (December 1988):

639–59; 'Education, Politics, Traditions, and the Future of Africa', Black History Month Lecture Series, Salisbury State University, 19 February 1992.

38. See 'Editorial', *West Africa* 3657 (14 September 1987): 1771; 'Falling Public Spending Reverses Gains in African Education', *Africa Recovery* 6, no. 1 (April 1992): 12–13; 'Dialogue or Force', *West Africa* 3628 (23 March 1987): 556–57; Helen Scadding, 'Junior Secondary Schools – An Educational Initiative in Ghana', *Compare* 19, no. 1 (1989): 43–48.

39. Morna, 'An Exercise in Educational Reform', 34–35.

40. 'Falling Public Spending', *Africa Recovery* 6, no. 1 (April 1992): 12–13.

41. Morna, 'An Exercise in Educational Reform', 34.

42. James Cobbe, 'The Political Economy of Education Reform in Ghana', in Donald Rothchild (ed.), *Ghana: The Political Economy of Recovery* (Boulder, CO and London: Lynne Rienner, 1991), 105.

43. Nwagboso, 'Nigeria', 2342.

44. Morna, 'An Exercise in Educational Reform', 35.

45. Cobbe, 'The Political Economy of Education Reform in Ghana', 104. The Nkrumah government's Seven Year Development Plan of 1964 had envisaged the reforms adopted by the PNDC government. The fact that both the 1964 and 1974 plans were shelved until now may provide fascinating insights into interest group struggles and crisis versus non-crisis situations policy making in Ghana as elsewhere in Africa.

46. Scadding, 'Junior Secondary Schools', 43–48; Cobbe, 'The Political Economy of Education Reform in Ghana', 101–115.

47. Morna, 'An Exercise in Educational Reform', 37.

48. A $140-a-year loan scheme had been established to assist indigent students. The loan was to be repaid at 3 per cent annual interest when students commenced working following graduation. The scheme had provoked vehement opposition by the students, who argued that it was a terrible idea at a time when salaries where insufficient to pay even a family food bill. Student graffiti at the University of Science and Technology (UST) dubbed the loan scheme as the 'devil's alternatives'. See Morna, 'An Exercise in Educational Reform', 37.

49. Ibid., 36. As part of the restructuring exercise, a six-member University Rationalization Committee was set up to make recommended changes. The Committee consisted of Esi Sutherland-Addy, Under Secretary for Education and Culture, three representatives of the three universities, a Legon-based education consultant and a nominee of the World Bank.

50. Scadding, 'Junior Secondary Schools', 45.

51. Bentsi-Enchill, 'Cost-recovery Costs', 193.

52. Scadding, 'Junior Secondary Schools', 45.

53. Bentsi-Enchill, 'Cost-recovery Costs', 193.

54. Scadding, 'Junior Secondary Schools', 45-46.

55. Bentsi-Enchill, 'Cost-recovery Costs', 192-93.

56. Scadding, 'Junior Secondary Schools', 48.

57. Ibid., 47.

58. Ibid., 44.
59. In its forty-year history, Legon had produced only two women mathematics honours students (one works at the West African Examinations Council in Accra and the other teaches at Achimota School). In an effort to correct this anomaly, the government organized a science, technology and mathematics clinic for girls under the auspices of the Ghana Education Services (GES) with the support of UNESCO from 22 August to 5 September 1987. See Ajoa Yeboah-Afari, 'Ghana: Science for Girls', *West Africa* 3661 (12 October 1987): 2018.
60. Robert W. Bailey, 'Uses and Misuses of Privatization', in Steve H. Hanke (ed.), *Prospects for Privatization* (New York: Proceedings of the Academy of Political Science, 1987), 151–52.
61. Cooke, 'The Nub of the Debate', 1792.
62. Philip Foster, 'Education and Social Inequality in Sub-Saharan Africa', *The Journal of Modern African Studies* 18 no. 2 (June 1980): 201–36.
63. Scadding, 'Junior Secondary Schools', 47.
64. Ibid., 47–48.

4

Can Sub-Saharan Africa Successfully Privatize Its Health Care Sector?

B. Ikubolajeh Logan

Introduction

The position taken in this chapter is that fundamental structural difficulties which are common to sub-Saharan African economies (subsequently referred to merely as Africa) preclude the widespread use of the market mechanism as an efficient allocator of scarce resources. Further, the allocative difficulties that typically ensue from these structural bottlenecks generally have lasting and far-reaching negative human resource consequences. Building upon these initial contentions, the chapter outlines the broad conceptual thesis that due to the heavy reliance of privatization on the market mechanism for its successful implementation, the strategy possesses a limited potential for initiating and sustaining improvements in health care delivery in Africa.

The discussion in the chapter is guided by three general arguments. First, that privatization is an economic and not a social welfare development strategy, and that its reliance on a benevolent market mechanism to generate positive ripple effects into the social welfare domain is problematic. Second, that privatization addresses resource ownership and distribution within a Western market environment but fails to accommodate the broader socio-cultural structures within which resource exchange occurs in Africa. Third, that privatization is not a political strategy, and that the implicit assumption that Africa's economic outlook can improve without dramatic reorganization of the political economy is problematic. In summary, the chapter follows the argument that, due to the inherent difficulties described above, privatization has limited potential for distributing health care in Africa. Further, that its implementation can neither correct present inequities and shortcomings in Africa's public health systems, nor can it provide a better distributive alternative.

Advocates of privatization question the justification of the hypotheses in the previous section for their intrinsic criticism of the capabilities of the market mechanism.[1] The view shared by such market liberalizationists is that many of the problems that have typically been attributed to the market are, in fact, caused by interventionist public policies. Their advocacy for the market is predicated on the supposition that low rates of economic performance under market strategies have been caused directly by public sector shortcomings: managerial incompetence within SOEs, market distortions through financial market regulations, control and misappropriation of equity funds, seriously manipulated foreign exchange allocative systems and crowding out by public sector borrowing. Although these arguments cannot be summarily dismissed, it is difficult to find definitive support for them in Africa's post-independence economic experience. In fact, the converse case can be made with equal justification; namely, that many forms of government intervention are necessitated by the rigidities of the market mechanisms, and its proclivity to bypass some political economy and social problems that are central to Africa's development crisis. The failure of market-based strategies (growth pole, vent for surplus, import substitution, to name a few) may be explained, therefore, by the need of governments to intervene and arbitrate in market structures that are, at best, nascent, and at worst, weakly developed or developing. Although the jury is still out, there is little theoretical or empirical ground to expect that, like its market precursors, privatization can operate effectively within the basic structural frameworks in Africa. Analyses of recent successes in Mauritius and Botswana with market-led economic policies are not quite conclusive.[2] Thus, it is difficult to determine whether economic progress should be credited primarily to the market or more directly to government intervention. The indeterminateness of the 'proper' mix of market and policy that will generate and sustain economic progress suggests that policy makers and institutional advocates of market-led development must demonstrate caution and pragmatism regarding their expectations concerning privatization. Deliberations about privatized health, for example, should be prescribed by concern over the abilities of the market to facilitate health care delivery to the mass of the population in the peasant and informal sectors where fully developed market structures are not yet in place.

Africa's health crisis

Most measures of basic health suggest that the substandard health and hygiene conditions which are now endemic to many parts of Africa are major threats to the development agenda going into the twenty-first century. Although rates of natural increase are high and are expected to continue to increase for much of the twenty-first century, total population growth is likely to be dampened by poor health conditions, amongst other factors. Mortality rates, especially for infants, are also far above world levels.[3] The population that survives childhood has become increasingly malnourished during the 1970s and 1980s as environmental, military and political difficulties have exerted their toll on different regions of the continent. For example, the World Health Organization estimates that in any given year, the nutritional status of most Africans is between 45 and 75 per cent of basic recommended levels. Other estimates are equally pessimistic. Espenshade places African countries amongst those suffering from serious malnutrition and/or hunger, with low caloric intake and low levels of animal and vegetable protein in typical diets.[4]

The health deficiencies described above are often compounded by poor access to preventive and curative health care. Africa, therefore, has one of the worst health conditions in the world. Medical managers and other human and physical health infrastructure are in short supply and are far below those of other developing regions. Africa's life expectancies are also amongst the lowest in the world. Even in relatively affluent economies like Côte d'Ivoire, Cameroon, Gabon and Kenya, life expectancies are below 60 years,[5] and the health outlook remains gloomy for the future.

Some assessments of African development suggest factors like domestic economic stagnation, misguided government policies, conspicuous public spending and a disproportionate allocation of resources to the military are at the root of Africa's poor health record.[6] The Economic Commission for Africa reports that average public expenditure on health care for African countries during the mid-1980s was only $7 per capita; compared to $26 per capita for Latin America and $75 per capita for Asia.[7] The International Monetary Fund (IMF) also reports that absolute government health expenditures and health expenditures as a percentage of total government expenditures have declined consistently through the 1980s and early 1990s for most African countries.[8]

Increasingly, however, some, both in academia and in policy formulation, are linking the human development woes of Africa to privatization and other economic adjustment packages that are being championed by the World Bank and the IMF.[9] Their major criticism is that austerity programmes impose harsh socio-economic conditions that are borne disproportionately by the poor, women and children – that very segment of Africa's population that is most in need of public assistance to meet its basic needs. Unfortunately, this line of enquiry has failed to associate Africa's recent human resource dilemma with some fundamental tensions that exist between the market system, on the one hand, and the economic/cultural background, on the other. It would seem that this aspect of the discourse must be addressed in its proper empirical context if the role, if any, of adjustment in undermining welfare conditions in Africa is to be established.

Public health care delivery in sub-Saharan Africa

In general, the health care system in many African countries is characterized by two separate, yet interrelated components – a traditional, private, informal subsystem made of herbalists, seers and midwives; and a modern, public/semi-private, formalized subsystem. The two are juxtaposed spatially and socially in a structure of medical pluralism which takes a variety of forms, as noted by Gesler.[10] In Zaire, they exist in equality; in Ethiopia, the links are more tenuous;[11] while in Sierra Leone, the two are mutually supportive. In this last and more common case in Africa, Western health care is dominant among the affluent (urban and rural) populations, while the rural and poor populations have access largely and primarily to traditional health care. Even among the urbanized populations, Western and traditional medicine may coexist as patrons migrate from one system to the other, depending on economic conditions, whether the disease is considered African or 'white men's', traditional beliefs, and the availability and renown of practitioners.[12]

Most of Africa's population, especially those in rural areas, have no access to modern health facilities and must depend on the traditional health sector for their basic health needs, even though traditional science is very general and can be extremely inaccurate in the case of some serious ailments. The widespread use of traditional cures, therefore, has serious limitations for improving health care. As a result, a vigorous modern health care system aimed specifically at the poor, must be seen to be a matter of urgent national and regional security.

Unfortunately, existing public health programmes throughout much of Africa show little promise of fulfilling these important mandates. Public programmes in Africa, almost without exception, are beset by a multiplicity of problems. Although the development plans coming out of Africa are regularly committed to the humanitarian attributes of health care delivery, what the 1978 Alma-Ata Conference of WHO and UNICEF declared to be 'a fundamental right',[13] capital scarcity has often limited the ability of governments to provide universal or satisfactory health care to a large proportion of their citizens. The post-colonial experience in health care delivery in Africa is typically a list of malfeasances: many establishments are understaffed; management is hindered by corruption; necessary equipment is not always available, and even when it is, it may not function properly. The following observation about the delivery of prescription drugs in West Africa captures the seriousness of the situation.

> [T]he problem with medical supplies like drugs is not that they are unavailable. The distribution and sale of drugs is usually not controlled. The places that should have supplies, like hospitals and clinics are chronically short of them. Drugs may be stolen or given away as favor to friends. . . . In these countries [in West Africa] people who went to government facilities for free or low cost treatment were often told that they must go to a pharmacy for drugs that the facility should have in stock.[14]

At present, subsidized medical care in Sierra Leone, even in Freetown, involves only diagnoses. Patrons must buy their own drugs and other supplies necessary for their treatment.

The public health programmes in much of Africa may also be indicted for a geographical bias, reflected first in the concentration of facilities in a few urban places and second in the pull of rural facilities toward regions that have political allegiance with the central authority. This type of endemic organizational and spatial dysfunction causes reduced accessibility (in travel time and cost), unnecessarily high costs for treatment and follow-up examinations, and a generally substandard service.

The inefficiencies of public health systems have allowed for substantial inroads by private practitioners. Consequently, there is a noticeable coexistence of public and private enterprises. Health components such as laundry, food and drugs are contracted and sub-contracted by governments to private companies, and private doctors, and other modern health professionals operate in the same market in which public health is provided. In spite of these developments, modern health care in Africa remains the purview of the public sector governments, and the quality of health care is tied directly to the efficiency of public programmes.

In summary, health care delivery in Africa may be divided into traditional, and modern Western systems. Most of the populations depend on the traditional system, which is cheap and easily accessible. Many at the margins of the urban sector and even some of the so-called urban élite utilize traditional cures – the former, depending on national economic conditions, the latter for what are considered to be 'non-white man' diseases and illnesses. The modern health sector, on the other hand, is dominated by governments, but services are bedeviled by serious management inefficiencies, a geographical bias against rural communities in favour of larger towns, and a general politicization of the location–allocation process. As a result, the private sector has become an important provider of modern health care, especially in major cities and towns.

An important question at this juncture is whether the market mechanism can spread its influence beyond the urban areas to facilitate modern health care delivery to rural communities and the poor. Essentially, will privatized enterprises be able to distribute modern health care to a larger population in a more efficient manner, in a shorter period of time than would occur under the existing public programmes? There is no definitive answer to this question, especially in the absence of hard empirical evidence. From a purely theoretical perspective, one should expect privatization to result in more efficiently operated facilities (better management and supplies). However, it is not clear that this will be translated automatically into improved social and geographic accessibility for the populations that are presently disenfranchised. The reasons for this pessimistic outlook are explored in more detail in the next two sections.

Privatization and public health:
some theoretical concerns

Privatization covers a wide range of social, economic and political activities.[15] It may also be described generally to include all methods through which public organizations, which were originally designed to provide goods and services to maximize social welfare objectives, are restructured (or change ownership) to provide the same or similar goods and services in response to market conditions. The rationale for the privatization of state-owned or operated enterprises (SOEs) is ostensibly to improve their efficiency by increasing their financial, economic and social profitability.[16] As Heald notes also, the transfer of ownership to the private sector to meet these ends may take one of several forms: 1) sale of an SOE as a single unit; 2) sale of all of the dismantled components of an SOE; 3) sale of only some of the dismantled components of an SOE; 4) sale of non-core units of an SOE.

Besides the sale of government assets, privatization may also be accomplished through liberalization or deregulation of government controls on industries, franchising, contracting and sub-contracting.[17] Walker emphasizes that privatization is a package that covers a range of complementary strategies.

> . . . privatization is not simply a matter of the full transfer of ownership from the state to private enterprises . . . privatization represents the introduction or further extension of market principles in the public social services . . . privatization may be said to take place when responsibility for a service or a particular aspect of service delivery passes wholly, or in part, to the private sector and when market criteria, such as profit or ability to pay are used to ration or distribute benefits and services.[18]

The aim of market liberalization strategies, including privatization, is to increase earning capacity through efficient management geared toward market optimization. Thus, under privatization, an inefficient SOE can be transformed into an entity that generates capital for overall economic development. Therefore, privatization is not merely geared toward market liberalization as an end in itself, it is seen as an important and critical means toward the end of development.

IS HEALTH CARE A MERIT OR A PUBLIC GOOD?

At the root of the debate over the privatization of health care and other social welfare facilities lies some serious ethical questions concerning the general attributes of private versus public goods and services.[19] Public goods are identified as those which are provided primarily to satisfy general social ends and are, therefore, closely associated with public sector provision of social services. In an earlier contribution, Townsend notes that public sector allocative mechanisms are:

> those means developed and institutionalized by society to promote ends which are wholly or primarily social. The ends include social justice; freedom from oppression; prevention of disease; abolition of poverty and squalor; integration in the community; harmony between races; equality of educational opportunity; full employment and especially social equality.[20]

Le Grand and Robinson point out that the state can engage in activities to meet these multifarious socio-political goals through outright provision of goods and services, subsidies, or regulations and legislation.[21] The objectives of the public sector and the methods employed to meet them are usually different from those of the private sector. In the latter, demand is often defined by purchasing power and not by the actual needs of different segments of society.[22] In fact, it has been observed that the market may actually promote inefficiency by allowing high-income segments of society to misuse services like electricity and water supply.[23] At the other extreme, the market can also engender poverty by reducing or eliminating the bidding power of low-income populations for important basic needs services.

Walker[24] suggests that it is too simplistic to employ a rigid distinction between public and private goods since most economies are characterized by a *mixed economy of welfare* which possesses three important attributes: i) some services, which may be defined as social in orientation, are offered by both public and private enterprises (for example, health, education, water, electricity and transportation); ii) both sectors are interlinked in terms of decision making; decisions made in the public sector have a direct impact on decision making in the private sector and vice versa; iii) many public enterprises operate under a market or quasi-market mechanism. Despite these areas of overlap, Walker reiterates that the mechanisms by which each sector operates and the bases upon which each is established are markedly different.

> In the public sector, benefits and services are funded wholly or predominantly on the basis of general taxation and administered partly on the basis of non-market criteria such as need. In the private sector, benefits and services depend on individual contribution, and are administered according to market principles, primarily the profit motive.[25]

Due to these somewhat diametrically opposed objectives, public and private sector allocative mechanisms should not be regarded as substitutes but rather as alternatives. To adopt one, by and large, therefore, entails the adoption of a set of societal goals that are usually inconsistent with those of the other. An important element of this discussion, then, rests upon determining whether the objective of an enterprise is to provide 'private goods', 'merit goods' or 'social/public goods'. As Leonard puts it:

> a pure private good exits when both the exclusion and rival principles are at work. . . . Pure social goods are those to which neither applies. . . . Any time exclusion is not possible, we are in a condition of market failure and there is a free rider problem. Pressure then exists to make the social good a public one, that is to involve the state in its provision.[26]

In the case of health care, Roth identifies pest eradication to be an example of a pure public good, while merit goods in this sector include immunization of children, and pre-natal and postnatal clinics.[27] The latter are services whose 'merit' qualify them for government involvement to ensure their proper and sufficient allocation to all segments of society.

Bokhari argues that distinctions based on government involvement lose much of their relevance in an age when most governments are actively engaged in domestic and international trade (providing pure private goods);[28] act as manipulators of trade mechanisms through protectionist policies; and are sometimes forced by political expediency to adopt an adversarial position against trade mechanisms (domestic social policies and some forms of international aid may fall under the last rubric). A further complication noted by Heald and Sugden is that public and merit goods are not restricted to statals and parastatals.[29] Non-profit organizations and even some private firms are involved in the provision of these types of goods, both in the domestic and international economies.

Ideological concerns also enter the debate.[30] Domberger and Piggott suggest, for example, that the *Berg Report* of 1981 established a political environment within which privatization became politicized.[31] In that climate, regimes that adopted privatization were associated not only with the free market, but also with democracy (the latter without much empirical justification). By contrast, reluctance to privatize was interpreted to be a Marxist or socialist disapproval of the free-market system.

How do these debates relate to the specific characteristics of health care delivery? The evidence from Britain, which has experimented with privatization, suggests that the shift from public to private health care can be quite a complex implementation task even in a developed market economy. According to Maynard and Williams,[32] conditions in the National Health Service (NHS) in Britain indicate that health care, like other areas of social welfare, experiences overlapping activities between the public and private sectors. They argue that it is difficult to distinguish between public and private health care because the NHS has always been complemented by privately practising physicians, and because traditionally, it has also sub-contracted the production of drugs, medical equipment and supplies to private firms. They link privatization to politics by suggesting that the debate about privatized health is not based on practice as much as on ideology. In this regard, two main positions are identified in Britain: the libertarian and the egalitarian. The *libertarian ideology* proposes that society is obligated to provide a basic level of health care for all citizens; beyond this, wealthy individuals may choose to purchase additional protection. In this mixed economy of welfare, the market is allowed to discriminate against the poor only after their basic health requirements have been satisfied. The *egalitarian ideology*, by contrast, perceives health care to be a right, and not a privilege. Advocates of this view suggest, therefore, that the private sector should withdraw completely from health care delivery.

The relevance of the egalitarian position for the African case rests on three contentions: first, that basic health care is a right which the market cannot be relied upon to distribute effectively; second, and relatedly, that all forms of health care fall under the rubric of public or merit goods, which, when once provided, should, in theory, be equally available to all segments of society; and third, that the definition of 'basic' under the libertarian position is a policy exercise which can be used to discriminate against the poor. Consequently, African governments need to be very cautious as they capitulate to World Bank and IMF pressures to privatize. Policy makers must be constantly cognizant of the fact that health falls under the aegis of national security. As such, the existing systems, ineffective as they are, must not be dismantled, merely to be replaced by one that has the potential to discriminate against large segments of the population. Africa's health care delivery systems need improvement, but not at the further expense of the disenfranchised.

PLACING THE MARKET PENETRATION DEBATE IN EMPIRICAL CONTEXT

One of the more fundamental structural problems facing an effective programme of privatized health in Africa is the distribution of the population into two sectors that do not interact as components of a single unit. African economies, thus, are often differentiated into a Western-oriented, modern sector and a rural, agricultural sector.[33] The former is composed variously of the political and educated élites in the urban areas and large-scale rural producers, while the latter is comprised of agrarian and nomadic peasants, hunters and gatherers.[34] Between these two 'extremes' lie an assortment of informal producers at the margin of the Westernized sectors, thereby creating a rural–urban continuum, rather than a dichotomy.

The differences in socio-economic characteristics along this continuum are seen to emanate primarily from degree of market penetration.[35] Thus, modernization theorists attribute the 'modernity' of urban activities to strong links to global capital.[36] On the contrary, the so-called backwardness of the indigenous sector is ascribed to its unadaptiveness;[37] namely, its inability to accommodate global capital.[38] A converse opinion would interpret the low level of market penetration into indigenous systems to be a strategy by which global capital relegates

Africa and other Third World regions to a state of dependency.[39] I shall not pursue these debates here since the nuances and subtleties that discriminate between the perspectives of development theory are not germane to the present study.

The point to be made in this chapter is that the continuum structure of African economics presents us with a set of different circumstances and conditions in which the impacts of privatized health will vary. At the more market-oriented end of the continuum, privatized health already exists and can be expanded. However, as we move toward the traditional end of the continuum the potential feasibility of market-led health care will taper off.[40] The continuum structure, therefore, cannot support broad-based market initiatives.

STRUCTURAL BOTTLENECKS TO PRIVATIZED HEALTH CARE IN AFRICA

Figure 4.1 is a schematic representation of the socio-economic linkages that underpin the continuum structure. The flows capture the point that sectoral differentiation in Africa is essentially a factor of strong versus weak market penetration. As a result of the dynamic interlinkages between the market and traditional institutions, at least three sub-populations may be identified along the continuum: 1) the urban political and educational élite and commercial farmers in the rural sector – these populations are completely integrated into the international market system; 2) the urban informal and underground economies and semi-subsistent rural producers – these populations are at the margins of the market system and tend to migrate between the traditional and market economies depending on social and economic conditions; 3) the rural indigenous, subsistent sector, which typically forms the bulk of Africa's population and which is the least penetrated (which is not being used here necessarily to mean affected) by the market system.

The two market enclaves have strong direct links with each other and with global capital. Unfortunately, the very links which bind the market enclaves together also operate to separate them from the larger domestic economy where decision-making is often dominated by socio-cultural rather than economic considerations. The populations in groups two and three often have stronger structural links with each other than with their enclaved counterparts in the modern Westernized sector. This condition is underscored by the fact that the population at the physical and social fringes of the urban sector (group two) comprises rural migrants, some of whom have yet to be absorbed into the mainstream economy, while others may have lost their place in that economy (temporarily or permanently) as a result of economic exigencies.

FIGURE 4.1
Structural linkages in African economies

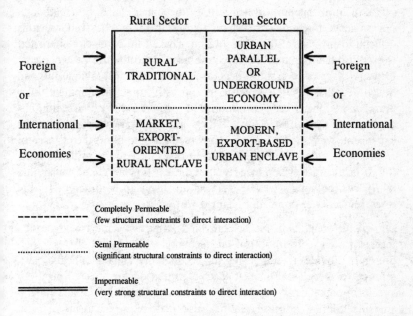

Flows of population, capital, products and services, therefore, occur more smoothly in a horizontal direction. This is not to suggest that vertical and diagonal flows do not occur. For example, linkages do exist between the urban informal and the rural export enclave, the urban mainstream and urban informal, and the rural export and rural indigenous sectors. However, such linkages are tenuous in nature, and are hampered by the friction of socio-economic distance.

POTENTIAL IMPLICATIONS OF PRIVATIZED HEALTH

Given the circumstances described above, privatized health will tend to be drawn to the market enclaves where infrastructural requirements such as piped water and electricity are already in place. The absence of these services in rural areas partly explains why government health programmes have been slow to diffuse to rural communities. Even ambulatory services which are predicated on the widespread dispersal of foot doctors have been bedevilled by poor transport infrastructure.

Infrastructural obstacles represent a major disincentive for the dissemination of privatized health. On the one hand, a modern health programme (public or private) cannot take off successfully without proper infrastructural support systems. On the other hand, even though governments might undertake such projects for public welfare, it is difficult to envisage a scenario in which private capital might be impelled to establish them primarily as a requirement for health care development. Cowan's study of several less developed countries,[41] including Kenya and Sudan, emphasizes the salience of infrastructural development as a prerequisite for market penetration. He concludes that privatization has a greater potential in Kenya, which has the framework for market expansion, while Sudan's weak infrastructural base limits the chances of a successful programme of government divestiture to the private sector.

If health care is privatized within the existing structural constraints in Africa, the human welfare impacts are likely to be different for the three segments of population defined earlier.

Group one (populations that are fully and permanently integrated into the market system). The political and economic dominance of this group presently provides it with the highest accessibility to modern health care. Political exigencies also often focus attention on the specific needs of vocal sub-populations, for example, the military, trade unions and college students. Similar political realities also underlie some forms of rural health care (for example, inoculation programmes) which are provided more extensively for ethnic and regional supporters.

These government activities result in a social hierarchy of health care, similar to the trickle-down that privatization should accomplish, except that the market is incapable of making decisions relating to political and social stability. Socially polarized health care under privatization might, therefore, set the stage for political unrest. The only way for this to be avoided is for governments to remain active participants in health care by catering to the needs of powerful sub-populations. In this case, government intervention must be seen as an effect of market imperfection (at least, in terms of Africa's political economy), and not the other way around.

Group two populations, those close to the market margins in the rural–urban continuum, presently enjoy access to modern health care in limited cases where free or subsidized public programmes are available. However, due to the shortcomings associated with, and the insufficiency of such programmes, many of the critical health needs of this group are met by low-cost traditional care. Under privatization, the health status of this population is unlikely to improve as it continues to migrate in and out of the modern economy. During periods of prosperity it might be able to afford levels of health care similar to that presently enjoyed under government programmes. However, considering that privatization is typically implemented in conditions of economic austerity, it is reasonable to expect short-run increases in unemployment, and other forms of economic hardships. This pattern has been observed for Tanzania, where austerity measures weakened the status of the poor, with the cost of health care increasing by 52 per cent between 1979 and 1984.[42] Thus, it is realistic to expect that the aggregate purchasing power of this population will decline at the same time that many are forced to direct their resources more towards food and shelter. Curative health needs will increasingly be met by the cheaper services of the traditional and urban informal sectors, and preventive health care is likely to be totally abandoned.

It is possible, however, that in the long run the economy will expand as a result of austerity measures, as some evidence now shows in the case of Ghana. If this occurs, some of the population at the market margin will be reabsorbed into the mainstream modern economy. Unfortunately, even this outcome is not guaranteed to ensure improved accessibility to modern health care. Quite paradoxically, increased purchasing power of the poor might stimulate price increases in the cost of medical care. Since their margin for competition in the market is limited, the poor will be crowded out by the overwhelmingly stronger bidding power of the affluent classes. Privatization, therefore, will not result in an unambiguous improvement in the health status of the populations at the margin.

Group three (populations within the traditional rural subsistence sector). The size and status of this group demands that it should be the primary target of health programmes. To date, it remains the most disadvantaged in all social welfare services. It is also the most disenfranchised, having very little political leverage, and making little or no input into important decision-making processes. Since there is no political pressure for governments to place a high priority on the health needs of this population, it receives modern health care only when the programmes are underwritten by foreign donors, or when they are in the collective national interest (examples are eradication programmes for contagious diseases like cholera and typhoid).

In summary, it is clear that public health programmes have been slow to reach Africa's poor. Despite expectations of positive trickle-down, it is not clear that privatization can change these conditions. Certainly, market biases against the poor will aggravate, rather than ameliorate the status of the poor because the social and political incentives that drive public decision-making will be absent.

Conclusion

Public health programmes in Africa are plagued by a number of shortcomings which limit their effectiveness and their potential impacts on the poor, especially those in rural areas. The trickle-down process has been slow and laboured, but it has occurred in limited doses for various reasons that we have discussed. On the other hand, there are reasons to doubt the ability of the market to accelerate progress in health care delivery to the poor. First, the suitability of the market for distributing health care is questionable since many of the services qualify as merit and public goods. This is especially the case if basic health care is considered to be a national security priority. Second, and relatedly, the neediest population in Africa is marginalized from the market by lack of purchasing power. By itself, privatization is incapable of addressing the structural barriers which underpin subsistence production and which stand in the way of market penetration to this population. Thus, even if the market can distribute health care effectively, its ability to do so for Africa's poor is constrained. With these concerns in mind, it is difficult to advocate privatization as a superior alternative to the public sector for distributing health care in Africa.

The concerns mentioned above are compounded by the apolitical and asocial characteristic of privatization. The governments of Africa are concerned about a number of social and political imperatives which cannot be addressed through the market mechanism.[43] In fact, the market mechanism has the potential to exacerbate social inequities, causing increasing social polarization which can easily result in political instability. Looking at the problem from a different perspective, it is equally clear that some form of popular participation or democratization is an important complement of market distribution. These political reorganizations and realignments do not seem to be forthcoming in Africa.

The existing circumstances in Africa lead to the conclusion that even though the public sector might be inefficient in maximizing profit, it is better able to accommodate the unique socio-political structures that underpin Africa's economies. The opportunity costs associated with the lost revenues from health facilities must then be assessed against certain socio-political benefits, including the fact that certain forms of health care that reach the poor will be impossible under a market system.

Notes

1. For example, R. Agarwala, 'Price Distortion and Growth in Developing Countries', Working Bank Staff Working Paper no. 575 (Washington, DC: World Bank, 1983); B. Balassa, 'Adjustment Policies and Development Strategies in Sub-Saharan Africa', in L. Taylor and L. Westphal (eds), *Economic Structure and Performance* (New York: Academic Press, 1984), 316–40; K. Marsden and T. Belot, *Private Enterprise in Africa* (Washington, DC: World Bank, 1987); and E. Savas, *Privatization: The Key to Better Government* (Chatham, NJ: Chatham House Publishers, 1987).
2. G.R. Alter, 'Export Processing Zones for Growth and Development: The Mauritian Example', IMF Working Paper no. 122, December 1990; R.C. Kearney, 'Mauritius and the NIC Model Redux: Or, How Many Cases Make a Model?' *Journal of Developing Areas* 24 (January 1990): 195–216.
3. K. Zacharia and M. Vu, *World Population Projections 1988–89* (Baltimore, MD: Johns Hopkins University Press, 1989).
4. E. Espenshade, *Goode's World Atlas*, 18th edn (Chicago, IL: Rand McNally, 1990), 20–24; 26–27.
5. Zacharia and Vu, *World Population Projections 1988–89*; World Bank, *World Development Report 1990* (New York: Oxford University Press, 1990).
6. R. Sandbrook, 'The State and Economic Stagnation in Tropical Africa', *World Development* (March 1986): 319–32; World Bank, *Sub-Saharan Africa: From Crisis to Sustainable Growth* (Washington, DC: World Bank, 1989).
7. Economic Commission for Africa (ECA), *African Alternative Framework to Structural Adjustment Programmes for Socio-Economic Recovery and Transformation* (New York: United Nations, 1989).
8. International Monetary Fund, *Government Finance Statistics Yearbook* (Washington, DC: International Monetary Fund, various years).
9. G.A. Cornia, 'Adjustment Policies 1980–1985: Effects on Child Welfare', in G. Cornia, R. Jolly and F. Stewart (eds), *Adjustment with a Human Face* (Oxford: Clarendon Press, 1987), 48–72; H. Mosley and R. Jolly, 'Health Policy and the Programme Options: Compensating for the Negative Effects of Economic Adjustment', in Cornia, Jolly, and Stewart, *Adjustment with a Human Face*, 218–31; 'Privatization: The New Message for Africa', *Africa Now*, 8–11 August 1986; F. Cheru, 'Adjustment Problems and the Politics of Economic Surveillance: Tanzania and the IMF', paper presented at the 1987 annual meeting of the African Studies Association, Denver, Colorado; B.I. Logan and K. Mengisteab, 'IMF–World Bank Adjustment and

Structural Transformation in Sub-Saharan Africa', *Economic Geography* 69, no. 1 (January 1993): 1–24.

10. W.M. Gesler, 'Health Care in Developing Countries', Resource Publications in Geography, Association of American Geographers, 1984.

11. L.J. Slikkerveer, 'Rural Health Development in Ethiopia: Problems of Utilization of Traditional Healer', *Social Science and Medicine* 16 (1984): 1859–72.

12. B.I. Logan and K. Mengisteab, 'The Potential Impacts of Privatization on Health Care Delivery in Sub-Saharan Africa', *Scandinavian Journal of Development Studies* 8, no. 1 (March 1989): 133–53.

13. Gesler, 'Health Care in Developing Countries', 2.

14. Ibid.

15. R.H. Bokhari, 'Social and Other National Objectives of Public Enterprises', in *Subvention Policy and Practices for Public Enterprises* (Ljubljana, Yugoslavia: International Center for Public Enterprises in Developing Countries), 11–14; G. Cowan, 'Divestment, Privatization and Development', *The Washington Quarterly* (Fall 1985): 47–56; D. Heald, 'Privatization Policies, Methods and Procedures', Conference on Privatization Policies, Methods and Procedures, Manila, Philippines, 31 January–1 February 1985.

16. Heald, 'Privatization Policies, Methods and Procedures'.

17. Cf. S. Domberger and J. Piggott, 'Privatization Policies and Public Enterprise: A Survey', *The Economic Record* (June 1986): 145–62; Cowan, 'Divestment, Privatization and Development', 47–56; E. Savas, *Privatization*; G. Roth, *The Private Provision of Public Services in Developing Countries* (New York: Oxford University Press, 1987).

18. A. Walker, 'The Political Economy of Privatization', in J. Le Grand and R. Robinson (eds), *Privatization and the Welfare State* (London: George Allen and Unwin, 1984), 5.

19. D. Leonard, 'African Practice and the Theory of User Fees', *Agricultural Administration* 18 (1985): 137–57; D. Leonard, 'The Supply of Veterinary Services: Kenyan Lessons', *Agricultural Administration and Extension* 26 (1987): 219–36.

20. P. Townsend, *Sociology and Social Policy* (Harmondsworth: Penguin, 1975), 28.

21. J. Le Grand and R. Robinson, 'Privatization and the Welfare State: An Introduction', in Le Grand and Robinson, *Privatization and the Welfare State*, 1–18.

22. K. Moll, 'Performance Improvements of Public Sector Industries in Mixed Economy Countries', in P. Fernandes (ed.), *Control Systems for Public Enterprises in Developing Countries* (Ljubljana, Yugoslavia: International Center for Public Enterprises in Developing Countries, 1982), 109–22; P. Hartley and C. Trengrove, 'Who Benefits from Public Utilities?', *The Economic Record* (June 1986): 163–79.

23. D. Erlenkotter, M. Hanemann, R. Howitt, and H. Vaux, 'The Economics of Water Development in California', in E. Englebert (ed.), *California*

Water Planning and Policy (Berkeley: University of California Press, 1980).

24. Walker, 'The Political Economy of Privatization'.
25. Ibid., 24.
26. Leonard, 'African Practice and the Theory of User Fees', 137.
27. Roth, *The Private Provision of Public Services in Developing Countries*.
28. Bokhari, 'Social and Other National Objectives of Public Enterprises'.
29. Heald, 'Privatization Policies, Methods and Procedures'; R. Sugden, 'Voluntary Organization and the Welfare State', in Le Grand and Robinson, *Privatization and the Welfare State*, 70–94.
30. P. Mosley, 'The Politics of Economic Liberalization: USAID and the World Bank in Kenya, 1980–1984', *African Affairs* 85 (1986): 107–19; Mosley and Jolly, 'Health Policy and the Programme Options'; Sugden, 'Voluntary Organizations and the Welfare State'.
31. Domberger and Piggott, 'Privatization Policies and Public Enterprise'. See also Mosley, 'The Politics of Economic Liberalization'.
32. A. Maynard and A. Williams, 'Privatization and the National Health Service', in Le Grand and Robinson, *Privatization and the Welfare State*, 96–110.
33. Cf. G. Meier, *Leading Issues in Economic Development* (New York: Oxford University Press, 1978); M. Bell, *Contemporary Africa: Development, Culture and the State* (Hong Kong: Longman, 1987); S. Corbridge, *Capitalist World Development: A Critique of Radical Development Geography* (Totowa, NJ: Rowman and Littlefields, 1986).
34. A. Grove, *The Changing Geography of Africa* (New York: Oxford University Press, 1989).
35. Cf. C. Wilber (ed.), *The Political Economy of Development and Underdevelopment* (New York: Random House, 1988).
36. G. Hyden, *No Shortcuts to Progress: African Development Management in Perspective* (London: Heinemann, 1983); G. Hyden, 'Discussion: The Anomaly of the African Peasantry', *Development and Change* 17, no. 4 (1986): 677–705.
37. See Meier, *Leading Issues in Economic Development*, for a review of this position.
38. L. Talbot, 'Demographic Factors in Resource Depletion and Environmental Degradation in East African Rangeland', *Population and Development Review* 12, no. 3 (1986): 441–51; L. Becker, 'The Collapse of the Family Farm in West Africa? Evidence from Mali', *Geographical Journal* (November 1990): 313–22.
39. See Stuart Corbridge, *Capitalist World Development: A Critique of Radical Development Geography* (Hong Kong: Rowman and Littlefield, 1987), for a review of the various convictions within World Structures theory.
40. See Logan and Mengisteab, 'IMF–World Bank Adjustment and Structural Transformation in Sub-Saharan Africa', for a fuller elaboration of the continuum structure.
41. G. Cowan, 'Divestment, Privatization and Development', *The Washington*

    Quarterly (Fall 1985): 47–56.
42. Cheru, 'Adjustment Problems and the Politics of Economic Surveillance'.
43. See Bokhari, 'Social and Other National Objectives of Public Enterprises';
    M. Loutfi, 'Development Issues and State Policies in Sub-Saharan Africa',
    International Labour Review 128 (1989): 137–54.

5

Structural Adjustment, Labour Commitment and Cooperation in the Ugandan Service Sector

J. C. Munene

Introduction and background

Organizations in Uganda and their employees have, for a considerable time now, suffered from enormous stress. The long-term causes of this phenomenon appear to be a complex mixture of external and internal factors. The former is exemplified by the international debt crisis and the latter by lack of accountability and the frustrated aspirations of the workers. Some workers trace the substantive date of the 'unprecedented' organizational stress to the first year of the Obote II regime (1981). Other commentators point to the first phase of the stabilization and structural adjustment programme (SAP) initiated in 1980, when the annual wage declined by 26 per cent to rank as the worst decline in ILO countries.[1]

The familiar scenario in African countries that have implemented SAPs – for example, Nigeria, Uganda, and Zambia – is a failure of organizations to look after their employees; salaries are less than a living wage, and other basic necessities such as adequate health allowance are not covered. There is a break in the psychological contract between employer and employee accompanied by frustrated aspirations, diminished organizational commitment and institutionalized and non-institutionalized corruption at all levels. Office resources are frequently privatized and marketed elsewhere. Clientele may privately request to be served quickly for a fee or the public servant withholds the service unless a private fee is paid.

Structural adjustment in Uganda and elsewhere means the supremacy of the market over state intervention.[2] Structural adjustment programmes operate through a number of tools including devaluation of the exchange rate, reduction of tariffs, elimination of subsidies and controlling wage adjustments.

There seems to be a consensus among the proponents of SAPs[3] as well as the sceptics[4] that such tools have been used in Africa as a last resort because all else have failed and not necessarily because they will work. Despite the default nature of the programme, or in spite of it, the implementers seem to have made little determined effort to tailor them to the African condition, in general, or to the peculiar characteristics of Uganda, in particular. One such characteristic is the Ugandan labour market, whose response to the restructuring exercise is the focus of this study.

The influence of SAPs on organizations and people who work in them is both direct and indirect. An example of a direct effect on organizations is the reallocation of resources from one sector to another.[5] The reallocation concisely exemplifies the 'in-house' conception of SAPs as 'shock treatment'. This process directly affects workers, who experience a salary reduction or are laid off. The general strategy here is demand management, to whose outcome Ugandans have responded by becoming traders and distributors of services, goods, or both.[6] The effect of this response is at its most telling and counterproductive, in terms of its overall effect on the economy, when 'bureau workers' withhold a service until a fee has been exchanged or a promise to pay later has been extracted.

The central concern in this chapter is with the effect on agencies generally, and employees particularly, of the formal demand strategy of devaluation and the informal one of peddling of bureau services. A key assumption of the study is that widespread organizational failure can come in the wake of SAPs, and that if it persists, the failure will work counter to the objectives of SAPs.[7]

The concern expressed above is shared by several others. After a decade of application of orthodox macro-economic policy in Africa, the World Bank introduced a capacity-building initiative in sub-Saharan Africa.[8] The Bank's initiative came in the wake of harsh realities which included widespread poverty, social inequalities, labour-related insecurity, and chronic high unemployment.[9] The pattern in Uganda after 1980 has, in addition, been one of low productivity, high absenteeism, unrealistically low wages and widespread moonlighting.[10]

The problem

A central concern of this chapter is the supply of discretionary cooperation, understood here to mean organizational citizenship behaviour, and commitment.[11] Discretionary cooperation refers to an agent's behaviour that the principal is not in position to demand or to enforce, but which is essential for the success of an enterprise or organization.[12] Commitment is the relative strength of an individual's identification with, and involvement in, a particular employment relationship or organization.[13] In examining these micro-level behaviours, we will initially accept the fundamental neo-classical macro-economic position of enthroning the market and leaving it to determine and control micro-level behaviour. The study will then seek to show that labour markets in sub-Saharan Africa generally, and Uganda in particular, do not behave according to theoretical predictions. Even when constraints and incentives are altered, the market will not, on its own, supply cooperation and commitment. This is because labour markets in sub-Saharan Africa are not anything like markets in industrialized countries, which act impersonally and rationally.[14] Instead, they are relational, differentiated, and complex while simultaneously operating along various, often contradictory dimensions.[15]

By combining insights from the new institutional economics and organizational psychology, the study proposes an alternative model of understanding to ensure commitment and discretionary cooperation. Three specific objectives are pursued within this general framework:

1. to examine and describe the perceived ability of organizations to meet their commitment to their employees, thereby honouring their part of the psychological contract;

2. to examine the workers' discretionary cooperation as an indicator of their service and their attitude toward the psychological contract; and,

3. to examine workers' expressed intention to leave their organization.

The study proceeds with a brief discussion of the labour markets in Uganda and sub-Saharan Africa in general. An eclectic model of discretionary behaviour and commitment is outlined, followed by methodology, data analysis and interpretation, discussion and conclusions.

Theoretical approach

INSTITUTIONAL CHARACTERISTICS OF THE LABOUR MARKET IN UGANDA

A labour-market definition of underdeveloped countries is that these are the countries where a large part of the labour force does not engage in formal wage employment.[16] This definition fits Uganda's situation, where 90 per cent of the population live in rural areas and engage in subsistence farming. This characteristic is in addition to the prevalence of undifferentiated activities where people regularly combine individual with exchange labour, and combine work across geographical areas.[17] These characteristics have long puzzled and frustrated employers who, during the colonial period, referred to Africans as 'target' workers.[18] Today's African employer faces a similar problem when workers, including senior executives, regularly take off for their 'village homes' on Thursdays, only to report for work the following Tuesday.[19]

The Ugandan labour market is neither homogenous nor dichotomous as the neo-classical theory underlying SAPs would assume. The prevalence of undifferentiated activities cited above means that such characteristics as formal and informal sectors, and rural and urban markets, break down and lose their descriptive and analytic powers when applied to Uganda and to most of sub-Saharan Africa.

The Ugandan labour market, like markets in most of sub-Saharan Africa, is a complex mixture of personal linkages developed for the purpose of survival.[20] It is very unlike the impersonal labour market of the West, where the employment relationship is limited to wage payment in return for productive services.[21] It is organized along different principles where the narrow economic base of the West is only peripheral. Instead you have a shopping-list of employment relations operating on different, perhaps conflicting, principles.[22] These relations have been referred to collectively as the 'economy of affection,' defined as 'a network of support, communications and interaction among structurally defined groups connected by blood, kin, community or other activities'.[23] Within this income-earning system people still pursue personal interests. However, the factors that come into play may require a different adjustive mechanism, which is not always economic.[24]

Throughout most of sub-Saharan Africa, including Uganda, wage differences, particularly within the public sector, contracted providing a more equal distribution between the highest and lowest paid from 1975 through 1985. The phenomenon of the accelerating unskilled/minimum wage was the result of a policy that advocated linking minimum unskilled wages to the average standard in rural areas and reducing differentials within the formal sector. The policy, though, simply served to make urban employment more attractive to the unskilled while demoralizing the skilled and the educated. The bias, however, was never quite felt while the exchange rate that subsidized imports was still kept at the nominal level. This helped to subsidize imports and enhance the value of real wages in Uganda.[25] The IMF–World Bank conditionality, coming with SAPs, removed the subsidy and exposed the skilled and the educated to the full force of the wage policy.[26] This was immediately followed by absenteeism, moonlighting and corruption, particularly within the established posts occupied by the more educated.[27]

THEORIZING LABOUR COMMITMENT AND COOPERATION

An understanding of the behaviour of labour and of organizations has recently been stimulated by fresh ideas from the new institutional economics (NIE). One of its major practical contributions is to provide a situational explanation of incentive structures and incentive management. Second, the model has brought a much-needed balance between market inefficiency and organizational and labour inefficiency (or X-inefficiency, as Leibenstein calls it[28]) in development analysis. Development analysts can now legitimately pose questions about the internal inefficiency of organizations and how this fits into the overall problem of underdevelopment. They can also make use of the findings of sociologists, political scientists, and psychologists who have traditionally examined the problems of organizations.

Briefly, NIE focuses on the problem of accountability and commitment by managing incentive systems and monitoring performance. Incentives are maximized, and commitment and accountability assured, if transaction and information costs are kept low,[29] and/or a high level of trust between interacting parties can be maintained.[30]

NIE provides us with new concepts and tools for understanding organizational behaviour in Africa. Three important additions include the importance of monitoring or supervision, the necessity for investing in information for the purpose of monitoring, and the direct influence of an uncertain environment on organizational commitment.[31] With regard to the first two concepts, there is ample evidence that information systems such as appraisals that could be used as monitoring devices are rarely used. In some Ugandan organizations they are actively discouraged.[32] The third addition is also important and has obvious links to the rise in malfeasance, shirking, and reduced commitment that are experienced in Ugandan organizations. The period under scrutiny (1980 onward) is characterized by a high level of environmental uncertainty, with observable implications for the future of most organizations and, therefore, the future of those working there. Apparently, the risk of working in organizations and jobs with uncertain futures has encouraged some of the corrupt behaviour so rampant in Ugandan organizations.

Three basic organizational forms are used to ensure accountability[33] by minimizing transactional, information, and monitoring costs. Under competitive conditions the market is most efficient. For reasons ranging from absence of competition to environmental complexity and uncertainty to lack of information, the market may fail. The hierarchy then becomes one efficient way of managing incentives, of monitoring and controlling behaviour, and of ensuring accountability.[34] Nevertheless, hierarchies are not automatic successes and Ugandan public hierarchies have mainly recorded failures.[35] To ensure success there should be sufficient hierarchies to guarantee accountability through competition.[36] Alternatively, other conditions such as those found in clans, the third organizational alternative, should be in place. The principal purpose of these conditions is to control or minimize opportunistic motivation that maintains exploitative structures. Among these are goal congruence backed by attitudinal commitment. When these are present, they must be maintained in a climate of reciprocity and trust. The two conditions and the social climate that must maintain them are indicative of a social exchange relationship.

Thus NIE gives us three ways in which to ensure labour effectiveness and efficiency. These are: 1) the market, based principally on getting the price of labour correct; 2) the hierarchy, which depends on a combination of careful pricing, monitoring, and control of labour; and 3) goal congruence, maintained by creating social exchange conditions.[37]

The present study takes cognizance of the outlined characteristics of the labour markets in Uganda and the rest of sub-Saharan Africa, where market pricing or ratio contracting are neither the basic nor the only motivation for relating. It begins from the assumption that only by considering all employment relationships as social exchanges can we include the multiplicity of assumptions and expectations that workers in Uganda bring to the employment situation. Similarly, the study considers pricing and hierarchy of limited validity in understanding and ensuring commitment and cooperation of labour in sub-Saharan Africa.

LABOUR COMMITMENT AS SOCIAL EXCHANGE

The central concern of the problem of commitment is the issue of moral hazard that is raised by the NIE. Commitment is 'the relative strength of an individual's identification with and relative involvement in a particular organisation'.[38] Workers committed this way experience a sense of unity and shared values of the object of their commitment. Such unity of purpose and value means that the need to monitor members of an exchange relationship such as employment is minimized. In this situation goal congruence is expected to be high and there is a convergence between self and group interest. When commitment is conceptualized in this fashion, it is generally referred to as emotional or affective commitment.[39]

Considerable effort is expended in determining the conditions that lead to commitment,[40] and researchers are increasingly adopting the social exchange model as the integrating framework.[41] As a social exchange, the employment relationship has the following characteristics: 1) unspecified obligations; 2) the return favour cannot be bargained about but must be equivalent and fair; 3) a need to prove trust by discharging obligations; and 4) generation of feelings of personal obligation, gratitude and trust.[42] These characteristics imply that an employment relationship is also a relationship of reciprocity requiring no supervision while generating mutual commitment to the fulfilment of each others' needs.[43]

A micro-economic view, articulated in principal–agent theory,[44] sees the relationship as rational and subject to ratio-contracting. Accordingly, one can draw up an enforceable contract by manipulating certain contextual conditions such as information availability, environmental uncertainty, and the self-interest of the parties of the relationship.

The social exchange view of commitment thus focuses on the importance of incentives and self-interest,[45] which are presented as the bases of social action, including economic action.[46] Here the work context is seen as a dual relationship composed of economic and social exchanges.[47] While economic exchange deals with bargains of wages in return for jobs defined in the job description, the social exchange aspect concerns an implicit expectation of 'consideration for services'.[48] Such services involve all discretionary activities that members of a work-force routinely perform on behalf of the organization, and for which no economic contract can be drawn – services beyond the call of duty.[49]

Without fully endorsing the interpretation of a paid job (a clearly economic activity) as at least partly a matter of returning favours, NIE, through its collective action variant,[50] acknowledges the role played by implicit personal contracts. It asserts that it is often too costly for one of the parties (principal or agent) to an exchange to enforce completely the formal, legal or economic contract. In reality, this type of contract can only be enforced to the level at which marginal costs are equal to marginal utility. Beyond this level, the other party to the exchange acquires property rights over his/her labour which is then exchanged at her/his discretion.[51] Since either party can monitor and enforce the formal contract only up to a level, mutual optimum benefit can only be realized if the said discretion is deliberately exercised in favour of the other party. Social exchange considerations determine the direction which the exercise of this discretion will take.

DISCRETIONARY COOPERATION AS SOCIAL EXCHANGE

The importance of cooperation in management and administration was recognized several decades ago by Chester Barnard[52] and by the Howthorne researchers. Recently the interest in discretionary cooperation has been increased through the study of organizational citizenship behaviour, which is spontaneous behaviour engaged in on the spur of the moment to deal with non-programmed activity.[53] The consensus concerning the nature of discretionary behaviour is that it is too nebulous for contractual purposes but, simultaneously, its absence can lead to measurable economic and/or psychological loss. For the purpose of this study discretionary behaviour will be taken to mean organizational citizenship behaviour.

Organizational citizenship behaviour is defined as 'individual behaviour that is not discretionary, not directly or explicitly recognised for the formal reward system, and that, in aggregate, promotes the effective functioning of the organisation'.[54] Organizational citizenship behaviour is considered a member outcome of the organization maintenance category.[55] It includes gatekeeping, encouraging, setting standards, experimenting and innovating. As with maintenance behaviour, organizational citizenship behaviour permits maximum use of organization resources by keeping the organization in good working order and providing a good climate for work and social relationships.[56] Such maintenance behaviour is an extra role which is freely put at the disposal of an organization and which managers are not in a position to demand.[57] It represents 'services beyond the call of duty', and cannot be enforced contractually since the marginal cost of enforcing such discretionary behaviour would exceed its marginal utility.[58] Rather, organizational citizenship behaviour or discretionary cooperation will be exchanged on social exchange rather than on economic exchange terms and the psychological contract, as a snapshot[59] of the status of the change, will play a significant role in the nature of organizational citizenship behaviour.

THE PSYCHOLOGICAL CONTRACT IN SOCIAL EXCHANGE

Central to a social exchange is the implicit personal contract, which is referred to here as the psychological contract. The psychological contract is defined as a dynamic set of implicit obligations and expectations continually negotiated between the organization and an individual.[60] As a network of expectations in employment relationships, the psychological contract refers to three main types of expectations.[61] The first includes general expectations which correspond to higher-order needs or expectations.[62] The second refers to role-related expectations. It is what an individual expects of another or of her/himself by virtue of a specific role that he or she plays within the relationship. The third set is referred to as comparative, and it is the one that is actually realized.

The psychological contract is broken or maintained depending on what happens to the expectations. The assessment of what transpires is governed by principles of distributive justice such as equality, parity and need. Which justice principle or principles are brought to bear depends on one's culture and socialization. For instance, societies that emphasize communal sharing as the basic mode of relating are likely to invoke the principles of equality or parity. Those that depend mostly on ratio contracting (market relating) are likely to invoke the principle of equity.[63] When an individual feels that the basic principle of relating is violated then he/she will consider that the psychological contract has been broken. Take for instance equity, which refers to a proportionate distribution of profits, where proportionate refers to the congruency between investments and profits, or between inputs and outputs. The psychological contract will be considered violated if what is taken as input by one of the parties to the exchange is not so recognized by the other. It is also violated if one outcome is recognized as reciprocal by one party and not the other.

CONSEQUENCES OF SOCIAL EXCHANGE FAILURE

The view is explicit about the options open to members who are dissatisfied with the exchange. For instance, they may decrease their inputs, leave the relationship, or force the other party out of the field.[64] In *Exit, Voice, and Loyalty* (EVL), Hirshman used the model to explain the responses open to individuals who are caught in unsatisfying productive and political relationships or, alternatively, in failing organizations. He showed that members of an unsatisfying exchange relationship can exit the relationship and look for better alternatives, they can voice their dissatisfaction in the hope of improving the relationship, or they can remain loyal and not attempt to rock the boat either through the voice or exit options. Later applications of the EVL indicate several things. The first is that members do have the fourth option of neglecting the relationship without physically quitting or trying to improve it.[65]

Exit and neglect are destructive processes that span indeterminate periods and lead to further deterioration of the exchange relationship. In romantic relationships the destruction may be exemplified by physical abuse or involvement with an outside party.[66] In productive relationships such as organizations on the African continent, the process is characterized by the phenomenon of capture, which is a tendency of members to engage in rent-seeking activities, particularly by those who control the allocation of organizational resources.[67] Those not in a position to 'capture' the organization practise shirking, malfeasance, tardiness, absenteeism, and other indications of moral hazard or non-commitment which are in daily evidence.

Thus it follows from the social exchange view that you do not expect to receive without giving, since commitment and cooperation based on the social exchange model are conceptually and practically two-way processes that must be seen as reciprocal. The model emphasizes the need to create a clear balance between obligations, rights, incentives and efforts. The precision with which this balance is struck, moreover, allows members of an employment relationship to pitch their expectations at an appropriate level.[68] In turn, this precision may reduce the incidence of shirking because individuals will know what is due to them and are less likely to spend time protecting their rights. The model implies a fundamentally symbiotic relationship between commitment, cooperation and equitability. That is, feelings of commitment depend on the decision rules people use to determine fairness.[69] This, in the last analysis, depends on the evaluation of the psychological contract. This type of contract *summarizes the complexity of real life as experienced within and without organizations. It mirrors the situation of multiple contracts.* People expect a number of rewards depending on the situation. Such rewards may include housing, educating of children at full or partial organization expense, sick leave, sick leave with pay, help with the kinship load burden, and so on. Those, for instance, who feel let down will not experience a moral obligation to be accountable. Instead, they will take the least-cost action that will restore the contract as they define it. Nurses on the hospital ward, for instance, may adopt a non-professional bedside manner. Teachers may assist their pupils to have access to national examinations for a fee, and every one may pursue all types of personal interests instead of organizational goals. Two hypotheses were tested:

1. There is a positive correlation between the psychological contract and discretionary cooperation.

2. There is a positive relationship between commitment, intention to exit, and the psychological contract.

Methodology

SAMPLE

The data were collected from rural and urban schools and health service organizations such as dispensaries, hospitals and health centres. Of 682 health workers including doctors, medical assistants, nurses and midwives, 357 worked in urban areas and 325 in the countryside. Of the 396 teachers who took part in the study, 226 were in urban and 170 in rural schools. A selected group of other personnel in the ministries and local administration of health and education who were considered to have a wider knowledge of their respective services were interviewed. These included, for instance, the head of the teaching services commission, professional hospital administrators, medical superintendents, chief nursing officers, head teachers, district medical and education officers, and a group interview with the Uganda Medical Association. Not all information collected will be used in this study.

INSTRUMENTS

The data were collected by means of a structured interview and a detailed questionnaire. The questionnaire sought four categories of information:

1. Objective information about the respondent and his/her organization such as education level, sex, magnitude of kinship responsibility, the length of service with a particular organization, and the size of the organization.

2. Income-related information including monthly take-home pay, distance between workplace and home, other income-generating activities. Under this category we also gathered information on absence incentives and barriers.

3. Respondents' psychological assessment and evaluation of their work experience conceptualized in this study as the psychological contract. It included the hypothesized consequences of the evaluation, namely organizational commitment and job satisfaction.

4. Supervisory rating of the respondents' discretionary cooperation operationalized as organizational citizenship behaviour.

A number of open-ended questions were asked concerning the major difficulties faced in health or education. These included a question seeking a general description of the state of the service. They requested a description of the foremost management problem and priority. They also included questions tapping the external and internal environments of the institutions and of the specific organization visited.

Another set of questions tried to tap what the respondent wanted to see done in order to deal with or respond to what had been described earlier.

MEASUREMENTS

Psychological contract: This was measured by a battery of items comprising the following:

a) Fairness (Justice): A five-item measure of distributive justice by Price[70] was adopted for the purpose of this research. The measure is based on social exchange and especially equity theories.

b) Expectations (Need): A seven-item measure adapted from Cook and Wall[71] of need non-fulfilment was used.

c) Trust (Trust): A six-item measure of organizational trust adapted from Cook and Wall[72] was used.

Items for all three were on seven-point Likert scales. The responses of the first two components ranged from strongly agree to strongly disagree. Responses on trust differed from item to item. For instance, the first item responses ranged from extremely sincere to extremely insincere. The second item responses ranged from extremely good to extremely poor.

The items were pooled and subjected to a reliability analysis. A coefficient of reliability (Cronbach alpha) of .85 was obtained.

Organizational commitment (Affect): An eight-item measure of affective commitment by Allen and Meyer[73] was adopted for use. The coefficient of reliability was .82.

Job satisfaction (Jobsat): Ten items from Cook and Wall were employed in the study. Cronbach alpha was .85.

Organizational citizenship behaviour: Sixteen items were compiled from Munene[74] and Organ and Konovsky.[75] Two components were measured:

a) Conscientiousness (Consc): Nine items measured general behaviour, such as seeking responsibility and always being ready to accept more work. The coefficient of reliability was .89.

b) Altruism (Altruism): Seven items were used to measure this component. The coefficient of reliability was .6.

Intention to exit (Intent): Three items were used to measure exit intentions.

Personal and role-related variables: Variables of education, tenure, salary, gender, age, and kinship responsibility were measured. The kinship measure required the individual to state the number of adults and children he or she is responsible for and whether the respondent was married or not.[76] Each affirmative answer was awarded 1 score. The total kinship index load was 13.

Income-generating activities: An open-ended question required the respondent to indicate what he or she does to make up for the difference between salary income and his/her expenditure.

Results

The first part of this section describes the non-psychological characteristics and responses of the sample and, in the process, sheds light on the state of Ugandan organizations. The second part examines the findings in terms of the hypotheses.

CHARACTERISTICS AND CHARACTERISTIC RESPONSES OF THE SAMPLE

Table 5.1 shows that just over 44 per cent and 26 per cent of respondents had worked for four years or less and above eleven years respectively. Thirteen per cent of the sample had worked for between eight and ten years.

The majority of our sample were relatively well educated, reflecting the professions from which it was obtained. Most had obtained post-secondary school training (56 per cent), a negligible percentage (3 per cent) had only primary education, and at least 10 per cent had a first or a second degree. Six hundred and forty-nine or 60.2 per cent of our sample were female, probably reflecting the predominance of women in health and education.

Of the sample who agreed to indicate their chronological age, over 50 per cent were 35 years and below. One (1 per cent) indicated that they had reached retiring age.

TABLE 5.1
Tenure

Years in organization	Count	%
< 4	480	44.5
5–7	173	16.0
8–10	141	13.1
11–13	123	11.4
14 and above	161	14.9

We calculated an index of kinship responsibility by adding up the number of relatives, including spouses, a respondent was directly responsible for. A full load of responsibility is indicated by 13 points and no responsibility at all by a zero (0). Table 5.2 summarizes the findings and shows that most of our respondents (45 per cent) have between eight and thirteen people to look after, which is above half the load (mean = 6; median = 6). The mean load is three times as much as the mean load (approximately 2) carried by a comparable group in the United States of America.[77] Those with half the load and more account for approximately 66 per cent.

The heavy kinship responsibility was found to compare unfavourably with what our respondents earned. To have an idea of how our sample fared, we asked them to indicate their monthly take-home pay including allowances, and their monthly expenditure. Table 5.3 summarizes the findings.

These figures indicate a clear imbalance between what our respondents earn from their organizations and what they have to spend. The figures are, however, in agreement with the World Bank report,[78] which indicates that the average expenditure in Kampala, for instance, is 60,000 shillings. As is clear from the table, the difference between incomes and expenditures is significant ($t = 23.62$; $df = 743$; $p < .0001$).

Most of the sample made up for the difference in activities that take them away from their paid work, as is shown in Table 5.4.

Asked when income-generating activities outside one's formal employment started, some respondents said that it was during Amin's time, when it paid more to practice *magendo* than to do a paid job. Others said that most people started after Amin. All agreed that these intensified after Amin (see Table 5.5).

TABLE 5.2
Kinship responsibility

Load	Count	%
0–1	67	6.2
2–3	142	13.2
4–5	247	23.0
6–7	214	19.9
8–13	405	44.9
no response	3	0.3

Our informants are in agreement with the findings of the report of the Public Service Review and Reorganization Commission, which found that 86 per cent of income-supplementary activities started in the 1980s.[79] They also confirm an important consequence of structural adjustment programmes in Uganda, namely, the deterioration of service as a result of the squeeze that accompanies austerity.

In the light of the finding that the largest percentage of the workforce were engaged in income-generating activities that took them out of their formal employment, we asked them what their organizations do about their behaviour (organizational misbehaviour). Table 5.6 summarizes the answers to the question.

The general conclusion we drew from responses to this question is that organizations exert very little control over the activities of their members. This is not surprising since organizations feel inadequate when it comes to remunerating their members and providing them with the resources for professional growth.

As Table 5.5 implies, the current organizational problems are traceable to the breakdown of the civil order as well as the introduction of the SAPs. One headmaster interviewed put the events affecting school performance in three clear phases:

(1) The Boom Time (1970–1980), which he said followed the expulsion of Asians and the turning of their businesses over to black Ugandans. Schools lost their teachers to the new opportunities created by Amin. (2) The period of instability (1981–1985) when people were living from day to day in real fear of their lives. Here teachers like any workers did as little as possible and moved to wherever was considered safe. (3) The period of inflation (1986 onward) which effectively reduced the salary power of teachers. Stability is experienced but people cannot survive with one job. The most significant cause of the deterioration in education is the cost of living.[80]

Table 5.3
Salaried and wage income and monthly expenditure ('000 shillings)*

Income	%	Expenditure	%
< 25	74.2	< 25	0
25–50	23.2	25–50	0.4
50–100	2.6	50–100	78.9
		> 100	20.7

Note: *1,200 shillings = \$1

The commissioner for education was also clear on the plight of teachers, particularly those of rural schools. He said that the SAPs have hit the rural teacher hardest of all (compared to the urban teacher). This is confirmed by the fact that many rural teachers cannot afford decent clothing. They come to school dressed in torn trousers and wearing sandals in a poor state of repair.

A direct reference to the influence of SAPs on organizational functioning was made by a number of interviewees. One said that the inflationary trend of SAPs has resulted in the diversion of funds from capital to recurrent budgets such as paying teachers and buying food. 'As a result we are unable to expand'.[81] SAPs have also ensured that teachers resort to coaching in a dishonest way. In order to attract more funds, they have to attract more parents. They therefore, give extra marks to children and to pupils they coach, and fewer to those they do not coach. This is done to encourage parents to participate or to continue to participate in coaching.

At the level of the organization, schools must also cultivate parents in order to survive. If no proper teaching can take place, schools must resort to forms of examination malpractice so as to get an acceptable level of first grades. It is the numbers of first grades that make parents happy and encourage them to send more children to high-performance schools.

Parallel instances of organizational failure leading to employment-related misbehaviour are to be found in the health sector as well. Because these have to do with life and death, they often make headline material, unlike those in schools. There is the case of the intern in Jjinja hospital who was alleged to have allowed the death of a patient, because the patient's relatives were unable to pay the young doctor a sum of money he had demanded. This kind of lack of professionalism and general undiscipline among health workers is recognized by all the medical superintendents we interviewed. Pilferage was reported to be endemic,

TABLE 5.4
Income generating activities

Category of activities	%
Advance, borrowing, begging from relatives/donations	35.6
Magendo, petty trade, tendering, briefcase business	40.6
Others: private practice, drug store, knitting, poultry, piggery, farming	57.5

doctors 'cut' ward rounds, and the bedside manner of nurses was found to be unprofessional.

The last example (bedside manner) was shown to have far-reaching consequences. We found, for instance, that relatives of patients have responded by taking on the nursing services themselves. This has often led to overcrowding. One superintendent reported that in her hospital, every patient had at least two full-time attendants, so that in a hospital ward of 100 children, she would find 300 people at one single moment. This number would stretch the capacity of the system to the limit with reference to water, sewerage and physical living space.

No direct connection between the SAPs and the problem of hospitals were made (unlike the case of the educators) by our informants. Several superintendents and other chief medical officers linked undiscipline and lack of professionalism to the fact that the services have been overwhelmed and to the loss of prestige that the health professions have experienced. Indirectly, though, they accepted that SAPs have played a role in exacerbating the stress levels of health organizations.

All of the health professionals agree that salary erosion has undermined the prestige of the medical field. One superintendent reported that doctors, in particular, are used more like servants by those with money. Since the undermining of the salaried class has come in the wake of SAPs, it is plausible to argue that part of the loss of professionalism among health workers, as with educationists, is related to adjustment programmes.

Examples of the impact of SAPs on the health services are not confined to remuneration only. Two case studies described below indicate how the services have been overwhelmed as a result of the reallocation of resources from the non-tradeable sector. The deprivation has been so complete in some cases that the services are hardly in a position to make proper use of donor-provided help.

TABLE 5.5
Period in which activities began

	%
Before or during Amin	15
After Amin	85
Intensified after Amin	100

Psychological correlates of organizational stress

The basic hypothesis of this study is that workers in formal employment relationships respond in a rational way to the work experience and environment we have briefly described. To test this hypothesis we proposed the concept of the psychological contract and stated that the way the state of the contract is perceived is related to the way workers behave in their organizations. To examine the hypothesis we correlated our measure of the psychological contract with the measure of discretionary cooperation operationalized as conscientiousness and altruism.

The results (Table 5.7) provide support for the importance of the psychological contract in employment relationships. Under the column marked conscientiousness (Consc) we can see the positive and significant correlation between contract and discretionary cooperation. Conscientiousness refers to general compliance or the willingness to perform general cooperative acts, including regular unfailing attendance, that are difficult for management to demand. Distributive justice, on its own, is also positively related to conscientiousness. Its independent status is also revealed in the second column marked Altruism. Altruism is an aspect of discretionary cooperation that specifically taps willingness to render help to colleagues or to clients waiting to be served. It is exemplified by a bank clerk who would temporarily abandon her/his post in order to attend to a waiting customer in the absence of a specific teller attendant.

Other relationships that are important to note in Table 5.7 are those between the psychological contract and intention to leave the organization (Intent), and between the contract, commitment, and job satisfaction. The negative results between intention to leave the organization and the psychological contract are to be interpreted positively, meaning that those

TABLE 5.6
Organizational sanctions

Sanctions	%
Withhold allowance	5
Warning	3
Withhold leave	4.3
Deny promotion	1
Delay salary	0.7
Not applicable	23.1

who enjoy a positive psychological contract with their employing organization are also those unwilling to leave. The relationship between commitment, job satisfaction and the contract are in the positive and expected direction, meaning that those who are committed or who pose little or no moral hazard are those who experience a positive contract. Job satisfaction is also a concomitant of a positive contract.

The same relationships can be indirectly examined by looking at the scores of the various groups that took part in the study. Table 5.8 summarizes our findings and takes location, i.e., whether the groups are rural or urban, as the independent variable. Significant differences are found in both aspects of discretionary cooperation. In both cases the difference is in favour of rural health workers, who were rated as relatively conscientious and altruistic. There was no difference between rural and urban teachers as well as between them and urban health workers on conscientiousness. On altruism, though, urban health workers were rated by their supervisors as the least helpful. With regard to intention to exit one's organization, the difference was in favour of urban workers of both education and health services. There was a strongly expressed desire by the rural workers in both sectors to exit their organizations. No difference exists between all the four groups on the measure of the psychological contract. This is to be expected as the non-profit-making nature of both services confines the employees to a monthly salary which, we have seen, is significantly less than the expenditure of the employees.

TABLE 5.7
Zero order correlation

Independent variables	Coefficients				
	Consc (n=389)	Altruism (n=389)	Intent (n=570)	Affect (n=570)	Jobsat (n=570)
Size	-.011	.179*	-.16*	-.09	-.07
Tenure	.044	.138*	-.14*	.11*	.00
Education	-.025	.046	.17*	-.15*	-.07
Kinship responsibility	-.023	.049	.18*	-.04	-.01
Psychological contract	.100*	.076	-.42*	.43*	.52*
Trust	.051	-.007	-.31*	.29*	.35*
Need	.078	.011	-.33*	.46*	.42*
Distributive justice	.096+	.172*	-.18*	.18*	.39*
Affective commitment	.069	.028	-.37*	1.00	.39*
Job satisfaction	.065	-.062	-.29*	.39*	1.00

Note: * p < .001; + p < .05

Evaluation of the findings

This chapter set out to show that one of the outcomes of demand management is to rob organizations of their ability to keep their side of the psychological contract. The argument used here is that employment relationships are ultimately exchange relationships, with expectations that a favour must be followed by a favour if the relationship is to continue.[82] The study has found examples of the failure of organizations to keep their side of the contract, particularly with regard to the living wage. The impression that this is the only problem is contradicted by other examples, such as those provided by the two case studies, as well as by others that we collected but have not reported here.[83]

These examples are illustrative of organizations stretched to the limit, and of people who work under experiences that few imagine until they are physically confronted with them. The nursing officer who has to sell off the drug kits she should be distributing is demonstrating that the

TABLE 5.8
Brief summary of analysis of variance (anova)

Variables	F Ratio	F Probability
Conscientiousness	2.5	> .05
Altruism	9.3	> .001
Intention to exit	21.6	> .001
Psychological contract	.6	< .10

service has deteriorated so much that it is hardly in a position to utilize donor help.[84] We suggest that these and similar experiences lead employees to evaluate the psychological contract as broken and, therefore, they feel no obligation to discharge their own part of the contract.

The data gathered here have provided other instances that stretch workers to their limit. The kinship load carried by most of our respondents is out of proportion to their income. This is a fact that is well known but to whose consequences organizations have paid little attention. However, as the zero order correlations show (see Table 5.7), kinship responsibility is a significant determinant of the worker's intentions to exit the organizations they work for.

According to the argument we try to advance in this study, part of the expectations our respondents bring to their employment is that somehow they will be able to take care of their kin if they work for a particular organization. This is part of the psychological contract they make with the organization. When they find that this expectation cannot be fulfilled, they consider the contract violated and plan to leave. Whether or not they actually leave or when they do is not the issue. The theory we have proposed suggested that damage to the goals of the organizations begins at the moment of deciding to leave, for it is at this moment that the disgruntled become destructive, either actively, for instance by embezzling funds, or passively, by neglecting their duties or working to rule. Doctors 'cutting' ward rounds, nurses displaying non-professional bedside manners, and teachers and schools participating in examination malpractice or forcing parents to have their children coached, are examples of destructive behaviour that this study has gathered.

The size of the failure of organizations keeping their side of the psychological contract can be deduced, albeit indirectly, from Table 5.1. It can be noted that 60 per cent have not worked for more than seven years in their organizations, and approximately 45 per cent have worked for only four years or under. If our sample is a good approximation of the working population in these two services, then the turnover rate is disproportionately high. It suggests that there is a steady stream of professionals leaving their organizations or their professions. Apart from depriving the profession or organizations of experienced individuals, it also means that the destruction that accompanies the process of exiting and/or neglecting, discussed above, is also high. In Ugandan organizations, this is witnessed by moonlighting, which is a fact we have come to accept in Uganda, and, indeed, which has been at one stage recommended by no less than the Vice-President (who was then the Prime Minister), who openly encouraged Ugandans to have more than one job. In this study we consider that holding more than one full-time job is a process of exiting or neglecting the organization, and is destructive. We also consider it as a failure in keeping the psychological contract, which would ultimately lead to the eventual break-up of the relationship.

When we turn to the psychological indicators used in the study, we confirm what the more objective data are telling us about the state of our organizations and that of the psychological contracts therein. We hypothesized that there would be a positive relationship between the psychological contract and discretionary cooperation of organizational citizenship behaviour. This hypothesis was supported, as Table 5.7 indicates. In this table, the psychological contract is significantly related to the conscientiousness aspect of discretionary cooperation. This means that those who positively evaluate the state of the psychological contract they made with their organizations are also those who are positively rated by their supervisors as more conscientious.

Psychologically meaningful and statistically significant findings are also found with regard to the altruism aspect of discretionary cooperation. The first is the positive relation between tenure and altruism. This means that those professionals who have stayed longer with their organizations were also those who were rated relatively more positively by their supervisor on helping behaviour (altruism). This is not surprising. Theoretically, if people who find their psychological contracts violated by their organizations exit and seek other opportunities, then among those who stay, you are likely to find those prepared to cooperate with the organization in fulfilling its objectives as well as their personal altruistic tendencies. Such people should be evaluated positively by their superiors.

The second psychologically meaningful finding is the positive relationship between distributive justice and altruism. Distributive justice has a certain obviousness, which suggests that it is a significant component of the psychological contract. More than any of the other two components – trust and need satisfaction – it taps directly into how one feels about what one gets in relation to significant others. If people feel that the distribution of rewards is proportionate, then they are more likely to accept what they get even if it may not be what they expect. Professionals in the services we have surveyed have been hardest hit, as the data from the interviews indicate. For the skilled and educated professionals, the issue of justice of distribution must rank relatively high in the way the psychological contract is evaluated. A medical doctor with a specialization and working in Mulago knows that when his/her professional and other allowances are added up, he/she takes home a pay packet that, at best, is only equivalent to that of a junior staff or a group employee in parastatal organizations such as foods and beverages. The importance of the justice in distribution is also observed with regard to conscientiousness. Here again it was found to be significant and positively related to the rating that supervisors awarded to the respondents.

An important finding with a significant statistical and psychological significance is found in Table 5.8. Here we indicated that when groups were compared on altruism, urban health workers were rated worst of all. Since the largest number making up this group were nurses, we may say that this statistic genuinely reflects the notorious bedside manner of the nursing staff in all government and non-government hospitals. Probably reflecting the general state of neglect of both services, there were no group differences on the measure of the psychological contract.

The other relationships concerning psychological indicators of interest to this study, and depicted in Table 5.7, are those between organizational commitment, job satisfaction, intention to exit, and the psychological contract. The last three columns show that relationships are in the predicted direction. Intention to exit is related to most of the variables in the table. We have already discussed its relationship with kinship responsibility. We can also note a similar relationship with education. Those who are more educated are those with the strongest wish to exit their organizations. This was also expected because of the anomaly in the institutional environment of the labour market, discussed above. The anomaly is the discrepancy between education/skill and wage income. That is, owing to the preferred policy of a protected minimum wage and unprotected maximum wage, the reality has been that the more educated and skilled you are, the less you are paid in proportion to the less educated, less skilled employee. The consequence of this policy was observed in a study that compared university graduate teachers with grade 2 and grade 3 teachers.[85] The latter scored highest on discretionary conscientiousness, altruism, psychological contract, commitment and job satisfaction. The two less educated groups (grade 2 and grade 3) of teachers were also highly praised by the ministry of education officials for being the only groups that have maintained professionalism in the service.

Summary and conclusions

This study undertook to investigate the response of labour to structural adjustment programmes by focusing on their professional behaviour, their behaviour in and attitudes about their organizations, and their attitude to the employment relationship. The specific behaviours of interest were discretionary cooperation, affective commitment, and their evaluation of the psychological contract.

The justification for a study such as this one is in recognizing that SAPs have a long gestation period, qualifying them as complex economic, social and political programmes. In effect, this means that the longer they take to mature, the more factors other than the purely economic considerations impinge on them and influence the final outcome. The recognition of this fact has led to several attempts to alleviate some of the outstanding consequences of SAPs. These efforts have been directed toward the poor and those groups most vulnerable to poverty, such as women and rural dwellers.

The efforts in this chapter have been directed at highlighting the vulnerability of organizations and of those who work there in the hope that both will be elevated to priority status. This has been done at two levels. The first level was theoretical. Here an attempt was made to make a case for a more serious application of behaviour determinants of economic activity than is normally the practice. To do this, it was argued that ongoing economic activities such as formal employment are essentially social exchange activities whose outcomes are never completely rationally determined. Following North,[86] it was pointed out that there is always an area of discretion that is not enforceable through legal or economic contracts and where behavioural considerations such as moods or temperament control the final outcome. In this study we proposed the concept of the psychological contract to define and measure this behavioural grey area. The concept was itself derived from social exchange theory, which highlights such determinants of behaviour as trust, distributive justice and need fulfilment.

On the second level we considered the current ability of organizations in the health and educational institutions to meet their side of the psychological contract, and concluded from available evidence that the organizations are hardly in a position to honour the contract. We have, in addition, given some evidence that failure to meet the contract leads to low commitment, and, therefore, to greater incidence of moral hazard. This is the case, since the psychological contract and commitment were positively correlated. This case has been further strengthened by providing evidence that the psychological contract is positively related to the actual behaviour of our respondents as seen in the eyes of their supervisors. Moreover, the relatively poor evaluation of the respondents by their supervisors seemed to concur with that which is generally experienced by the public, as was the case of nurses' bedside manners.

Discretionary cooperation, which was the major behavioural focus of the chapter and whose relationship to the state of the psychological contract the study has supported, could be considered as an aspect of the service ethic. There should be no contention concerning the centrality of either behaviour in the daily functioning of a service organization or any other organization. Thus no effort should be spared by organizations and institutions to ensure the supply of these behaviours.

The theoretical and the practical arguments we are putting forward have wider implications beyond SAPs and SAP objectives. It is important to restate the most significant implication of the general findings of this study, namely, that SAPs cripple the very mechanism that ultimately carries out or delivers the objectives of every macro and micro plan, by directly disabling organizations from carrying out their part of the implicit or psychological contract. The wider implication is that no economy succeeds when organizations, as delivery systems, experience an extended period of inability to keep their own side of the psychological contract.

Implications for policy

1. Considering the role that organizations play in the economic development of any nation, there is need to rethink much more carefully the effect of any macro objectives on organizations. With regard to SAPs, we have noted evidence that organizations may be adversely affected and have urged that prolonged organizational stress could cripple them beyond repair. Since our findings indicate that many organizational members estimate the stressful period to be about a decade, it is suggested that an organizational rescue programme similar to PAPSCA be put into place. This will relieve organizations and make it possible for them to deliver

the ultimate objectives of restructuring and revamping of the economy.

2.   The second implication comes from finding that distributive justice is positively related to the ratings that supervisors give to their employees. Some of the gaps in distribution are so obviously unjust that the prevalent labour behaviours of absenteeism, malfeasance, free-riding, and even embezzlement could be considered as direct responses to perceived and experienced injustice. It is such obvious distributive injustice that makes a PAPSCA-like organizational rescue plan even more urgent. This is essential for there is a limit at which any organization, including the government, can get services on the cheap, and the individual can be asked to make sacrifices.

3.   To deal with the above, the government must (a) reconsider its wage policy of subsidizing the minimum wage while exposing the maximum wage to market forces, and (b) consider public expenditure as complementary to private expenditure, particularly since most of the institutions and the environment required to support market forces are not in place in Uganda,[87] nor are they likely to be, in the foreseeable future.

4.   The problem that the government is likely to face while attempting to remedy the position of the highest grades is political rather than economic, since there is evidence that improvement to the pay packets would add relatively little to the total pay bill.[88] The real problem is one of dealing with the repercussions elsewhere in the labour market. This is a tough political problem that has to be faced because of equity, productivity, and humanitarian considerations.

On humanitarian grounds we have only to recognize that it is at the level of the household that the fierce struggle for survival is centred in Uganda and elsewhere in the Third World.[89] The skilled and the educated must also be assisted in this struggle. The equity problem is highlighted by the fact that the professional demands of a professor at Makerere and a consultant surgeon at Mulago teaching hospital leave very little time for supplementary income activities, compared to a group employee in one of the public enterprises whose take-home pay compared very favourably with that of the highest-paid medical doctor or professor.

On productivity grounds, SAPs have inadvertently brought about a situation where especially favourable terms have to be given to certain public service employees in order to maintain functional levels of morale, motivation, and efficiency. This, as we have seen, is because the supply of commitment and discretionary cooperation has been directly affected by the contradictory impact of the programmes. At the same time, competent public service is as crucial as the building of economic infrastructure.[90]

Notes

1. M. Mamdani, 'Uganda: Contradiction of the IMF Programme and Perspectives', presented to the Meeting of the Economic Association of Uganda, Kampala, Uganda, 1989.
2. G. Standing, 'Structural Adjustment and Labour Market Policies: Towards Social Adjustment?', in G. Standing and V. Tokman (eds), *Towards Social Adjustment* (Geneva: ILO, 1991).
3. See, for instance, T.E. Mutebile, 'Selected Issues in Stabilization and Adjustment Policy in Uganda', Discussion Paper no. 3, Uganda Ministry of Planning and Economic Development.
4. Mamdani, 'Uganda: Contradiction of the IMF Programme and Perspectives'.
5. Mutebile, 'Selected Issues'.
6. V. Jamal, 'Coping Under Crisis in Uganda', *International Labour Review* 127, no. 6 (1988): 679–701.
7. R. Amjad and G. Edgren, 'The Role of Labour Markets in Employment Generation and Human Resources Development in Asian Countries', in Standing and Tokman, *Towards Social Adjustment*.
8. World Bank, *The African Capacity Building Initiative* (Washington, DC: World Bank, 1990).
9. Standing, 'Structural Adjustment and Labour Market Policies'; D. Robinson, 'Labour Market Implications of Public Expenditure Constraints and Privatisation', in Standing and Tokman, *Towards Social Adjustment*.
10. Republic of Uganda, *Report of the Public Service Review and Reorganisation Commission*, vol. 1 (Kampala: Uganda Government, 1989).
11. C.I. Barnard, *The Functions of the Executive* (Cambridge, MA: Harvard University Press, 1938); C.D. North, *Institutions, Institutional Change, and Economic Performance* (New York: Cambridge University Press, 1990); D.W. Organ, 'The Motivational Basis of Organisational Citizenship Behaviour', *Research in Organisational Behaviour* 12 (1990): 43–72.
12. Organ, 'The Motivational Basis of Organisational Citizenship Behaviour'; North, *Institutions, Institutional Change, and Economic Performance*.
13. R.T. Mowday, L.W. Porter, and R. Dubin, 'Unit Performance, Situational Factors, and Employee Attitudes in Spatially Separated Work Units', *Organisational Behaviour and Human Performance* 12 (1974): 231–48.
14. J. Weeks, 'The Myth of Labour Market Clearing', in Standing and Tokman, *Towards Social Adjustment*.
15. Geller, 'Labour Market Adaptation'.
16. Weeks, 'The Myth of Labour Market Clearing'.
17. Standing, 'Structural Adjustment and Labour Market Policies'.

18. See Olakunle A. Ogunbameru, 'The African Proletariat in Industrial Employment: A Reappraisal', *International Social Science Journal* 36 (1984): 341–54 for a good summary of this problem.

19. J.C. Munene, 'Not-on-Seat: An Investigation of Some Correlates of Organisational Citizenship Behaviour in Nigeria', *Applied Psychology: An International Review* (forthcoming).

20. T. Franks, 'Bureaucracy, Organisation Culture and Development', *Public Administration and Development* 9 (1989): 357–68; G. Hyden, *No Short Cuts to Progress* (London: Heinemann, 1983).

21. Weeks, 'The Myth of Labour Market Clearing'.

22. C.C. Onyemelukwe, *Men and Management in Contemporary Africa* (London: Longman, 1973).

23. Hyden, *No Short Cuts to Progress*, 9.

24. Weeks, 'The Myth of Labour Market Clearing'.

25. Bibanganbah, 'The Impact of Structural Adjustment Programmes on Agriculture in Uganda'.

26. C. Colclough, 'Wage Flexibility in Sub-Saharan Africa: Trends and Explanations', in Standing and Tokman, *Towards Social Adjustment*.

27. Republic of Uganda, *Report of the Public Service Review and Reorganisation Commission*.

28. H. Leibenstein, 'Organisational Economics and Institutions as Missing Elements in Economic Development Analysis', *World Development* 17, no. 9 (1989): 1361–73.

29. O.O. Williamson, 'The Economics of Organisation: The Transaction Cost Approach', *American Journal of Sociology* 87 (1981): 548–77.

30. See for instance M. Olson, *The Logic of Collective Action* (Cambridge, MA: Harvard University Press, 1965); and North, *Institutions, Institutional Change, and Economic Performance*.

31. K. Eisenhardt, 'Agency Theory. An Assessment', *Academy of Management Review* 14, no. 1 (1987): 57–74.

32. In a recent study of commitment in public enterprises (Munene, forthcoming) we were told, when looking for information on absenteeism, that no such data were available since collecting them would have led to low morale. I have also been reliably informed that the administrative arm of Makerere University has consistently resisted any form of appraisals, often leading to inconsistent and contradictory promotion decisions.

33. There is an alternative form that is gaining relative success. The form is based on altruism and participation. The non-governmental organization (NGO) is an example. However, this form suffers from the problem of institutionalization. That is, most NGOs start out with a particular philosophy such as that of altruism or participation, which they nevertheless eventually abandon or severely dilute due to the pressures of success or expansion. Many northern NGOs suffer, for instance, from the problems of overcentralization, bureaucratic red tape, and genuine lack of participation. Many southern NGOs become exploitative of donor agencies and of the

clients they set out to help. Theoretically this indicates that this form could in the end gravitate to one or the other of the basic forms outlined.

34. Williamson, 'The Economics of Organisation'; W.G. Ouchi, 'Markets, Bureaucracies, and Class', *Administrative Science Quarterly* 25 (1980): 129–41.

35. Republic of Uganda, *Report of the Public Service Review and Reorganisation Commission*; E.A. Brett, *Cost Effective Services for the Rural Poor: Policy and Institutional Reform in Uganda* (Sussex: Institute of Development Studies, 1992).

36. A. Hirshman, *Exit, Voice, and Loyalty* (Cambridge, MA: Harvard University Press, 1970); S. Paul, *Accountability in Public Services. Exit, Voice, and Capture* (New York: World Bank, 1990).

37. Ouchi, 'Markets, Bureaucracies, and Clans'.

38. Mowday, Porter and Dubin, 'Unit Performance, Situational Factors, and Employee Attitudes'.

39. N.J. Allen and J.P. Meyer, 'The Measurement and Antecedents of Affective, Continuance, and Normative Commitment', *Journal of Occupational Psychology* 63 (1990): 1–18.

40. R.T. Mowday, L. Porter and R.M. Steers, *Employee-Organisational Linkages, the Psychology of Commitment, Absenteeism, and Turnover* (London: Academic Press, 1982); H.L. Angle and J.L. Perry, 'An Empirical Assessment of Organisational Commitment and Organisational Effectiveness', *Administrative Science Quarterly* 26 (1981): 1–14; and J.P. Meyer and N.J. Allen, 'Links Between Work Experiences and Organisational Commitment During the First Years of Employment: A Longitudinal Analysis', *Journal of Occupational Psychology* 61 (1988): 195–209.

41. P.M. Blau, *Exchange and Power in Social Life* (New York: John Wiley, 1964); J.C. Adams, 'Inequality in Social Exchange', in L. Berkowitz (ed.), *Advances in Experimental Social Psychology* 2 (New York: Academic Press, 1965), 267–99; D.W. Organ and M.A. Konovsky, 'Cognitive versus Affective Determinants of Organisational Citizenship Behavior', *Journal of Applied Psychology* 74 (1989): 154–64; and R. Eisenberger, P. Fasolo and V. Davis-Lamastro, 'Perceived Organisational Support and Employee Diligence, Commitment, and Innovation', *Journal of Applied Psychology* 75, no. 1 (1990): 51–59.

42. Blau, *Exchange and Power in Social Life*.

43. A. Gouldner, 'The Norm of Reciprocity. A Preliminary Statement', *American Sociological Review* 25, no. 2 (1960): 161–79.

44. K. Eisenhardt, 'Agency Theory. An Assessment', *Academy of Management Review* 14 (1987): 57–75; M. Jensen and W. Meckling, 'Theory of the Firm: Managerial Behaviour, Agency Costs, and Ownership Structure', *Journal of Financial Economics* 3 (1976): 305–60.

45. Adams, 'Inequality in Social Exchange'.

46. See for instance literature on equity theory (e.g., J. Greenberg and R.L. Cohen, *Equity and Justice in Social Behavior* (New York: Academic Press,

1982), the most developed branch of the social exchange framework; L. Berkowitz and E. Walster, Preface in L. Berkowitz and E. Walster (eds), *Advances in Experimental Psychology*, vol. 9, *Equity Theory: Toward a General Theory of Social Interaction* (New York: Academic Press, 1976); C.G. McClintock and L. Keil, 'Equity and Social Exchange', in Greenberg and Cohen, *Equity and Justice in Social Behavior*.

47. B. Hvinden, 'Exits and Entrances. Notes on a Theory of Socialisation and Boundary Crossing in Work Organisations', *Acta Sociologica* 27, no. 3 (1984): 341–49.

48. Hvinden, 'Exits and Entrances', 193.

49. D. Katz and R.L. Kahn, *The Social Psychology of Organisations* (New York: Wiley, 1978); Organ, 'The Motivational Basis of Organisational Citizenship Behaviour'.

50. Olson, *The Logic of Collective Action*; North, *Institutions, Institutional Change, and Economic Performance*.

51. North, *Institutions, Institutional Change, and Economic Performance*.

52. Barnard, *The Functions of the Executive*.

53. Organ, 'The Motivational Basis of Organisational Citizenship Behaviour'.

54. Ibid., 4.

55. C.A. Smith, D.W. Organ and J.P. Near, 'Organisational Citizenship Behaviour: Its Nature and Antecedents', *Journal of Applied Psychology* 68 (1983): 653–63.

56. D.A. Kolb, I.M. Rubin and J.M. McIntyre, *Organisational Psychology. An Experiential Approach* (New York: Prentice Hall, 1974).

57. Organ and Konovsky, 'Cognitive versus Affective Determinants'.

58. See North, *Institutions, Institutional Change, and Economic Performance*.

59. P. Herriot, *Recruitment in the '90s* (London: IPM, 1989).

60. Kolb, Rubin, and McIntyre, *Organisational Psychology*.

61. Blau, *Exchange and Power in Social Life*.

62. A. Maslow, *Motivation and Personality* (New York: Harper, 1970).

63. P.A. Fiske, 'The Cultural Relativity of Selfish Individualism: Anthropological Evidence that Humans Are Inherently Sociable', in M.S. Clark (ed.), *Prosocial Behaviour* (New York: Sage, 1991).

64. Adams, 'Inequality in Social Exchange'.

65. D.D. Rusbult, I.M. Zembrodt and K. Gunn, 'Exit, Voice, Loyalty, and Neglect: Responses to Dissatisfaction in Romantic Involvements', *Journal of Personality and Social Psychology* 43 (1982): 1230–42.

66. Rusbult et al., 'Exit, Voice, Loyalty, and Neglect'.

67. Paul, *Accountability in Public Services*.

68. G.R. Jones, 'Transaction Costs, Property Rights, and Organisational Culture: An Exchange Perspective', *Administrative Science Quarterly* 28 (1987): 454–67.

69. D. Krebs, 'Prosocial Behaviour, Equity, and Justice', in Greenberg and Cohen, *Equity and Justice in Social Behaviour*.

70. J.L. Price and C.W. Mueller, *Absenteeism and Turnover of Hospital*

Employees (London: JAI Press, 1986).

71. J. Cook and T. Wall, 'New Work Attitude Measures of Trust, Organisational Commitment, and Personal Need Non-Fulfillment', *Journal of Occupational Psychology* 53 (1980): 39–52.
72. Cook and Wall, 'New Work Attitude Measures'.
73. N.J. Allen and J.P. Meyer, 'The Measurement and Antecedents of Affective, Continuance, and Normative Commitment', *Journal of Occupational Psychology* 63 (1990): 1–18.
74. J.C. Munene, 'Basic Clerical Disciplines, Attitudes, and Competences', Working paper, Birkbeck College, Department of Occupational Psychology, University of London, 1979.
75. Organ and Konovsky, 'Cognitive versus Affective Determinants'.
76. M.A. Blegen, C.W. Mueller, and J.L. Price, 'Measurement of Kinship Responsibility for Organisational Research', *Journal of Applied Psychology* 73, no. 3 (1988): 402–9.
77. See Blegen et al., 'Measurement of Kinship Responsibility'.
78. World Bank, *The African Capacity Building Initiative* (Washington, DC: The World Bank, 1990).
79. Republic of Uganda, *Report of the Public Service Review and Reorganisation Commission*.
80. Headmaster, Ggayaaza Primary School.
81. Headmaster, Ggayaaza Primary School.
82. Gouldner, 'The Norm of Reciprocity. A Preliminary Statement'.
83. See J.C. Munene, 'Organisational Pathology and Accountability: Their Relationship to Personal and Professional Accountability in Health and Educational Services in Rural Uganda', a report to ESCOR; ODA.
84. Drug kits are supplied by the Danish Red Cross on a quarterly basis. During this study we confirmed that in many districts, the kits do not last up to three months as they are supposed to.
85. Munene, 'Not-on-Seat'.
86. North, *Institutions, Institutional Change, and Economic Performance*.
87. Brett, *Cost Effective Services for the Rural Poor*.
88. Robinson, 'Labour Market Implications of Public Expenditure Constraints and Privatisation'.
89. L. Beneria, 'Structural Adjustment, the Labour Market and the Household: The Case of Mexico', in Standing and Tokman, *Towards Social Adjustment*.
90. Robinson, 'Labour Market Implications of Public Expenditure Constraints and Privatisation'.

6

Devaluation: The Response
of Exports and Imports

Kidane Mengisteab

Objectives of the study

There is very little disagreement that the valuation, in terms of local currencies, and the allocation of foreign exchange in sub-Saharan Africa as in other low-income undiversified economies should reflect its acute scarcity. There are, however, vocal disagreements on how best to do this in order to bring about external equilibrium and also to promote economic growth. One side of the argument is to devalue local currencies to reflect the scarcity of foreign exchange and to leave the allocation to the market mechanism. Another argument is that, in the case of low-income undiversified economies, the valuation and allocation of foreign exchange are best managed by government policies such as import controls, subsidies, taxes and multiple exchange rates.

The first argument is championed by the IMF and the World Bank. Devaluation is an integral component of the structural adjustment programmes they have prescribed for developing countries. In the past, sub-Saharan African states, by and large, have resisted devaluation. In the 1980s, however, burdened by the debt crisis and strapped for external funding, they have found compliance with the conditionalities of the IMF and the World Bank unavoidable. By the end of the 1980s, only three sub-Saharan African states, Ethiopia, Liberia and Rwanda, had not devalued.

Proponents expect devaluation to stimulate the expansion and diversification of exports by raising their prices in terms of domestic currency, and to expand their market share in the international market by

106

lowering their prices. The expansion of the volume of exports, in turn, is expected to more than compensate for the decline in prices and to raise export earnings, making the export sector the leading sector for general growth. On the import side, devaluation is, in the short run, expected to bring about a downward change by raising the prices of imports in terms of the domestic currency. In the long run, the export-led higher income is expected to drive imports upwards to a new equilibrium level at a higher standard of living.

The above views of devaluation have faced some serious challenges. For some, the relationship between devaluation and external balance of payments is at best inconclusive.[1] For others, the usefulness of devaluation as a tool for correcting external disequilibrium cannot be generalized to all types of disequilibria, much less to all types of economic structures.[2] Its relevance is thus qualified by a number of conditions among which are: 1) the level of competition (including responses of competitors to a given country's devaluation) and export restrictions such as quotas, that a country's exports face; 2) the elasticity of the supply of export commodities; 3) the elasticity of foreign demand for the devaluing country's exports; 4) the elasticity of the demand for foreign products in the devaluing country; and 5) the nature of the causes of the external disequilibrium, i.e. whether it is caused by uncompetitive costs of production or by external factors such as declining demand and prices at the international market.

Moreover, critics claim that as devaluation fails to increase export earnings it creates new economic and social problems, among which are the following:

1. It leads either to inflationary conditions through a wage-price spiral (if governments allow nominal wages to follow increases in prices of imports and their substitutes) or to reverse income redistribution and political conflict if governments suppress the wage increase pressures.[3]

2. By reducing the imports of intermediate goods, including machinery, spare parts, fertilizers, etc., and also by shifting income from wage earners to profit earners who generally have a lower propensity to consume,[4] devaluation leads to contraction of economic activity.

This study is an attempt to contribute to the debate on the relevance of devaluation in the case of sub-Saharan Africa by examining the responses of exports and imports of goods and non-factor services to devaluations.[5] The hypothesis to be tested is that in the low-income undiversified economies of sub-Saharan Africa, changes in real exchange rates (RERs) do not lead to significant changes in exports and imports, thus rendering devaluation ineffective as a mechanism for correcting external disequilibria. An attempt is also made to examine briefly the impacts of devaluation on inflation, income redistribution, economic growth, and broader structural changes of sub-Saharan African economies such as the transformation of the subsistence sector into a surplus-producing exchange economy and diversification through selective import substitution.

METHODOLOGY I

Testing the hypothesis raises several problems. The response time for both imports and exports to devaluation varies depending on the nature of the goods. The response time for imports of consumer goods can be expected to be rather short, while that of capital goods and inputs can be long since it takes considerable time for the production process to change to less import-intensive techniques. In countries where the chief exports are mineral products and perennial agricultural crops, the response to devaluation can also be expected to materialize within a year provided there is under-utilized capacity. However, in countries where the chief exports are tree crops such as coffee, cocoa and tea there is a considerable time lag between devaluation and the possible responses of such exports, since these products take up to five years between planting and harvest. In order to deal with these problems three testing approaches are selected.

The first test examines 1) the relationships between the dependent variable, annual changes in the values of exports (Y_1) and the annual changes in the independent variable, annual changes in RERs (X_1) in fourteen sub-Saharan African countries, and 2) the relationships between the dependent variable, annual changes in the values of imports (Y_2) and the independent variable X_1 in the same fourteen countries.[6] In order to determine if exports and imports respond to changes in the values of real exchange rates, the values of the independent variables are regressed against the values of the dependent variable of a year later. For the hypothesis to be rejected, changes in the values of RERs should be accompanied by significant changes in the values of exports and imports. The fourteen countries selected for inclusion in this test for reasons of availability of consistent data are: Cameroon, Congo, Côte d'Ivoire, Ethiopia, Ghana, Kenya, Malawi, Nigeria, Sudan, Tanzania, Uganda, Zaire, Zambia and Zimbabwe. The time period under study is 1966–83. The sources for the data used are Adrian Wood, *Global Trends in Real*

TABLE 6.1
Responses of the values of exports to devaluation

Country	Coefficients			
	b_1-y_1	PR	F-Value	Adj. R^2
Cameroon	-1.75	0.585	0.327	-0.092
Congo	1.41	0.500	0.506	-0.066
Côte d'Ivoire	1.33	0.476	0.567	-0.057
Ethiopia	-0.96	0.330	1.094	0.012
Ghana	-0.84	0.272	1.421	0.050
Kenya	-1.55	0.539	0.418	-0.079
Malawi	1.55	0.539	0.416	-0.079
Nigeria	1.68	0.571	0.354	-0.088
Sudan	-7.01	0.891	0.020	-0.140
Tanzania	2.52	0.703	0.158	-0.118
Uganda	9.49	0.919	0.011	-0.141
Zaire	0.34	0.022*	8.673	0.490
Zambia	2.79	0.731	0.128	-0.122
Zimbabwe	-3.66	0.793	0.074	-0.131

Note: * significant at 0.05 level of confidence.

Exchange Rates, 1960 to 1984, World Bank Discussion Paper, No. 35 and IMF, *International Financial Statistics Supplement on Trade Statistics*, 1988.

RESULTS OF THE FIRST TEST

The results of the first test show that, with the exception of Zaire's exports, the impacts of changes in the values of RERs are not accompanied by significant changes in the values of either exports or imports. Despite the exception (which appears to be a fluke with no clear explanation), the results of this test do not support the contention that devaluation through its impacts on exports and imports brings about the correction of external disequilibria in sub-Saharan Africa. These results are hardly surprising since even if devaluation has strong impacts on exports and imports, the impacts would, especially in the case of

TABLE 6.2
Responses of the values of imports to devaluation

Country	Coefficients			
	$b_2\text{-}y_1$	PR	F-Value	Adj. R^2
Cameroon	-1.66	0.566	0.363	-0.087
Congo	1.73	0.582	0.333	-0.091
Côte d'Ivoire	1.26	0.454	0.628	-0.049
Ethiopia	0.89	0.301	1.247	0.030
Ghana	-1.99	0.632	0.251	-0.103
Kenya	-0.87	0.287	1.331	0.040
Malawi	0.78	0.240	1.646	0.075
Nigeria	-2.69	0.721	0.138	-0.121
Sudan	0.53	0.102	3.550	0.242
Tanzania	0.43	0.055	5.306	0.350
Uganda	-1.26	0.455	0.626	-0.049
Zaire	-0.76	0.228	1.742	0.085
Zambia	-2.28	0.669	0.200	-0.111
Zimbabwe	4.44	0.828	0.051	-0.135

developing countries, take several years to materialize. We now try another approach that tests the responses of exports and imports over a longer period of time.

METHODOLOGY II

The second approach is made up of two tests. The first compares average annual growth rates of exports (x_1) and imports (x_2) of five years before and after devaluation for twenty-three cases of devaluations in sub-Saharan Africa. Averages of five years are selected since some of the exports such as coffee, cocoa and tea take up to five years between planting and harvesting. An analysis of variance is then utilized to determine whether the differences in the growth rates of exports and imports in the two time periods are significant. A second test is conducted in order to control the impacts of external factors, such as changes in commodity prices, during the two time periods. The growth rates of exports and imports of countries with real devaluations are compared with those of countries with only nominal devaluations. All other factors being common to both groups of countries, the exports of those with real devaluation can be expected to do better.

The same data sources as in the first test are used for this test. The data we have for imports and exports go up only to 1987 and since a five-year period is required for the response of exports of some commodities, the last devaluations that are included in this test are those of 1982. The IMF–World Bank-sponsored devaluations of the 1980s are thus excluded from consideration. However, the third test attempts to overcome this drawback.

RESULTS OF THE SECOND TEST

A glance at Table 6.3 shows that none of the nine nominal devaluations between 1966 and 1970 was accompanied by real devaluation. Yet with the exception of Ghana (see Table 6.4) all of the countries recorded rising export earnings during this period. This improved export performance is unlikely to be due to nominal devaluations. Rather, it might be explained better by the generally high commodity prices during this period.

Table 6.3 also shows that only seven of the fourteen nominal devaluations during the 1976–82 period were accompanied by real devaluations. A comparison of the performances of exports and imports of five years before and five years after devaluation for these seven cases with real devaluations shows no significant differences (see Table 6.5). In fact, with the exception of Madagascar, all of these real devaluations were accompanied by a decline in export performance which can be attributed to the general decline in commodity prices during this period. Even with such a decline in general commodity prices and other unfavourable external factors, the exports of the countries with real devaluations would be expected to perform better (or less badly) than those of countries with only nominal devaluations, since the external factors can be regarded as common to all. However, there are no significant differences in the exports of these two groups of countries. Thus, the second test also fails to support the hypothesis that devaluation of RERs improves the performances of exports. Even in this case, the absence of support for the hypothesis may be attributed to the failure of the devaluing countries to consistently maintain undervalued exchange rates for an extended period of time.[7]

TABLE 6.3
Selected devaluations vs. the US$ 1966–82

Devaluating country	Date of devaluation	Nominal devaluation in %	Changes in RERs in %*
Rwanda	1966	75.0	-24.29
Ghana	1967	21.5	-23.90
Zaire	1967	101.5	-26.43
Cameroon	1970	6.9	-5.20
Congo	1970	6.9	-9.36
Côte d'Ivoire	1970	6.9	-6.12
Madagascar	1970	6.9	-6.00
Senegal	1970	6.9	-10.35
Togo	1970	6.9	-13.23
Kenya	1976	13.9	1.14
Malawi	1976	5.7	0.80
Zambia	1976	12.2	-2.41
Burkina	1977	2.8	5.88
Niger	1977	2.8	6.14
Zaire	1977	8.2	17.69
Ghana	1978	53.4	-3.59
Sudan	1979	13.7	0.53
Madagascar	1982	23.1	2.93
Cameroon	1981	20.9	-8.48
Nigeria	1981	12.9	-3.18
Côte d'Ivoire	1981	20.9	-16.78
Somalia	1982	70.8	-33.44
Tanzania	1982	12.1	-0.64

Note: *Negative signs represent appreciation of real exchange rates.

Source: Computed from the figures in Adrian Wood, *Global Trends in Real Exchange Rates, 1960 to 1984* (Washington, DC: World Bank, World Bank Discussion Paper no. 35, 1988).

TABLE 6.4

Growth rates of the values of exports and imports of five years before and after devaluation

Country	Before devaluation		After devaluation			
	X	M	X	% change	M	% change
Rwanda	-21.9*	142.2	14.4	165.7	7.9	-111.9
Ghana	19.3	0.04	8.7	-54.9	0.9	2150.0
Zaire	7.9	2.6	11.8	49.4	20.8	700.0
Cameroon	11.0	10.5	17.5	59.1	20.5	95.2
Congo	-6.8	-4.9	47.4	797.1	24.4	597.9
Côte d'Ivoire	11.5	10.5	22.5	95.7	25.2	140.0
Madagascar	10.1	22.8	16.0	58.4	17.8	-21.9
Senegal	4.4	3.5	31.8	622.7	24.9	611.4
Togo	16.1	7.8	37.8	134.8	22.6	189.7
Kenya	22.1	13.7	10.0	-54.8	19.7	43.8
Malawi	18.4	15.7	11.1	-39.7	13.5	-14.0
Zambia	14.3	7.2	3.9	-72.7	11.6	61.1
Burkina	22.8	30.9	6.7	-70.6	11.4	-63.1
Niger	27.7	25.7	22.8	-17.7	22.5	-12.5
Zaire	9.2	2.1	-6.2	-167.4	-2.1	-200.0
Ghana	11.9	21.4	28.0	135.3	34.3	60.3
Sudan	10.5	12.5	4.9	-53.3	2.7	-78.4
Madagascar**	-4.8	1.4	1.9	139.6	-5.1	-464.3
Cameroon	18.9	19.8	-6.3	-133.3	5.6	-71.7
Côte d'Ivoire	10.7	14.9	6.7	-37.4	-1.7	-111.4
Nigeria*	-4.1	25.9	1.8	143.9	-21.1	-181.5
Somalia*	21.9	13.5	-0.3	-101.4	-10.2	-146.6
Tanzania**	-0.7	0.03	-4.1	-485.7	-2.4	-242.9

Notes: *Three years average is used due to missing data.
**Four years average is used due to missing data.

Source: IMF, *International Financial Statistics Supplement on Trade and Statistics* (Washington, DC: IMF, Supplement Series no. 15, 1988).

TABLE 6.5
Impacts of real devaluations on imports and exports

	Exports X_1	Imports X_2
F Value	2.12	0.94
PR	0.17	0.35
R^2	0.15	0.07
Mean B_d	15.13	14.57
Mean A_d	7.31	8.94
Mean difference between $B_d - A_d$	7.82	5.63

Notes: B_d represents before devaluation and A_d represents after devaluation.
The differences in the performances of exports and imports before and after devaluation are not significant at the 0.05 level of confidence.

METHODOLOGY III

A third approach utilized is a comparison of the growth rates of the values of exports (x_1), values of imports (x_2), GDP (x_3) and average annual changes of current account balance (x_4) of four groups of countries. The first group (GP1) is comprised of countries with an average of over 10 per cent rate of devaluation of RERs for the period between 1980 and 1987. The second group (GP2) consists of countries with real devaluation rates of less than 10 per cent and more than 5 per cent, the third group (GP3) consists of countries with below 5 per cent average real devaluation rates and the fourth group (GP4) consists of countries that have not devalued or have revalued. The time period under consideration in this test is 1980–87, a period that was essentially excluded from the previous two tests. Devaluations in the later years of this period do not allow sufficient response time for some of the exports. However, each of the selected devaluing countries began a series of devaluations in 1980 or 1981. Therefore, this approach can detect a trend on the impact of real devaluation on exports, imports and consequently, on current account balance (CAB) as well as on gross domestic product (GDP). The data for this test are acquired from IMF, *International Financial Statistics* (several years), IMF, *International Financial Statistics: Supplement on Trade Statistics*, 1988 and United Nations Development Programme and the World Bank, *African Economic and Financial Data*, 1989.[8]

The results of the third test also do not reject the null hypothesis, as the four groups of countries do not show any significant difference in any

TABLE 6.6
Input

Country	Devaluation rate in %	X (x_1)	M (x_2)	GDP (x_3)	CAB (x_4)
GP1					
Nigeria	16.7	-11.1	-17.6	-2.6	298.7
Burkina	15.9	5.6	-1.2	5.2	-265.9*
Côte d'Ivoire	10.7	-0.3	-6.8	0.7	13.5*
GP2					
Ghana	5.6	2.8	2.2	0.9	-237.3
Zaire	8.2	3.0	-5.0	1.5	-23.0
Zambia	6.4	-2.2	-8.4	-0.1	-0.8
Madagascar	8.0	-7.4	-10.4	0.03	20.5*
Malawi	7.2	1.1	-4.9	2.0	-778.5
Cameroon	9.5	9.5	2.9	6.2	210.0*
Kenya	6.0	2.4	-2.8	3.3	-88.1
GP3					
Sierra Leone	4.4	-7.6	-24.7	-0.3	23.8*
Sudan	4.6	-3.5	-8.0	0.9	12.1
Tanzania	4.3	-4.1	-2.0	1.6	-1.9*
GP4					
Ethiopia	0.0	-0.02	7.9	3.5	-826.9*
Liberia	0.0	-3.9	-6.1	-1.4	59.1
Rwanda	-2.3	3.5	5.8	2.2	-24.2

Note: *Average of six years is used due to missing data.

Source: Computed from IMF, *International Financial Statistics Supplement on Trade and Statistics*, 1988; United Nations Development Programme and the World Bank, *African Economic and Financial Data* (Washington, DC: World Bank, 1989).

TABLE 6.7
Results of the third test

	Exports X_1	Imports X_2	GDP X_3	CAB X_4
F Value	1.06	-2.05	0.21	0.53
PR	0.4006	0.1609	0.8904	0.6717
R^2	0.2101	0.3386	0.0489	0.1165
Mean GP1	-1.933	-8.533	1.100	15.433
Mean GP2	1.314	-3.771	1.976	-128.171
Mean GP3	-5.067	-11.567	0.733	11.333
Mean GP4	-0.140	2.533	1.433	-264.000
Mean Difference				
GP1-GP2	-3.248	-4.762	-0.876	143.600
GP1-GP3	3.133	3.033	0.367	4.100
GP1-GP4	-1.793	-11.067	-0.333	279.400
GP2-GP3	6.381	7.795	1.242	-139.500
GP2-GP4	1.454	-6.305	0.542	135.800
GP3-GP4	-4.927	-14.100	-0.700	275.300

of the variables tested (see Table 6.7). None of the three tests thus rejects
the hypothesis that devaluation of RERs did not bring about the correction
of external disequilibrium in sub-Saharan Africa during the period
between 1966 and 1987. It may be argued that the reason for the
ineffectiveness of devaluation is that the devaluation rates in sub-Saharan
Africa were not sufficient and that higher rates would correct the
problem. Higher rates, however, while capable of depressing imports, are
not likely to raise export earnings (see the next section on reasons for the
ineffectiveness of devaluation). And without raising export earnings,
further devaluations tend to lead to adverse economic conditions that are
discussed in the section below on the negative impacts of devaluation.

Reasons for the ineffectiveness of devaluation

There are a number of plausible explanations for why devaluation has not
been effective in correcting external disequilibria in sub-Saharan Africa.

TABLE 6.8
World demand elasticities of selected primary commodities

Product	Demand elasticity
Cocoa	-0.300
Coffee	0.230
Tea	-0.250

Source: Pasquale L. Scandizzo and Dimitris Diakosawas, *Instability in the Terms of Trade of Primary Commodities, 1900-1982*, Economic and Social Development Paper no. 64 (Rome: FAO, 1987).

One reason is the low demand elasticities of primary commodities at the international level. Coffee, cocoa and tea have faced a near saturated demand at the international market (see Table 6.8).[9] Copper continues to be displaced by other metals. Synthetic substitutes have also affected cotton. Recession in the industrialized countries in the early 1980s contributed to the stagnation of demand and the decline of prices of primary commodities. Projected increases in the volume of world commodity exports are also hardly promising.[10]

Given such low elasticities, devaluation can hardly be expected to increase the global consumption of these commodities. Individual devaluating countries can certainly raise their market share at the expense of other commodity exporters. In the 1980s, however, devaluation has become a common occurrence among large numbers of primary commodity exporters. Attempts by a large number of countries to increase the volume of their exports through devaluation has worsened the over-supply of primary commodities in the world market, culminating in the fall of their prices. Thus, contrary to increasing the volume and thus earnings of exports, devaluation results in the loss of export earnings when the size of the share of the devaluing groups of countries together in total world supply is significant and when the price-elasticity of the exports is low.[11]

Sub-Saharan Africa's foreign exchange problems and its economic crisis are generally more serious than those in other regions of the developing world. This has often been attributed by many to the overvaluation of sub-Saharan Africa's currencies. However, trends of real exchange rates do not provide a strong support for this argument. Between 1960 and 1984, sub-Saharan African currencies significantly depreciated relative to those of industrial and middle-income economies

TABLE 6.9

Actual real exchange rate trends by country groups (1980–84 average as ratio of 1960–64 average)

Region/country	Official rate	Black market rate
India	0.62	0.83
China	0.40	0.96
Other low-income econ.	0.60	0.58
Low-income Africa	0.76	0.71
Low-income Asia	0.59	0.74
Oil-importing middle-income economies	0.87	0.95
High-income oil exporters	3.52	3.66
Industrial economies	1.00	–

Source: Wood, *Global Trends in Real Exchange Rates*, 66.

and only modestly appreciated relative to those of other low-income economies (see Table 6.9). Furthermore, such a claim requires the support of comparative data not only on exchange-rate trends but also on the rates of subsidies, export taxes, import tariffs as well as direct controls, variables for which data are not available. In any case, it seems that sub-Saharan African countries suffer the most from the decline of the prices and market share of primary commodities primarily because their exports are more dominated by non-oil primary commodities than are those of the other regions of the Third World. In 1986, for example, the percentage of exports of non-primary commodities to total exports for twenty-seven sub-Saharan African countries averaged only 13.8 per cent compared to 43.3 per cent for thirteen Asian and Pacific countries (excluding Japan, Taiwan, Singapore, Hong Kong, and the two Koreas) and 25.1 per cent for twenty Latin American and Caribbean countries.[12]

Proponents recognize the limitations of the effects of devaluation on export earnings in the short run due to the inelastic world demand for primary commodities. However, they expect devaluation to alter the internal terms of trade between tradeable and non-tradeable goods and thus to increase the incentives for export production, including non-traditional commodities, and to promote less import-intensive production methods. Devaluation of real rates certainly shifts the internal terms of trade in favour of internationally tradeable goods. A combination of devaluation and price deregulation has, for example, raised the producer price for cocoa in Ghana from 12,000 cedis per tonne in April 1983 to 174,000 cedis per tonne in 1989.[13] Whether this redistribution of income will promote export diversification remains to be seen, although the third approach of this study, which tested export earnings over a period of seven years, gives little indication that the process of export-diversification has begun to make a difference in export earnings.[14] Moreover, the process of diversification would depend on a number of factors such as production and marketing capabilities in addition to exchange-rate incentives.

Negative impacts of devaluation

As already noted, high rates of devaluation can depress imports and reduce external disequilibrium even without raising export earnings. This type of adjustment is, however, likely to fuel several economic and social problems. Among such problems are inflation, contraction of economic activity, reverse income redistribution, social conflict and slowing of structural changes. We now briefly examine the impacts of devaluation on each of these problems.

IMPACTS ON INFLATION

Increases in the local currency value of imports spark a general price increase by raising the prices of imported consumer goods, of capital goods, imported raw materials and other intermediate goods. The pressure for higher prices is followed by pressure for wage increases. The higher the devaluation rate the higher the inflationary pressure is. The inflationary ramification of devaluation is evident from Table 6.10 where the increases in the consumer price index correspond with the nominal devaluation rates.[15] As Gulhati et al. argue,[16] the inflationary impact of devaluation may be preventable by budgetary and monetary restraints, and wage controls. However, such policies, which reinforce the redistribution of income in favour of the export sector and against the domestic sector (including urban consumers, civil servants and even small food producers), may prove politically difficult to maintain for long unless devaluation quickly increases export earnings and thereby generates economic growth or is accompanied by significant resource inflows from aid-donors. Authoritarian governments may be expected to be more successful in sustaining such policies. However, such governments would also have to divert resources from economic to security concerns, which undermines the objectives of devaluation.

TABLE 6.10

Devaluations and changes in consumer price index of selected African states, 1980–87

Country	Nominal devaluation in %	Average annual changes in consumer prices in %
GP1		
Ghana	5490.3	49.9
Sierra Leone	2836.9	74.0
Zaire	3914.4	53.4
Zambia	1106.8	27.5
GP2		
Madagascar	406.1	18.5
Malawi	171.1	15.2
Nigeria	634.5	16.4
Sudan	500.0	28.6
Tanzania	683.9	30.4
GP3		
Cameroon	42.2	10.7
Kenya	81.9	10.9
Côte d'Ivoire	42.2	5.8
Burkina	42.2	4.9
GP4		
Ethiopia	0.0	21.2
Liberia	0.0	3.6
Rwanda	-14.2	5.4

Source: Computed from the IMF, *International Financial Statistics Supplement*, and UNDP and the World Bank, *African Economic and Financial Data*.

IMPACTS ON OVERALL ECONOMIC ACTIVITY

That devaluation can lead to economic contraction has been widely recognized.[17] One reason why devaluation can lead to a decline in real output is because it raises the value of imported inputs of production, which tends to lower capacity utilization. Most sub-Saharan African countries already face large current account deficits and huge debt obligations that have lead to import strangulation which, in turn, has led to contraction of production and development projects. Singh, for example, points out that import strangulation has forced Tanzania's manufacturing industry to operate at only 20 per cent of capacity, while agricultural production has been hampered by scarcity of inputs such as fertilizers.[18] While the degree of import strangulation varies from country to country, many other sub-Saharan African countries, including Uganda, Sudan, Zaire and Madagascar, have suffered severe capacity under-utilization.[19] In the short run, devaluation can only worsen the problem of import strangulation since, as our three tests indicate, exports have not responded to devaluation to offset the increases in import prices brought about by devaluation.

Recent experiences of some sub-Saharan African states suggest that devaluation, in company with import decontrols, is also likely to undermine the efforts of these countries to diversify their economies through import-substitution industrialization. In Nigeria, closures have become rampant, with manufacturers often blaming the difficulties on reduction of protectionist barriers and on the sharp cost increases for imported raw materials and spare parts brought on by devaluation.[20] In Côte d'Ivoire, the number of workers employed in textile industries dropped from 12,000 in 1982 to 8,000 in 1987.[21]

Another reason why devaluation is contractionary is its impact on income distribution. It shifts income from wage earners to profit earners, who generally have a lower propensity to consume. Devaluation's impacts on the prices of inputs also affects producers, especially the small ones. Subsistence peasants are, for example, likely to be excluded from access to imported inputs such as fertilizers by higher prices. Both these factors depress aggregate demand and thereby lead to economic contraction.[22]

IMPACTS ON INCOME REDISTRIBUTION

Reliable and consistent data on income distribution are not available for sub-Saharan Africa. Our analysis in this regard is thus essentially conceptual. Some have argued that overvaluation of currencies leads to skewed income distribution since it discriminates against agriculture in favour of import-substitution industry, which employs only a small percentage of the population.[23] Implied in this argument is that devaluation, by favouring agriculture over industry, will bring about a more equitable distribution of income. There is, however, a problem with this analysis. Devaluation improves the relative prices of cash crops in local currency. It also raises the prices of imported agricultural products, which in company with price decontrols may raise the demand for and the relative prices of local food products. Both these developments raise the incomes of cash crop producers and those of surplus-producing farmers. However, the impact of devaluation on the subsistence sector can very well be negative. There is lack of data on what percentage of the peasantry in sub-Saharan Africa is engaged in the production of export-oriented cash crops, what segment of it is capable of producing surplus food and what portion of it is essentially subsistent. It is thus not clear what percentage of the peasantry might benefit from devaluation. If Ghana's experience is indicative, however, only a small segment benefits. As already noted, devaluation in Ghana contributed to the increase in the producer price of cocoa from 12,000 cedis per tonne in April 1983 to 174,000 cedis per tonne in April 1989. However, only about 18 per cent of Ghana's farmers grow cocoa and 94 per cent of the gross cocoa income has gone to the 32 per cent of cocoa producers who are large farmers.[24] The small size of the marketed portion of the produce of the farmers of sub-Saharan Africa may also indicate that its peasantry is essentially subsistent, and that it needs to have access to productivity-raising agricultural inputs and raise its productive capability before it can benefit from devaluation and price decontrols.[25] Devaluation, by raising the prices of imported inputs such as fertilizers and thus denying the subsistence peasantry access to such inputs, may worsen income maldistribution and impair the transformation of the subsistence sector into a surplus-producing exchange economy. It may also worsen the discrimination against food production relative to cash crops since it is geared to making exports more profitable than non-traded goods, although it may also increase the competitiveness of domestic food production against imported food products.

Devaluation, through its impact on general prices, also shifts resources from wages to profits and thereby promotes reverse income redistribution. For instance, with three steep devaluations in Mozambique between January 1987 and January 1988, the official exchange rate against the US dollar was slashed from MT40 to MT450.[26] With these devaluations overall prices rose about 210 per cent, while wages rose by only about 70 per cent.[27] This reverse income redistribution affects the general level of output by lowering aggregate demand. It also leads to increased social conflict which, in turn, leads to increased appropriation of resources for security.

Conclusion

A comparative analysis of the performances of devaluation and state intervention in the valuation and allocation of foreign exchange was beyond the scope of this chapter. Considering the self-serving nature and sometimes the sheer incompetence of many governments in sub-Saharan Africa, allocation of foreign exchange by government policy through rationing of foreign exchange or through other policies such as a multiple exchange-rate policy, import controls, and subsidizing of exports has often been ineffective, as proponents of devaluation point out. However, the findings of this study also do not justify the importance that devaluation has been given in the adjustment programmes for the recovery of African economies. First, evidence does not support past appreciation of real exchange rates being at the root of Africa's economic problems. Second, due to the low demand and price elasticities of primary commodities on the world market, devaluation is unlikely to lead to significant improvement of balance of payments as long as African economies remain undiversified. Third, while the results of the tests do not allow us to conclude that devaluation does not lead to export diversification in the long run, it is likely that its impact in this regard is also exaggerated since diversification requires much more than devaluation. In the light of these findings, and also considering that devaluation may aggravate many of sub-Saharan Africa's economic problems by fuelling economic contraction, inflation and reverse income redistribution when it fails to increase export earnings, the importance that devaluation has been given in the economic reform programmes may need to be scrutinized more carefully.

Notes

(This article reprinted with permission from *Africa Development* 16, no. 3/4 [1991].)

1. Michael Mussa, 'The Theory of Exchange Rate Determination', in J. Bilson and R. Marston (eds), *Exchange Rate Theory and Practice* (Chicago: University of Chicago Press, 1984).

2. Alfred Maizels, 'The Impact of Currency Devaluation on Commodity Production and Exports of Developing Countries', Discussion Paper no. 86-07, University College London, 1986, 20.

3. Ajit Singh, 'Tanzania and the IMF: The Analytics of Alternative Adjustment Programs', *Development and Change* 17, no. 3 (July 1986): 425–54.

4. Carlos F. Diaz-Alejandro, 'A Note on the Impact of Devaluation and the Redistributive Effect', *Journal of Political Economy* 71, no. 6 (December 1963): 577–80.

5. Exports are better indicators of the impacts of devaluation than imports, since high levels of imports could be maintained due to aid or accumulation of debt despite devaluation. For the same reason, exports are also better indicators than balance of payments. So, while the impact of devaluation on imports is also tested in this study the emphasis is on the response of exports to changes in real exchange rates.

6. The two equations tested in the first test are $Y_1 = a + bX_1 + E$ and $Y_2 = a + bX_1 + E$ where a stands for the constant, b stands for the coefficients and E represents the standard error. These two equations are run separately for each of the fourteen countries.

7. Richard D. Fletcher, 'Undervaluation, Adjustment and Growth', in John F. Weeks (ed.), *Debt Disaster? Banks, Governments and Multilaterals Confront the Crisis* (New York: New York University Press, 1989), 126.

8. Real exchange rates are estimated on the basis of the equation, $RER = EP^*/P$, where E = nominal devaluations, P^* = foreign price index (consumer price index of industrialized countries, which are the most important trading partners of sub-Saharan African countries) and P = consumer price index of each sub-Saharan African country in the test.

9. Ravi Gulhati, Swadesh Bose and Vimal Atukorala, 'Exchange Rate Policies in Africa: How Valid is the Scepticism?', *Development and Change* 17, no. 3 (July 1986): 412.

10. World Bank Staff, *The Outlook for Primary Commodities*, Commodity Working Paper no. 9 (Washington, DC: World Bank, 1983).

11. M. Godfrey, 'Trade and Exchange Rate Policy: A Further Contribution to the Debate', in T. Rose (ed.), *Crisis and Recovery in Sub-Saharan Africa* (Paris: OECD, 1985), 168–79; Maizels, 'The Impact of Currency Devaluation'.

12. World Bank, *The World Bank Annual Report 1988* (Washington, DC: World Bank, 1989).

13. John Araka et al., 'Farmers Adjust to Economic Reforms', *African Farmer* 3 (April 1990): 7.

14. Perhaps the strongest case for devaluation is its expected impact on export diversification. However, we may have to wait well into the 1990s before we can determine this impact of the devaluations of the 1980s.

15. The causal relationship between devaluation and inflation is not unidirectional since the pressure to devalue may also be instigated by inflation. However, whatever its initial causes are, devaluation increases the

inflationary pressure.

16. Ravi Gulhati, Swadesh Bose and Vimal Atukorala, *Exchange Rate Policies in Eastern and Southern Africa, 1965-1983*, World Bank Staff Working Papers, no. 720 (Washington, DC: World Bank, 1985), 22.

17. R. Cooper, 'Currency Devaluation in Developing Countries', in G. Ranis (ed.), *Government and Economic Development* (New Haven: Yale University Press, 1971), 472-513; Paul Krugman and Lance Taylor, 'Contractionary Effects of Devaluation', *Journal of International Economics* 8 (1978): 445-56; Sweder van Wijnbegen, 'Exchange Rate Management and Stabilization Policies in Developing Countries', in S. Edwards and L. Ahamed (eds), *Economic Adjustment and Exchange Rates in Developing Countries* (Chicago: University of Chicago Press, 1986), 17-41; Sebastian Edwards, *Real Exchange Rates, Devaluation, and Adjustment: Exchange Rate Policy in Developing Countries* (Cambridge, MA: MIT Press, 1989); Sebastian Edwards, 'Are Devaluations Contractionary?', *Review of Economics and Statistics* 68 (August 1986): 501-8.

18. Singh, 'Tanzania and the IMF', 429.

19. Gulhati et al., *Exchange Rate Policies*, 30.

20. Ernest Harsch, 'Privatization: No Simple Panacea', *Africa Recovery* 2, no. 4 (December 1988): 14.

21. Harsch, 'Privatization', 14.

22. Diaz-Alejandro, 'A Note on the Impact of Devaluation and the Redistributive Effect'.

23. Kevin M. Cleaver, *The Impact of Price and Exchange Rate Policies on Agriculture in Sub-Saharan Africa*, World Bank Staff Working Papers no. 728 (Washington, DC: World Bank, 1985), 24.

24. Araka et al., 'Farmers Adjust to Economic Reforms', 7.

25. D. Ghai and L. Smith, *Agricultural Prices, Policy and Equity in Sub-Saharan Africa* (Boulder, CO: Lynne Rienner Publishers, 1987), 60-67.

26. 'Mozambique: The Economic Rehabilitation Programme One Year On', *Africa Recovery* 2, no. 1 (March 1988): 9.

27. Ibid., 12.

PART 2

Other Ways Forward:
Democratization and Regional Integration

7

Overcoming Africa's Crisis:
Adjusting Structural Adjustment Towards
Sustainable Development in Africa·

Hartmut Krugmann

Introduction

The nature and impacts of structural adjustment programmes (SAPs) in
Africa and elsewhere in the developing world is a hotly debated theme.[1]
A lot has been written about the topic, and the literature continues to
grow. The environmental implications of SAPs have emerged as a
relatively recent concern.

The purpose of this chapter is to arrive at some general conclusions,
for (sub-Saharan) Africa as a whole, about the relevance and effects of
SAPs on social, economic, institutional, political and environmental
aspects. I do not wish to ignore the significant differences across different
African countries. They are real and must be taken into account, notably
in policy reform. But there are also striking similarities in the history,
culture, structural features, and development prospects and constraints of
societies throughout Africa that distinguish this continent from other
developing regions. It is my intention to focus on the common elements
and the unique situation of Africa *vis-à-vis* other regions – primarily at
the conceptual level but building on accumulated experience.

In the next section, I analyse Africa's multi-faceted development
crisis. I attempt to make a distinction between underlying causes and
mere symptoms, both internal and external. The third section deals with

---

·The views expressed in this chapter are those of the author and do not
represent or reflect those of the International Development Research Centre.

the SAPs as designed and prescribed by the IMF and the World Bank. Their main features are described, and the various aspects of critiques that the SAPs have been subjected to are examined. Environmental aspects are assessed, among other things. A number of shortcomings in the SAP approach are identified. The final section of the chapter presents some principles for an alternative adjustment approach.

Africa in crisis: symptoms and causes

Africa is in the midst of a difficult and complex development crisis. A variety of economic, social, environmental, political, institutional and cultural factors have been identified as having influenced or helped bring about the present crisis. However, in pinpointing these factors, it is often the case that not enough effort has been made to try to distinguish between underlying causes and mere symptoms of the crisis. In this section, I will attempt such a distinction, with a view to isolating the principal structural causes and past policy approaches that are likely to have been mainly responsible for Africa's present malaise. This analysis will naturally provide clues as to what kind of structural change and policy adjustment might be needed to turn things around on the continent.

SYMPTOMS

When it comes to analysing Africa's development crisis, there is a widespread tendency to start with, and sometimes restrict attention to, *economic* problems. The literature is replete with relevant information, and it is not difficult to catalogue a number of such problems, internal or external. Among the *internal* economic problems that are usually mentioned are: declining economic performance as measured by conventional indicators such as national income or GDP per capita; excessive public-sector spending; burgeoning government budget deficits; expanding urban informal sector;[2] rising inflation; substantial capital flight (hard currency) from individuals/companies in the region to the North;[3] and rampant corruption.

Frequently cited *external* economic problems include: declining terms of trade; resulting trade deficits; lack of direct foreign investment; virtually no new loans from foreign commercial banks; high and fluctuating international interest rates; negative balance-of-payments accounts; a crippling foreign debt burden;[4] mounting debt service payments;[5] and a resulting decapitalization in Africa.[6]

Some of the 'external' problems actually have a clear domestic policy component. The accumulated mountain of foreign debt, for instance, has its origin, in part, in irresponsible borrowing by Southern élites (as well as reckless lending by Northern banks) for dubious projects and outright speculation. This happened in the early 1970s, when foreign exchange markets were flooded with so-called Eurodollars,[7] and excess liquidity in international capital markets drove international interest rates to record lows.

Likewise, most of the 'internal' economic problems mentioned above are influenced by external policy- and decision-making processes. Generally, African countries are now firmly integrated into the international economic/financial order (see next sub-section) and African governments have increasingly been forced to run their economies under a system of aid conditionalities which severely constrains freedom of economic policy choice. The Fund/Bank-designed SAPs are a good example of such aid conditionality. Specifically in regard to the interconnectedness of the 'internal' problem of capital flight to the North, foreign banks do not seem to mind accepting fugitive hard currency resources while at the same time insisting on debt service payments which could have been met, in part, by using the lost foreign exchange.

In addition to economic factors, there are a host of other problems indicative or reflective of the crisis. For instance, in most African countries per capita food production has been declining dramatically and food imports have become an important drain on available foreign exchange. Food insecurity has risen, both nationally and at the local level. In most African countries, social variables in the areas of health, nutrition and education have been deteriorating. Large and increasing segments of the population suffer from material *poverty* and lack of longer-term choices. *Urbanization*, in part a reflection of both precarious conditions in rural areas and government policy bias in favour of urban areas, is proceeding at a very rapid pace.[8]

At the political level, governments have tended to intervene in self-serving (and inefficient) ways, with limited accountability and without much popular participation in decision-making processes. All over Africa highly centralized political authority, and often autocratic rule, have reflected governments' perceived need to exercise tight control over people and resources. In some sub-regions (e.g., the Horn of Africa or Lusophone Southern Africa), ethnic strife and armed conflict have created large internal and external refugee populations. Ethnic tensions, perceived insecurity, and armed conflict have meant increased military expenditures and arms imports by African governments, consuming valuable foreign exchange.[9]

Last but not least, the bio-physical environment and natural resource base, on which the well-being of people, communities and countries depends very directly, is being degraded at an alarming rate – in spite of the undeniable potential and despite the fact that it is still far from being fully exploited. The symptoms of widespread natural resource degradation and environmental decline are readily apparent. Overall in Africa, some 3.7 million hectares of forest and woodland are disappearing every year. Removal of vegetation cover exposes the continent's fragile soils to the forces of erosion. Losses of 20 to 50 tonnes of topsoil are not uncommon in areas under cultivation.[10] Habitat loss is leading to significant reductions in biodiversity. Clean water is becoming a scarce commodity in the region. And air pollution (indoor and outdoor) is already greatly affecting the well-being of most rural and urban poor.[11]

It is clear that most of the problems listed above are both complex and interdependent. It is equally evident that they have contributed significantly to Africa's development crisis. Nevertheless, these problems have been largely symptoms, rather than fundamental causes of the crisis. What then are the causes of the crisis?

CAUSES

In the following diagnosis of the causes underlying Africa's development crisis, it seems useful again to use the categories 'internal' and 'external'. The fundamental *external* systemic cause of the crisis, I suggest, lies in profound and far-reaching changes in the international economic and political order and in the global policy environment that have taken place in the recent past, particularly since 1980. The global context within which we find ourselves today has little in common with the international order shaped after the Second World War. Some have argued that the very idea of global development which emerged from that post-war order is collapsing.[12] They say that global forces have been unleashed to forge an international system in which there seems to be no place for the notion that Third World countries can and will be lifted up to the level of developed countries if they adopt the right policies and receive required international assistance. Let us look at some of the dimensions of the changed global context.

The globalization of the world economy. The production and distribution of goods and services increasingly transcend national borders. Likewise, market competition has become internationalized and is fuelling economic competition between the dominant economic powers. This is motivating a search for opportunities to exploit economies of scale, reduce costs, and increase productivity so as to gain the upper hand in the economic race. In the process, corporate economic power is being concentrated in fewer and fewer hands. A small number of powerful transnational companies have come to dominate worldwide production and distribution of goods and services, operating more and more outside the control of nation-states. Financial markets largely function independently of the production and distribution of goods and services. New communication technologies have allowed financial markets to become integrated worldwide. Capital flows freely across national borders.

International trade is changing in nature, direction and content. The principles of balanced trade and comparative (cost) advantage are losing their significance.[13] The current trade situation is characterized rather by countries seeking absolute advantage over others, a situation which is prone to lead to trade imbalances. Prevailing economic wisdom calls for 'free trade', i.e., the greatest possible removal of trade barriers, worldwide. The current (Uruguay) round of trade negotiations under GATT is discussing proposals to extend the principle of free trade to sectors hitherto governed by special rules, namely agriculture, food, and service sectors such as banking. An ever greater proportion of the trade is taking place within emerging regional trading blocks[14] as well as within and between transnational companies.[15] At the same time, the content of international trade (measured in terms of exchange values) is shifting away from primary commodities (primarily exported by developing countries) to high-technology products (typically exported by developed countries).

The globalization of the economy and financial markets, coupled with far-reaching trade liberalization, present certain opportunities to some of the more advanced developing countries.[16] However, the least developed countries, many of them in Africa, may find themselves increasingly unable to participate in the global economic 'supermarket', for one or more of the following reasons. Their levels of infrastructure, technology and managerial skills are not sufficient to attract direct foreign investment; their primary export commodities fetch ever less in the world market and increasingly face artificial substitutes being developed in industrial countries; and they are exposed to the forces of international economic competition but their infant industries cannot compete with efficient transnational companies.

Global technological revolution. The last decade has seen a revolution in technological and technical change,[17] largely confined to the industrialized countries. Discoveries and applications primarily in micro-electronics, biotechnology, and new material technologies, as well as novel information and communication systems based on these technologies, are beginning to stimulate parallel social and institutional change, and to transform the way advanced economies and societies work. Among other applications, biotechnology and advanced technologies are being harnessed in the North to develop substitutes for the South's principal agricultural and mineral commodities. Those countries who are not able to participate in the technological revolution, and continue to be largely dependent on exports of primary commodities, risk being marginalized. This risk is particularly great for Africa.

New environmental awareness. The past few years have seen the emergence of a new awareness that the capacity of local and global ecosystems to support ever-growing human economic activity is finite and already approaching its limits. The importance of maintaining the integrity of the biophysical environment as the principal life-supporting system is being increasingly recognized. The new consciousness is a result of mounting evidence of both widespread local environmental degradation (soil erosion, deforestation, etc.) and global environmental change (climate, ozone holes, etc.). In the industrialized countries, the perceived global environmental limits have prompted renewed demands for checking population growth in the South and led to additional environmental conditionalities being attached to development aid to the Third World. But there is also an incipient feeling that continued economic growth and material progress based on advances in science and technology – a cornerstone of the Western ethos – cannot be taken for granted any more, and that lifestyles as well as consumption and production patterns may have to be changed fundamentally to ensure environmental sustainability. In the Third World, there is great concern that Northern environmental demands and conditionalities will hinder badly needed economic growth and thus lead to yet greater underdevelopment and poverty in the South.

This situation presents a real danger that developing countries, in particular Africa, might be caught between the fire and the frying pan: reluctance in industrial countries to change lifestyles and consumption patterns and a system of international economic relations which perpetuates subsidization of the North by the South[18] on the one hand, and powerlessness of the South to expand available environmental and economic 'space' and respond to explosive social demands in their own hemisphere on the other.

A changed geopolitical order. The collapse of the Communist system in the Soviet Union and Eastern Europe and the end of the Cold War have fundamentally altered the balance of power in the world. Previously monolithic political blocks are dissolving, and the rigid ideological alternatives that these blocks represented have all but disappeared. As the political rationale for maintaining previous political alliances is being eroded and as global economic competition intensifies, there is a growing risk of geopolitical fragmentation as well as inward-looking behaviour among the major powers. Changes may be ushering in an era of 'cold peace' characterized by heightened geopolitical instability. What we are witnessing, partly as a result of the current geopolitical rearrangements, are shifts in global ideological and socio-cultural value systems, toward Westernized market-based consumerism and popular culture.

At the same time, global economic forces and environmental problems call into question the effectiveness of conventional political systems based on the concept of the nation-state. The trend toward economic transnationalization (see above) is increasingly eroding the ability of the nation-states – particularly weaker states – to exercise control over what happens within their boundaries. The emergence of regional trading blocks and economic communities implies willingness on the part of member states to give up some of their sovereignty in favour of regional institutions. Similarly, global environmental problems such as climate change and loss of biodiversity require collective solutions which cannot be effective unless nation-states agree to accept and enforce global agreements and conventions which curtail national autonomy and sovereignty in the common global interest.

There are major implications for the Third World and for Africa in particular. The end of the East–West polarization and stand-off and the focusing of Western interests on assisting the East and integrating it in the current economic order appear to be leading to far-reaching disengagement of the North from Africa. Africa's perceived geopolitical and global economic significance is decreasing as a result. Furthermore, the forces of economic transnationalization and environmental globalism are hitting Africa at a time when a number of its countries are only starting to leave behind their colonial past and trying to form a national identity. Africa is under threat to lose out on both Northern assistance and internal cohesiveness in the process.

The relationships between a dramatically changed global system and a component of that system (Africa) which is being marginalized as a result of global forces has its mirror image at the national level in Africa. I suggest that the *internal* systemic cause of Africa's development crisis is associated with structural rigidities operating within most countries of the continent.

I wish to start from the apparent fact that the debt crisis has hit Africa harder than other developing regions. This can be seen by looking at some indicators. The ratio of total debt to GNP in the period 1980–87 in Africa was at least twice that in other developing regions. Or, the ratio of the average growth rate of total debt stock to that of the average growth rate of GDP was at least four times higher in Africa than in other developing regions.[19] Proponents of SAPs have tended to attribute the differential impacts of external shocks, such as the debt crisis and the resulting greater disequilibria in Africa, to the higher degree of state intervention in this continent's economies. Reference is made to government practices like setting prices and (often overvalued) exchange rates, owning assets and regulating foreign trade, and attention is drawn to the inefficiency and self-serving nature of such practices.

However, surely African economies differ from those of other developing countries in more than just the extent of state intervention. There are also differences in modes of production, degrees of economic diversification, international division of labour, etc. Furthermore, not all types of government intervention are inefficient and/or self-serving (more on this later). Therefore, I argue that the answer to the question concerning the principal reason behind Africa's poor economic performance and vulnerability to shocks lies more likely in the pervasiveness of some fundamental structural constraints.[20]

To begin with, it has been pointed out that Africa, more than any other region, is characterized by a peasant mode of production – near-subsistence resource-poor household-level activity geared primarily to ensuring survival. In most countries on the continent, the traditional peasant sector comprises the vast majority of the people but has very weak links with the so-called modern sector.[21] The peasantry does engage in some exchange of goods and services, essentially offering cheap labour and basic natural-resource-based commodities (food, livestock, charcoal, etc.) against farm inputs and basic consumer goods (clothing, oil, sugar, etc.). Yet such exchange is relatively limited and does not normally influence allocative decisions very much. Rather, it is self-sufficiency in providing the food needs of the family that is often the primary goal shaping household expenditure patterns among the peasantry. This distinguishes the traditional 'sector' from the modern capitalist system. Furthermore, the near-subsistence peasantry generally also has little access to goods and services provided by the state. Thus, it is deprived of resources allocated by both the market and the state.

The large size of the near-subsistence sector and its weak connections with the modern exchange system, taken together, typically give rise to the following disarticulations of African economies. On the one hand, domestic markets are small and modern exchange systems generally operate as enclaves within their domestic economies, with private enterprises being oriented towards international markets for inputs, outputs, growth and capital accumulation. On the other hand, the use of available resources is often dissociated from social needs. Political power and economic resources are concentrated in the modern urban-based sector, while the peasantry is unable to raise productivity and participate in the market by translating their needs into effective demand. Emphasis on producing goods and services for the international market – first introduced during colonial times – has continued to prevail even after independence. Declining (per capita) food production and rising food imports, an important drain on foreign exchange earnings, are a reflection of this structural problem.

Diminishing food production has often been ascribed to policy failure to provide sufficient economic incentives for food producers to expand production, with particular reference to price controls and low producer prices. However, price controls have not only affected food crops, and even without price controls it is doubtful that market-oriented producers would choose food crops over non-food cash crops. Moreover, producer price increases would provide incentives only to surplus-producing farmers; near-subsistence producers would require productivity-raising changes before they can benefit appreciably from higher prices. The above analysis suggests that the problem is fundamentally related to the lack of coordination between market-guided allocation of available resources and social needs and to the continued marginalization of large segments of near-subsistence peasants. This is tantamount to market failure, in terms of ignoring the needs of the majority of the population, rather than in narrow terms of economic efficiency. In most cases, the African state has failed to correct this problem, by advancing the interests of the ruling élite, allowing corruption, and failing to promote representative and participatory political structures. Neglecting the concerns of the peasantry and the food sector has also contributed to internal conflicts and civil strife and hence exacerbated allocation of resources by providing incentives for increased military expenditures.

The disarticulation of African economies has been accentuated by their weak position in the international division of labour. Most African countries emerged from colonialism as economically the least diversified worldwide and they continue to rely, more than any other region, on a few non-oil primary commodities for their export earnings. The other side of the coin is that because of their narrow technological, managerial and production base, African countries are highly dependent on foreign technology, capital, know-how and services. The terms of trade between these imports and the commodity exports has continually worsened since the mid-1970s, for the following reasons. In their desperate search for foreign exchange, developing countries out-compete each other in the same export markets and oversupply these markets with basic commodities whose income and price elasticities are generally low. Moreover, as pointed out above, for a number of the principal export commodities substitutes are being developed in more developed countries. This puts additional downward pressure on international commodity prices.[22]

It thus appears that Africa's economic crisis and the severity of its external debt situation are a reflection of deep-seated structural problems. The continued marginalization of the peasantry, the neglect of their social needs, the limited size of domestic markets, the dependency on international markets for economic growth, and very unfavourable terms of trade have made African countries extremely vulnerable to fluctuations and adverse changes in global economic conditions. The logical conclusion from this analysis is that the economic and debt crisis can only be overcome through consistent aggressive policies towards greater economic diversification (and hence a more favourable position in the international division of labour) as well as much greater emphasis on targeting available resources to meeting social needs with a view to transforming the peasantry by increasing their productivity and effective participation in the domestic marketplace. Selected protection from imports and subsidies, especially in food production, may have to be part of such policies.

None of the outlined economic objectives will be possible to achieve without far-reaching political reforms. Economic transformation and diversification requires (and fosters) political liberalization and pluralism. The vast numbers of people in the near-subsistence sector must also be enabled to form their own representative institutions and participate, as directly as possible, in political decision-making processes at local and national levels. Also, for reasons of avoiding tensions and conflict along ethnic lines and not putting the fragile nature of nationhood under further pressure, it is mandatory that the political economy of exclusion be alleviated and more democratic systems be evolved.

The fundamental external and internal causes identified above are also responsible for the general trend of environmental decline in Africa. Marginalization of African countries in the global system and of the peasantry within African countries has given rise to unsustainable natural resource export patterns (from the continent) and to local resource overexploitation associated with poverty.

IMF/World Bank-prescribed structural adjustment programmes

Structural adjustment can be defined as a process of deliberately adjusting the structure of an economy to mitigate the effects of negative (external or internal) shocks or to take advantage of new opportunities.[23] Most structural adjustment, particularly in Africa, is defensive in nature. It is intended to put a country in a position to deal effectively with adverse changes and shocks (like drought), whether anticipated or unexpected. It is widely accepted that structural adjustment is necessary to adapt to changing external and/or internal circumstances. Where people disagree, however, is what constitutes the most appropriate kind of structural adjustment. In Africa, since about 1980, virtually all countries have embraced SAPs designed by the IMF and the World Bank to strengthen the countries' capacity to overcome the crisis and resume growth and development. The first section described some of the symptoms and causes of Africa's crisis. This section is intended to analyse the main features of the IMF/World Bank-designed SAPs, with a view to determining their suitability and limitations for Africa. I will address environmental aspects and implications in a separate subsection.

Essentially, the Fund/Bank approach to structural adjustment has combined the following elements: austerity, stronger export orientation in domestic production, greater reliance on markets to set prices, and institutional reforms (notably privatization). Strictly speaking, the Fund and the Bank have followed somewhat different approaches, in line with their institutional mandates.[24] The Fund-prescribed medicine has aimed for short-term demand stabilization of the economy through drastic measures designed to restore equilibrium quickly between supply and demand in the internal and external accounts. By contrast, the Bank has taken a longer-term and somewhat more flexible approach. Emphasis has been not only on bringing aggregate consumption down to equilibrium levels but also on promoting supply-side changes to improve the efficiency of resource allocation, expand output, and restore economic growth.[25]

In a nutshell, the principal policy measures of SAPs, in their conventional time sequence, have been:[26]

1. reductions in aggregate demand and government expenditure, using fiscal and monetary policy instruments;[27]

2. expenditure switching both within the government budget and, through exchange-rate devaluation, from foreign to domestic goods (in consumption) as well as from domestic goods to tradeable goods and import substituting goods (in production);

3. reduction of trade barriers and controls;[28]

4. market and price liberalization;[29]

5. institutional reforms.[30]

How effective have the SAPs been to date? Judging from ten years of experience, their success has been very mixed. Assessments vary in their conclusions, depending on the criteria used for evaluation. Most countries have improved their balance-of-payments performance though much of this, particularly in Africa, has come from reducing imports rather than increasing exports.[31] The World Bank has undertaken at least two reviews of their experience with adjustment lending.[32] The first review examined the effects of adjustment lending to nine developing countries in Africa, Asia, Latin America and Europe in the period 1980–83. The review concluded, among other things, that virtually none of the countries improved the competitiveness of the exchange rate at the start of the SAP or made much progress in getting the government deficit under control. The second review, a ten-year evaluation of adjustment lending, was more positive, pointing to improvements in economic growth and trade balances among those countries implementing SAPs versus others. But it also concluded that on average investment ratios declined and that debt service as well as debt export ratios increased. These results cast doubt on the economic sustainability of the SAPs.[33]

Critics have pointed to a number of perceived flaws in the SAPs: nature of conditionality;[34] timing and pace of implementation;[35] inconsistencies in the mix and sequencing of policies;[36] lack of flexibility in adapting the policy packages to the particular realities of individual countries;[37] too much reliance on market and price mechanisms alone; ideologically inspired privatization; ideologically based weakening of the role of the state; the export-led growth model; neglect of the social, environmental, and political costs of adjustment; corresponding conflicts with domestic development goals such as income redistribution, maintaining environmental quality, and promoting political reform, more democratic decision making at different levels, and a strong civil society.

Heeding some of this criticism and as a result of learning from experience, the Fund/Bank have adjusted their packages over the years. In fact, since 1980, the SAPs have evolved significantly. They have generally become softer and somewhat more flexible, moving away from the hard-nosed retrenchment and pricist-type recipes applied early on. For example, mindful of problems posed by non-price supply-side constraints (weak infrastructure, market rigidities, etc.) to the success of price reforms, particularly in poor African countries, the Bank has begun to introduce sectoral adjustment loans for specific reforms in key sectors of the economy.[38] However, real concerns about many of perceived weaknesses of the Bank/Fund adjustment approach remain.

PRIVATIZATION

This is a controversial issue on which positions often differ on ideological grounds, rather than on the basis of empirical evidence. SAPs usually promote privatization of public enterprises, property rights, etc., as a matter of principle. In the case of *land tenure*, for instance, the privatization school of thought dismisses public land ownership as ineffective (which is widely accepted), and relies on Hardin's 'tragedy-of-the-commons' concept, first publicized in 1968,[39] to rule out forms of common-property regimes. According to Hardin's economic theory, common-property schemes inevitably disintegrate into open-access regimes because it is assumed that individuals put their personal advantage ahead of collective benefit and thus have an intrinsic incentive to increase their share of the collective resource. However, there is now considerable evidence from anthropological studies that common-property regimes operate under rules enforced by local institutions and that if these institutions function well, the common-property schemes can be superior, environmentally and economically, to private property, in particular in marginal lands and fragile ecosystems.

The idea of privatizing public enterprises under SAPs has gone through a learning process. It is understood today that privatization does not necessarily mean the selling off of public enterprises to reduce the government deficit. There would be little point in simply replacing a public monopoly by a private one. Therefore, a privatization programme must ensure, above all, greater competitiveness. This may take the form of abolishing a public monopoly and letting public and private firms compete. Or it may mean setting performance standards for public enterprises.[40]

MARKET LIBERALIZATION AND FAILURE

The principle of letting markets set prices and allocate resources has been central to all Fund/Bank-prescribed SAPs. This is not surprising, given that the design of the SAPs is profoundly inspired by neoclassical economic theory. Accordingly, these programmes concentrate heavily on 'getting the prices right'. However, for a variety of reasons, economic liberalization is not always effective or relevant in poorer Third World countries. Moreover, in countries with a poor infrastructure and poorly functioning markets, as in most African countries, price signals by themselves cannot be expected to elicit the desired supply response.

A case in point are price incentives to agricultural producers, which formed a central part of the early SAPs. The objectives were to stimulate agricultural production (and exports) and raise the incomes of the rural poor in the process (at the expense of the urban middle class). This, it was anticipated, would also counteract, at least in part, the widespread policy bias in favour of urban areas. Today, we know that price measures alone can be quite ineffective, or even counterproductive, particularly under near-subsistence conditions. As pointed out in the second section, small farmers usually put household food security first, which tends to make them indifferent to rising prices.

Further, where smallholder families' livelihoods depend (in part) on engaging in salaried work, producer price increases may actually lead to reductions in production, aside from adversely affecting income distribution. For food price increases will hit these families hard and may lead to loss of land to bigger farmers whose productivity may be lower. It has been pointed out that in order for price *in*centives to work in poor countries, they must be preceded or accompanied by at least five other *in*'s: *in*puts, *in*novation, *in*formation, *in*frastructure, and *in*stitutions[41] – each of them, in particular infrastructure and innovation, strongly depending on effective government support. The latter, however, is not compatible with SAP philosophy of minimal government and therefore likely to be handicapped, in practice, by government spending cuts. Thus under typical African conditions, SAPs are likely to be inconsistent in their offsetting effects on agricultural output and rural incomes of reduced public-sector support for the above five 'in's' (resulting from advocated lower government) on the one hand and of producer price increases on the other (see note 36 for other inconsistencies).

This inconsistency is closely related to the disarticulations of African economies discussed in the second section. It was pointed out that the weak linkages between the typically large near-subsistence peasant sector and the commonly small modern market-based export-oriented enclave prevent market allocation of resources from meeting the social needs of the vast numbers of peasants who cannot convert their needs into effective market demand. Under these conditions, markets tend to organize available resources to respond primarily to the demands of the élite. The failure of markets to reach the resource-poor (and the associated failure of price signals to elicit the desired supply response and raise rural incomes) can only be overcome by targeted government intervention to lift the productivity of the peasants by providing the kind of support indicated above in terms of the other five 'in's'. This highlights the complementarity between effective markets and effective public-sector support, as opposed to the assumption of inevitable market-state trade-offs underlying the design of SAPs.

Aside from this fundamental market failure in undeveloped economies, there are other types of intrinsic market failure, arising from the dynamics of the market itself. These inherent failures are therefore of relevance to the so-called modern sector in African economies. They include the following phenomena:

- the inability of markets fully to internalize social and environmental costs in prevailing price;[42]

- the divergence between private and social discounting;[43]

- imperfect competition – or the tendency of markets to erode their own competitive foundation;[44] and

- the allocation of resources to provide so-called public goods.[45]

The important thing here is that none of these intrinsic market failures can be addressed effectively without active assistance or mediation of the state.

THE FAILURE AND PROPER ROLE OF THE STATE[46]

These considerations seem to suggest an important role for the state in economic development. By contrast, the 1980s have witnessed the rise of a new orthodoxy (neoclassical liberalization school) that views state intervention as the primary cause of economic problems in developing countries, particularly in Africa, and hence calls for curbing the state and placing greater reliance on markets (see second section above). This view is largely reflected in the Fund/Bank-prescribed SAPs that are being implemented in Africa and elsewhere.

Africa's recent (post-colonial) history, indeed, reveals relatively strong state intervention. The post-independence African state resulted in many cases from armed liberation struggles and, therefore, was expected to play a liberating role, with heavy investments in social advancement of all citizens. Not surprisingly, active state involvement in economic affairs was considered vital. In the 1960s, there was a consensus in development thinking, including even the World Bank and other proponents of the market approach, that what was needed was *state-led* industrialization. Impressive gains were made in the development of social infrastructure (hospitals, school, etc.) and in general socio-economic well-being. Some economic diversification was achieved and an African capitalist class emerged, but never strong enough to challenge the dominance of the state. Since the mid-1970s external shocks (oil price hikes, worsening terms of trade, escalating debt burden) combined with internal conflicts (ethnic tensions, civil strife) to expose Africa's vulnerability and undermine economic development.

The post-independence African state has certainly not lived up to early expectations of state-led economic and social liberation. It did not succeed in its early attempts to provide the poor with access to resources and raise their productivity. Instead, the African state soon succumbed to special interests and became generally élite-oriented and often corrupt. Thus, the diagnosis of liberal economists of a self-serving and inefficient African state which has aggravated distortions and hampered socio-economic development is by and large correct, and there is little disagreement on this aspect. It is the recommended solution to the problem which has given rise to disagreement. The recipe of simply replacing the state by the market has serious flaws.

The fact that the African state has tended to be inefficient and to cater for special interests does not necessarily imply that state intervention by necessity is unhelpful and counterproductive. There are important types of intervention and functions that can only be undertaken or fulfilled by the government. The Korean experience suggests that the state, if sufficiently autonomous and capable, can have a crucial function in identifying a dynamic economic niche in the international division of labour, directing investment to move toward this niche, and promoting necessary technological innovation. For constructive state intervention to happen in Africa, the state must be reformed to become more democratic and competent and pay greater attention to the needs of the poor. Political reforms are vital to this end and must accompany economic reforms.

Earlier in this chapter, we saw that several types of market failure all seemed to require a strong active state for their correction. This suggests that the dichotomy and trade-offs of market versus state, emphasized by the advocates of economic liberalization, are artificial and unhelpful for policy design. And it also suggests that a minimal state – just providing basic services and infrastructure and an enabling environment for private business – is incompatible with current needs. In Africa, both a strong (competitive) market and a strong state are required; the two are often complementary and hence must work in tandem. Beyond the issue of how market and state should relate to each other looms the still larger question of the role of civil society – the range and diversity of institutions (and corresponding interests) that lie outside government, have more than a mere market role, and are crucial in expressing competing opinions, facilitating consensus-building, as well as legitimizing and controlling both market and state. It is civil society to which the state is ultimately accountable and which must give the market social legitimacy, through regulatory mechanisms via the state.[47]

In Africa, civil society is generally only beginning to evolve. But a strong and dynamic civil society is urgently needed to fulfil its important functions. How are the SAPs affecting Africa's incipient civil society? This is difficult to say – though it is possible that an excessive shift towards market freedom will strengthen unregulated market forces to the point where corporate interests prevail over people's interests. The current transition in Africa from authoritarian to more democratic structures is most welcome, but the risk remains that unbridled market forces and powerful corporate interests will come to erode the social fabric of society, threaten the integrity of ecosystems, hinder the evolution of a strong civil society, and at the same time weaken the state as an instrument for society's affairs in the public interest. The ultimate goal must be balanced and mutually reinforcing triangular relationships among the three pillars of society – civil society, market and state.

THE EXPORT-LED GROWTH MODEL

We indicated earlier that export-oriented resource exploitation in the interest of foreign consumers has predominated in Africa since colonial times. In the early post-independence years, considerable efforts were made to build up in indigenous industry using import control and substitution, but this period was short-lived. Around the mid-1970s, when foreign debt started to accumulate, the import-substitution model was abandoned in favour of the export-led growth model. One reason for this change lay in the necessity to generate foreign exchange to pay off the foreign debt. The SAPs implemented since 1980 have certainly sought to enhance outward-looking economic behaviour, through systematic exchange-rate devaluations and removal of trade barriers.

The wisdom of attempting to generate sustained trade surpluses at the current low levels of development in Africa has been questioned. It has been argued that the export-led policy approach increases the exposure of developing countries to the uncertainties of international commodity price trends and to the whims of protectionist sentiments in industrialized countries. With international commodity agreements (e.g., the coffee agreement) collapsing and commodity prices falling, African countries have earned less and less for their exports. If it were not for the creditors, African countries would probably be better off using some of the exported resources for reinvestment at home, trying to achieve greater value-added and more economic diversification as well as more attractive longer-term dynamic economic niches in the international marketplace. This strategy, while probably requiring some measure of protection against cheap imports to assist infant industries, would, if successful, increase flexibility and adaptability in the longer run and hence lessen the vulnerability to future shocks – a more fundamental purpose of adjustment than generating growth and meeting creditors' demands in the short run.[48]

By contrast, insisting, as the SAPs do, on an export-led economic strategy and on sustained trade surpluses is likely to enhance structural rigidities in the developing economies – such as the weak linkage between the neglected peasant economy and the modern sector which receives most of the available resources but responds primarily to signals from the global marketplace[49] – and may lock countries into unsustainable patterns of natural resource use, especially the lowest-income countries, which are entirely dependent on natural resource consumption. Admittedly, few people would suggest, and it is not the idea of SAPs, that developing countries should specialize in simple commodities for ever. But the question is how to get from the present production and export pattern to one with a more viable longer-term niche, at a time when debt obligations are rising and when progressive trade liberalization exposes domestic enterprises to the forces of international competition and thus renders any industrialization and economic diversification difficult.

SOCIAL AND ENVIRONMENTAL COSTS

The social dimension of the SAPs has become a subject of intense debate in the last few years. This aspect was forcefully put on the table by UNICEF, with their study entitled 'Adjustment with a Human Face'.[50] It was also at the centre of ECA's critique of the SAPs, as presented in its 'African Alternative Framework'.[51] Since then, the social question has been consistently flagged by numerous assessments as an issue that is largely glossed over by the SAPs. Essentially, the critics have pointed to the SAPs' tremendous social costs, which are evident in adjusting countries and hit poor segments of the population particularly hard. And they have called for mechanisms to cushion the social impact which threatens to undermine the ultimate adjustment goal of resumed economic growth and long-term development.

In Africa, governments that are responsible for the prevailing political economy of exclusion cannot be expected to implement deflationary policies in a manner that will spare the poorer segments of society from further deprivation.[52] In most cases, spending cuts are concentrated on politically easy targets – health, education and support for small farmers while the interests of the powerful and the wealthy are protected by the state. The downward redistribution of resources that is necessary for the transformation of the near-subsistence sector is unlikely to occur under these circumstances. And hoped-for trickle-down to alleviate poverty and increase the productivity of the near-subsistence sector as a result of more vigorous economic growth in the longer term is doubtful, as retrenchments in public expenditure on health, education, nutrition, credit for small farmers, etc., tend to undermine the human resource base which is essential for long-term growth.

The Fund and the Bank have responded to this criticism by instituting the 'Social Dimensions of Adjustment Program' (under which the social effects are analysed and recommendations for action are made) and generally paying greater attention to the social dimension in recent adjustment packages. Most recently, the Bank has announced a programme of undertaking systematic poverty assessments in developing countries. Nevertheless, SAPs still lack built-in social objectives. The current approach is essentially a 'curative' one, dealing with undesired social effects as they occur. Efforts seem focused on identifying and trying to compensate the biggest losers. However, adjustment is unlikely to lead to (socially) sustainable development, unless this limited social welfare approach gives way to measures and policies that actively seek to engage the people in the adjustment process and aim for the social advancement and economic transformation (empowerment) of the poor, in particular the peasantry, as an explicit objective.

ENVIRONMENTAL COSTS

Compared to the social dimension, it is even more recent that the environmental dimension of structural adjustment is catching people's attention. It was the publication of 'Our Common Future' by the Brundtland Commission in 1987 that focused global attention on the critical environmental implications of and constraints on current development patterns and popularized the notion of 'sustainable development'. Since then the global environmental debate has intensified, culminating most recently in the UN Conference on Environment and Development (UNCED) as well as its action programme for the next century (*Agenda 21*). In this context, it is natural that the SAPs would also come under increased scrutiny from an environmental angle. The Bank has responded in so far as it seems to be paying more specific attention to the performance of natural resource sectors under SAPs, how to deal with environmental problems as a result of export pressures, and generally how to enhance both economic and environmental performance through sectoral lending.[53]

The literature of SAPs and the environment is still small, but several studies and papers now exist that allow a more informed discussion of the linkages between the two.[54] While the empirical material on the interrelationships between SAPs and environment for particular countries is still very sparse and weak,[55] the conceptual linkages can be traced with greater confidence. Because of this constraint and because of the interest in this chapter to come to generalized conclusions for (sub-Saharan) Africa as a whole, I will keep my analysis primarily at the conceptual level, yet draw on the accumulated wisdom from information that is available. I will examine the environmental implications for each of the SAP policy measures, as listed above, and then try to derive overall conclusions. Because of the preliminary nature of the analysis, my points will tend to be hypotheses (for further research and validation) rather than definitive conclusions.

To begin with, like social aspects, environmental considerations have not been incorporated in the design of the SAPs. As pointed out earlier, the SAPs reflect neoclassical economic thinking, which in essence holds that the economic system is a closed system that, while using natural resources, is not constrained in any way by natural resource supply. For these reasons alone, it cannot be expected that the SAPs will be able to put countries on a path towards sustainable development.[56] While SAPs were designed without any explicit environmental objective in mind, their implementation certainly impacts upon the environment in a number of ways. This is because SAPs strongly affect levels and mixes of public-sector investment and spending, absolute and relative prices throughout the economy, and the way a range of institutions work. At the same time, because of the lack of environmental goals, it is probably fair to say that SAPs are likely to have *mixed* effects on the environment. Some policies may be beneficial for environmental conservation and sustainability, while others can be assumed to add to existing pressure on natural resources.

In what follows, I will explore the environmental implications for each of the SAP measures, with a view to suggesting modifications from an environmental point of view.

Public sector spending cuts. First of all, spending on environmental quality-related goods and services often does not have high priority, particularly in low-income African countries. This makes such spending prone to suffering disproportionately large reductions during times of fiscal austerity. The second generic observation is that in so far as public spending cuts are socially regressive and augment poverty, their overall environmental implications are likely to be negative as well. For it is often the case that a trend towards more poverty among many cum more influence among some (as opposed to a more even income distribution) tends to put more pressure on the environment (because of greater natural resource over-exploitation by both the poor and the rich, on different scales and for different reasons) which may lead to a downward spiral of poverty and environmental degradation, particularly in marginal rural areas.

The specific impacts on the environment will depend on the relative size of the cuts in recurrent expenditure and public investment, respectively, and on the changes in spending level as well as intersectoral mix in each of the two categories. Public investments and recurrent expenditures that are important from an environmental angle include those on maintenance of certain infrastructure (sewage systems, water purification, waste recycling programmes, etc.), public services such as (environmental) education and health, and provision of particular public goods (national parks, forests, etc.). Reductions in all of these items are likely to have negative effects on environmental quality (as well as social welfare).

A second important way of reducing government expenditure is by lifting subsidies. Depending on the particular kind of subsidy, this may have positive or negative effects. Clearly, reducing fiscal subsidies on the consumption of natural resources (energy, water, etc.) will drive up their price to the consumer and hence lead to economically more efficient use of the resources, with generally positive environmental effects. But where subsidies are essential to the social well-being of the poor, as with food subsidies, reducing them may enhance poverty and induce further environmental degradation (see general point above on the social regressiveness of measures).

Monetary austerity. Interest rate increases, the main instrument for curtailing credit expansion, will generally dampen private (and, perhaps to a lesser extent, public) investment. The impact on private investors will be largely confined to the small modern sector in African countries. It has been estimated that in Africa only about 5 per cent of the population has access to commercial credit.[57] Therefore, monetary austerity will tend to constrain very limited modern commercial activity but will leave the vast majority of near-subsistence families largely unscathed. Aside from some (positive) scale effects (less consumption of natural resources), the negative effects on the environment include reductions in on-farm investment which are key to sustainable agriculture.

Market liberalization and privatization. Superimposing policies of market liberalization onto the current system in Africa is likely to bring 'more of the same' and is apt to exacerbate, rather than alleviate, structural constraints. For one, market liberalization in and of itself will not expand, create and diversify domestic markets. Rather, its impact is likely to be largely confined to the modern sector and may thus reinforce its nature as an enclave within the larger developing economy. Thus, in the near-subsistence sector, 'getting the prices right' will not in itself lead to sustainable resource management, if the economic agents are not able to respond to price incentives.

Within the exchange economy, SAP-induced pervasive price adjustments are likely to result in complex changes in natural resource use. However, the environmental outcome will also depend on actual management practices, and the significance for environmental sustainability will depend on how close the economic system is to its ecological limits. Furthermore, the 'right prices' should be those that internalize the full social and environmental costs of production – something which the market alone cannot achieve (see below under environmental market failure). But relative prices and associated resource use patterns will also reflect income-dependent demand patterns and hence be influenced by the redistributive effects of SAPs. The net result for the environment cannot be predicted, but depends on the particular circumstances.

Environmental problems are clearly caused by the lack of markets or (perceived) property rights for a range of environmental goods and ecosystem services. A good example for Africa is the widespread deforestation resulting from timber exploitation or expansion of agriculture. Some of the environmental goods and ecological services provided by forests (secondary forest products, watershed protection, micro-climate regulation, etc.) don't have markets and are not priced, nor often traded. Their loss through deforestation is thus not registered in the (formal) exchange economy. It can only be the responsibility of the government to use tax instruments to see to it that the values of the lost non-priced goods and services are factored into the price of those marketed products whose production causes the non-priced loss, namely timber and agricultural products. This way 'external' environmental effects would be internalized.

Public policy – failure and proper role. Governments often fail to address and correct environmental market failures, particularly in low-income African countries, for lack of information, administrative capacity, or resolve. Of course, environmentally consequential public policy failure goes beyond not correcting environmental market failure. Take rangeland policy, for example. The rangelands (arid and semi-arid areas) in Africa cover a good part of the African territory and have been inhabited by (agro) pastoralists for centuries. Government policy in Africa often assumes that these lands are 'empty' territories that are 'undeveloped', or even 'wastelands'. Accordingly, development approaches tend to ignore the traditional land-use and tenure systems and put in place modernization schemes or let cultivators encroach. This leads to environmental damage and human suffering because traditional land-use systems are disrupted and become unsustainable, and the modern schemes themselves are often not sustainable.[58] The proper public policy role would be to build upon, not dismiss, traditional systems.

Interactions between market failure and public policy failure. The above considerations suggest that environmental market failure and public policy failure interact in multiple ways. The SAPs generally concentrate on providing remedies for what they see as public policy failure, but often on enhancing the potential for market failure in the process. Markets as well as governments have both weaknesses and strengths. Policy reform should take advantage, wherever possible, of complementarities in strengths, or in correcting weaknesses ('win-win' situations), but in some instances, trade-offs (e.g., for environmental quality) between market failure and government failure are inevitable and require a balanced approach.

An example of an environmental win-win situation is a change in government policy towards lifting fuel subsidies that had been intended to promote industrial development and in parallel reforms to let markets set prices. An example of a trade-off is a reduction in export taxes to promote greater exports. In Africa, these exports will typically consist of agricultural commodities. If the incremental production takes place at the margin (through clearing of land belonging to the producers or by encroachment on common-property land) environmental damage is likely to occur. Likewise, if the additional output is achieved by intensifying ongoing production, the environmental costs associated with using more inputs could be considerable (in the absence of relevant information among the farmers and of effective government regulations). In the case of substitution of export crops for food crops, there is a clear nutritional and social implication, and in so far as food and social stress is forced upon the natural resource base the environment will suffer.

Institutional reform. SAPs tend to create or promote institutional arrangements that are market-oriented and privatized. Privatization policies will have environmental effects. In particular, the privatization of property rights deserves attention. As we saw earlier, private land tenure is not superior to collective forms of tenure on lower-potential land, such as in arid and semi-arid areas. Its promotion in these areas is likely to lead to land degradation. In the area of intellectual property rights, protecting the commercial-level inventions of plant breeders and biotechnology firms through patent systems while allowing open access to local genetic material such as indigenous plants and animals and to the associated indigenous management information (all results of innovations over long periods by traditional farmers), discriminates against the small farmers and contributes to genetic erosion and environmental decline.

In Africa, institutional reform, particularly in the near-subsistence economy, must respect and build upon traditional local institutions and non-market mechanisms or risk being destructive and/or irrelevant. This implies a flexible approach to adjustment by accepting (and even promoting) diversity in markets, technology, credit, knowledge, and tenure systems.

Expenditure switching, exchange-rate devaluation, export promotion and trade liberalization. As I have argued in the second section above, African economies have all along been biased in favour of exports. Trade liberalization will expose African economies (the modern enclave, that is) even more to the forces of international competition than has been the case so far. This threatens further to entrench the current international division of labour, further weakening the global position of African economies while deepening their dependency on global forces and increasing their vulnerability to external fluctuations and shocks. In the absence of changes in the mix of exports and economic diversification, a shifting emphasis towards tradeables will perpetuate Africa's weak position in global markets, and will redistribute income further in favour of domestic exporters, to the detriment of small-scale food producers. And together with the mandatory import decontrols which tend to expose infant industries to the competitive strength of efficient overseas exporters, devaluation is likely further to narrow the production base of African countries. Moreover, devaluing exchange rates simultaneously in many developing countries that export the same primary commodities risks oversupplying world markets and causing international prices to fall. Under these conditions, and given the low price elasticities of international demand for the African export commodities, there is no clear empirical evidence that devaluation will indeed increase exports and growth.[59]

What are the implications for the natural resource base and environment? The fact that the necessity of repaying foreign debt and the SAPs locks Africa into a position of primary commodity exporter under worsening terms of trade means that African countries are forced to increase natural resource exports to ensure national survival. Under these conditions, it is likely that checks and balances on how these exports are to be achieved take second place. There is a great risk, therefore, that environmental demands and regulations are relaxed or ignored in the desperate attempt to cut costs and increase exports at any price. Declining export prices reflect ever less the social and environmental costs of the export commodities. These costs are borne primarily locally, while the benefits (in terms of lower prices) accrue to Northern consumers. While the potential for ecological damage in African countries is great, the extent and nature of environmental degradation depends on the exact mechanisms by which production of export goods is promoted and expanded (expanding land under cultivation at the margin, intensified production, substitution for food crops, etc.) and on the precise management practices adopted.

To counteract this adverse situation would require modifying the export-led growth model towards policies stressing economic diversification and some measure of protection to allow industrial development. It would likely also require far-reaching debt forgiveness (to reduce pressure on African countries to export in order to meet debt service payments) and renewed commodity agreements to stabilize and raise international commodity prices as well as efforts to internalize the social and environmental costs of primary commodities through fiscal policy (e.g. taxes) in industrial countries.

Towards a different adjustment approach in Africa

The analysis of the underlying causes of Africa's crisis, and the assessment of the Fund/Bank-prescribed SAPs which are designed to help overcome this crisis, provide strong arguments to adopt a different approach to structural adjustment and policy reform in Africa. In fact, rather than improving the capacity of African countries to respond to shocks, the SAPs may well diminish this capacity. It is quite clear from the foregoing discussion that the adjustment approach must be broader, more flexible, long-term, and more equitable and sustainable. Below I list some of the principles that might be followed in designing the alternative policy package. The policies themselves would need to be carefully thought out and adapted to specific realities.

Perhaps the greatest difference in approach lies in the suggestion that structural adjustment should not be confined to developing countries. The conventional SAPs, it has been pointed out, amount to adjustment of the weak to a situation that is out of control due to the policies of the strong.[60] I strongly argue that adjustment in the South cannot succeed without parallel adjustments in the industrialized countries and in the global system of economic/financial relations. For instance, the current *annual* US trade deficit alone is considerably bigger than the whole accumulated debt of Africa. The US deficit tends to drive up world interest rates and thus exacerbates the debt burden of the South. Global structural adjustment would also make it difficult to blame the lack of success of structural adjustment in the South on the adverse external conditions.[61]

Here then are the suggested principles for a different adjustment approach in Africa:

1. *Flexibility* – adapting policy packages to the particular realities of different countries, building flexibility into the packages themselves, and viewing adjustment as an evolutionary process (learning from experience).

2. *Long-term time horizons and gradual phasing in of policy measures* – allowing the policies to work their way through the structure; because of rigidities in the economies and deep-rooted structural constraints it will take time for a response to emerge.

3. *Build on traditional systems and emphasize diversity* – all too often in Africa's recent past 'modern scientific' policy and management concepts, models and methods, usually imported from the North, have not worked because they were alien to indigenous local cultures; at the same time, they have weakened traditional forms of management because they have failed to build on them; this has created confusion, marginalization, and inefficiency; there is a need for identifying constructive and participatory ways to combine and effectively integrate traditional (informal) and modern (formal)

systems; this applies to a variety of dimensions including marketing (local near-subsistence markets versus national/international markets), technological innovation (traditional versus modern technologies), credit systems (informal versus formal), knowledge systems (indigenous versus formal), and tenure systems (customary versus statutory, and in particular common-property versus privatization); implicit in a strategy of building on traditional systems is an emphasis on diversity, socio-cultural and environmental, which has tended to be eroded through indiscriminate application of imported approaches and packages.

4. *Focus on transforming the peasantry, strengthening domestic markets and promoting economic diversification* – this will involve targeted support to smallholders to increase their productivity and allow them to express their needs as market demand; strategic public-sector investments in perceived dynamic growth sectors (crowding in of private business), with emphasis on value-added activities and gradual industrialization; some level of protection against imports to allow domestic infant industries to develop (without letting them become inefficient).

5. *Systematically promote technological innovation* – this includes support to R&D to improve the science and technology base; development of patent systems to protect and encourage innovation; focus on the development of technologies providing a possible dynamic advantage in international commerce (such as certain biotechnologies); without strenuous efforts in this area Africa will be marginalized technologically.

6. *Emphasis on food production and relative food self-sufficiency* – providing economic incentives to increase food production; government support to small farmers; land reform and land-tenure reforms as necessary; maintaining a level of import control to protect domestic food production.

7. *Incorporate social and environmental objectives into the design of policy packages* – here the aim is to build on complementarities and carefully balance trade-offs between economic, social, and environmental objectives; the ultimate goal is social well-being and sustainable development.

8. *Build on the strengths of both markets and public policy* – a false dichotomy between markets and public policy should be avoided; both markets and government intervention are prone to failure; the

aim is to combine market mechanisms and public policy measures to achieve the adjustment objectives.

9. *Political reforms* – generally towards more democratic structures, competent governance and a strong civil society.

10. *Shift responsibilities for adjustment from external agencies to the countries themselves* – in design, implementation, monitoring and evaluation; in other words, adjustment should be internally based (with the greatest possible popular participation) rather than externally prescribed.

11. *Global economic and financial reforms* – Africa's and the Third World's debt must be cancelled (using as models previous debt-cancellation agreements which benefited countries such as Germany and Indonesia) as a precondition for improving prospects for Africa and the Third World; mechanisms must be found for Africa to receive renewed international finance and direct investment, reversing the present capital outflow; prices of primary commodities must be stabilized and increased through international agreements and through mechanisms leading to greater internalization of social and environmental costs; technology transfer to the South must be encouraged; beyond that, any measures to promote more balanced and fair trade will help, but trade liberalization should not be pursued indiscriminately (the assumption that free trade benefits all trading partners does not correspond to the present reality).

Notes

1. The term 'Africa' is used here, and henceforth in the chapter, for the sake of brevity to refer primarily to sub-Saharan Africa. There are significant historic, socio-cultural, and economic differences between sub-Saharan Africa and the rest of the continent.
2. This is sometimes referred to as a 'solution', rather than a problem.
3. There seems to be agreement that capital flight is both substantial and serious. It is, however, quite difficult to measure with any degree of accuracy the accumulated foreign deposits and the annual flow arising from capital flight.
4. Already approximately equal to annual GDP for Africa as a whole and further increasing.
5. Often eating up much or most of foreign exchange earnings.

6. For the past few years, there has been a net flow of billions of dollars annually from Africa to the developed countries. The current annual net outflow from the Third World as a whole amounts to several tens of billions of dollars.

7. This was a result of several factors, including: 1) the then US President Nixon's decision to abandon the Bretton Woods international currency reserve system based on gold as the standard and to delink the US dollar from the value of gold, and 2) tremendous international liquidity from Arab oil sales following the first oil price shock in 1972–73.

8. Unlike Latin America and more than Asia, Africa is still predominantly rural. But the rate of urbanization is higher here than elsewhere.

9. While in Africa military expenditures as a proportion of GDP are lower, on average, than in other developing regions, the ratio of arms imports to total imports are higher, except for the Middle East. US Arms Control and Disarmament Agency, *World Military Expenditures and Arms Transfers* (Washington, DC: 1987).

10. See Paul Harrison, *The Greening of Africa: Breaking Through in the Battle for Land and Food* (New York: Penguin Books, 1987).

11. See World Bank, *World Development Report 1992* (Washington, DC: Oxford University Press, 1992).

12. See, for example, Keith Bezanson, 'The Collapsing Vision of Global Development', in *A World Fit for People*, Uner Kirdar and Leonard Silk (eds), (New York: New York University Press, 1994), 211–216.

13. The reason is that the basic assumption underlying comparative advantage in international trade, namely international immobility of capital, obviously does not correspond to today's reality any more. (Herman E. Daly and John B. Cobb, *The Common Good – Redirecting the Economy Towards Community, the Environment and a Sustainable Future* (Boston: Beacon Press, 1989).

14. Like the EEC and the North American Trade Zone. But regional trading blocks are also starting to form in the South. Examples are the Preferential Trade Area (PTA) comprising more than half of the African countries and Mercosur (Argentina, Brazil, Paraguay, and Uruguay) in Latin America.

15. Intra-corporate trade is now estimated to account for some 30 per cent of reported international trade. David Korten, 'Beyond the Market Versus State', *Human Economy Newsletter* 13, no. 2 (June 1992).

16. For instance, as a low-cost environment (offering cheap but sufficiently skilled labour and possibly also access to often underpriced natural resources such as water, biomass and hydro-electricity) they may attract foreign direct investment, provided the public infrastructure is considered good enough.

17. Technological change can be defined as the output of potentially useful discoveries and innovations. By contrast, technical change refers to the introduction, diffusion and exploitation of the discoveries and innovations.

18. Aside from current net capital outflow to Northern creditors arising from mounting debt service payments *vis-à-vis* shrinking foreign assistance, loans and direct investment, subsidization proceeds in at least three ways: first, supply by the South, at worsening terms of trade, of luxury goods and primary commodities whose true ecological costs are not paid for by the Northern consumers; second, access by the North to biological resources, genetic diversity and associated traditional knowledge at little or no cost while innovations of Northern companies (e.g., biotechnology) are covered by intellectual property protection systems and thus have restricted access; and third, the poor of the South are not using their legitimate share of the global commons like the atmosphere, thus permitting people of the North to expand their share and build up their economies. Centre for Science and Environment (CSE), 'Environmental Policy: An Agenda for South Asian Social Scientists', *Annexure* 4 (1992).

19. See Kidane Mengisteab and B.I. Logan, 'Are Structural Adjustment Programs Relevant?', *Africa Development* 16, no. 1 (1991): 95–113.

20. This line of argument draws significantly on Mengisteab and Logan, 'Are Structural Adjustment Programs Relevant?'.

21. Of course, the peasantry is not a homogeneous group. It spans a spectrum from market-oriented middle-income families to the much larger low-income subsistence-level population. However, a common denominator is immediate dependence on access to natural resources for livelihood.

22. In addition, African countries receive less for their exports and pay more for their imports relative to other developing countries, for a number of reasons including small market size limiting economies of scale in production, and lack of effective control of transnational companies in transactions between parent companies and subsidiaries located in developing countries.

23. David Glover, 'A Layman's Guide to Structural Adjustment', *Canadian Journal of Development Studies* 12, no. 1 (1991).

24. While short-term stabilization was traditionally the preserve of the Fund while the Bank focused more on medium-term supply enhancement (through structural adjustment), this division of labour has partly broken down with the introduction of the Fund's Structural Adjustment Facility (1986) and Enhanced Structural Adjustment Facility (1987). See Mearns, 'Environmental Implications of Structural Adjustment', 3–6.

25. It has not always been easy to make the short-term stabilization efforts compatible with the longer-term structural adjustment measures. For one thing, stabilization programmes also involve price-induced measures which may not be successful prior to market, price and institutional reforms (the longer-term programme). For another, cuts in government spending may hit expenditures on health and education hard and thus contribute to the erosion of the very human resource base that is required for longer-term recovery and growth.

26. Mearns, 'Environmental Implications of Structural Adjustment', 3–6.

27. This includes cuts in recurrent government expenditures (reductions in public-sector wages, food subsidies, etc.) and in public sector investment and lending on the fiscal side, and curbing domestic credit expansion by raising interest rates and through other possible measures on the monetary side.
28. This includes reductions in import tariffs and export taxes.
29. This focuses on removing price controls and subsidies that have often been used to stabilize markets and for income support of poorer segments of the population.
30. This comprises reforms such as in land tenure, credit, marketing and distribution, research and extension, and privatization of state enterprises. In some cases, infrastructural developments and technological innovation are also supported.
31. Glover, 'A Layman's Guide to Structural Adjustment'.
32. World Bank, 'Experience with Structural Adjustment Lending', draft February 1986, as cited in London Environmental Economics Centre (LEEC), 'Macroeconomics Adjustment and the Environment', report prepared for WWF, November 1991; World Bank, 'Adjustment Lending: An Evaluation of Ten Years of Experience', Policy Research Series no. 1 (Washington, DC: World Bank, 1988), as cited in LEEC, 'Macroeconomics Adjustment and the Environment'.
33. These conclusions are from the mentioned Bank reports, but as summarized in London Environmental Economics Centre (LEEC), 'Macroeconomic Adjustment and the Environment'.
34. In order to receive structural adjustment lending, recipient countries must agree to meet a number of specific targets within tightly defined time frames. Further disbursements are made, contingent on satisfactory progress toward these time-specific targets. Not all of these targets are immediately related to the overall goals of the programme and some targets (such as privatizing public enterprises) appear ideologically inspired and/or ends in themselves. Also, the effort and cost of monitoring performance towards these targets is heavy. This has led to suggestions to adopt fewer and more aggregate targets and looser deadlines, and to leave it more up to the country to see to it that targets are met. Beyond these implementational details, there is the larger question of the extent to which adjustment based on externally-imposed conditionality, which is often perceived to be one-sided and not subjected to domestic debate and consensus-building, can lead to sustainable development.
35. The Fund and the Bank have advocated 'shock treatment' and designed their SAPs to be implemented within a short time period (a few years). There is a widespread feeling, however, that shock treatment increases, rather than decreases, adjustment costs without the likelihood of improvement in the longer term. Arguments for more gradual approaches are generally justified by pointing to prevailing structural rigidities in developing countries, particularly in Africa.

36. Different instruments in the policy package may compete and have mutually offsetting effects on particular targets. Likewise, the combined net effect of the package may differ, depending on the sequencing of policies. An example of potentially offsetting effects on economic growth is the combination of public investment reductions as a result of advocated government spending cuts on the one hand and of price reforms to encourage increased supply and growth on the other. An example for the sequencing problem is that most SAPs used price-policy instruments for short-term demand reduction and expenditure switching, while medium-term non-price supply-side reforms often appear necessary to increase the efficacy of price policy, particularly in the agricultural sector (see section below on market liberalization and failure).

37. The Fund and, to a lesser extent, the Bank have tended to apply a standard SAP recipe to all countries, despite marked differences in particular circumstances. Several possible reasons for this attitude have been suggested, including limited knowledge or appreciation of differences across countries, the ideological content of the programmes, the perceived immunity of simple solutions (like the pure market approach) to political and administrative complications, and the desire to avoid the appearance of favouritism *vis-à-vis* particular countries (Glover, 'A Layman's Guide to Structural Adjustment').

38. Mearns, 'Environmental Implications of Structural Adjustment', 5–6.

39. Garrett Hardin, 'The Tragedy of the Commons', *Science* 162 (1968): 1243–48.

40. Glover, 'A Layman's Guide to Structural Adjustment'.

41. Paul Streeten, 'Structural Adjustment: A Survey of the Issues and Options', *World Development* 15, no. 12 (1987): 1469–82; and L.D. Smith, 'Structural Adjustment, Price Reform and Agricultural Performance in Sub-Saharan Africa', *Journal of Agricultural Economics* 40, no. 1 (1989): 21–31.

42. Examples of social and environmental externalities are: the distributive effects of market-based activity – who benefits (social); and land degradation or pollution as a result of agricultural production (environmental).

43. This leads to investment decisions that are not in the public interest.

44. There is massive evidence worldwide that in unregulated markets the stronger (more influential) actors tend to gain at the expense of the weaker (less influential) ones, with economic power becoming concentrated in ever fewer hands. Witness the formation of monopolies and oligopolies in many markets, as a result of the recent global trend towards greater market deregulation. (Unregulated) economic globalization, in particular, has produced imperfect competition, very visible in the existence of few and powerful transnational companies which often practice collusion and segment markets among each other so as to increase profits.

45. Examples of public goods are: information, knowledge, public infrastructure, national parks, air and water. Because the marginal opportunity cost of using such goods is essentially zero, markets alone cannot supply them. The help of governments is required to provide public goods efficiently. Investment

in public goods is often based on estimated willingness of individuals to pay for the use of such goods.

46. This section draws heavily on Kidane Mengisteab, 'Partnership of the State and the Market in African Development', paper presented at the annual meeting of the Association of African Studies, Atlanta, Georgia, 2–5 November 1989.

47. Korten, 'Beyond the Market Versus State'.

48. Hartmut Krugmann, 'Social and Environmental Impacts of Structural Adjustment Programs in Africa – A Framework for Analysis, May 1990', paper presented at the 9th Annual Conference of the International Association of Impact Assessment, Lausanne, Switzerland, 27–30 June 1990.

49. Mengisteab and Logan, 'Are Structural Adjustment Programs Relevant?'.

50. G.A. Cornia, R. Jolly and F. Stewart (eds), *Adjustment with a Human Face* (Oxford: Clarendon Press, 1987).

51. Economic Commission for Africa (ECA), *African Alternative Framework to Structural Adjustment Programmes for Socio-Economic Recovery and Transformation* (Addis Ababa: E/ECA/CM.15/6/Rev.3, 1989).

52. Mengisteab and Logan, 'Are Structural Adjustment Programs Relevant?', section 3.

53. Three recent SAPs in African countries explicitly address environmental question: the Gambia (fisheries, agricultural diversification to improve soil fertility, and groundwater management); Ghana (forest resource management); and Guinea-Bissau (sector policy reviews in agriculture, forestry, and fisheries). Mearns, 'Environmental Implications of Structural Adjustment'.

54. These studies/papers include: James P. Lassoie and Stephen C. Kyle et al, 'Policy Reform and Natural Resource Management in Sub-Saharan Africa', College of Agriculture and Life Sciences, Cornell University, mimeo, 1989; Krugmann, 'Social and Environmental Impacts of Structural Adjustment Programs in Africa'; Mearns, 'Environmental Implications of Structural Adjustment'; LEEC, 'Macroeconomic Adjustment and the Environment'; Charles Abugre, 'Structural Adjustment and the Environment', *Third World Economics* (1–15 February 1992): 14–19; Fantu Cheru, 'Structural Adjustment, Primary Resource Trade and Sustainable Development in Sub-Saharan Africa', *World Development* 20, no. 4 (1992): 497–512; David Reed (ed.), *Structural Adjustment and the Environment* (Boulder, CO: Westview Press, 1992).

55. Mearns, 'Environmental Implications of Structural Adjustment', discusses the case of Malawi, but without (as he admits) sufficient empirical data and information. LEEC, 'Macroeconomic Adjustment and the Environment', and Reed, *Structural Adjustment and the Environment*, both focus on the Ivory Coast, Mexico and Thailand as case studies. For each country, particularly the Ivory Coast, the lack of available data and information is deplored as rendering difficult in-depth empirical analysis.

56. LEEC, 'Macroeconomic Adjustment and the Environment'.

57. Mengisteab and Logan, 'Are Structural Adjustment Programs Relevant?'.
58. A good example is the establishment of wheat farms in the rangelands of Tanzania, on territory formerly inhabited by the Barabaig pastoralists. Charles Lane, 'Barabaig Natural Resource Management: Sustainable Land Use Under Threat of Destruction', UNRISD Discussion Paper no. 12, June 1990.
59. Mengisteab and Logan, 'Are Structural Adjustment Programs Relevant?', section 3.1.
60. Jan Pronk, 'Adjustment and Development: Bridging the Gap', *Development, Journal of the Society for International Development* 1 (1989): 59–63.
61. A good part of the debate about the SAPs has focused on external versus internal origins of the crisis in Africa (and elsewhere in the developing world). Obviously, from the analysis in this chapter it is clear that internal constraints and policies as well as external factors have played a role. Failure to be able to assign clear responsibility between the two has been likened to piling bricks on top of a cardboard box. When the cardboard box finally collapses, is it the fault of the bricks or the box? Glover, 'A Layman's Guide to Structural Adjustment'.

8

A Partnership of the State and the Market in African Development: What Is an Appropriate Strategy Mix?

Kidane Mengisteab

The appropriate roles of the two devices of political economy – the state and the market – have become highly controversial in sub-Saharan Africa (henceforth simply Africa). Unlike many states, the post-independence African state, in most cases, emerged as a result of popular struggle for self-determination. It was thus expected by the general population to play a liberating role, which included not only national independence but also the freeing of all citizens from poverty, disease, hunger and illiteracy. Thus, the newly independent state considered active participation in economic activity imperative. State intervention in economic activity has since been significant in Africa. By some estimates, the public sector's share of total output is 15 per cent relative to 3 per cent in (non-socialist) Asia and 12 per cent in Latin America. Its share of investment is estimated at 25 per cent relative to about 17 and 19 per cent in Asia and Latin America respectively.[1] Public enterprises account for as much as 40 to 45 per cent of the manufacturing value-added while public sector employment in Africa in 1980 was also estimated to account for 50 to 55 per cent of non-agricultural wages, relative to an average of 36 per cent in Asia, 27 per cent in Latin America and 24 per cent in OECD countries.[2]

Since the late 1970s and early 1980s, with the rise of conservative macro-economic orthodoxy in the industrialized countries, especially the US and the UK, many analysts (we will refer to them as the liberalization school) have attributed much of Africa's economic malaise to the magnitude of state intervention in economic activity.[3] Balassa, for example, suggests that the prevalence of interventionist policies might explain the poor performance of African economies relative to the economies of other developing areas.[4] The liberalization school views state intervention as self-serving and inefficient, crowding out available productive resources from the more efficient private sector. Proponents of this school advocate the curtailment of the role of the state and the expansion of the market mechanism. Among their specific suggestions are the reduction of public expenditures, elimination of subsidies, privatization of publicly owned enterprises and decontrolling prices, interest rates, exchange rates and imports. Sponsored by the IMF, the World Bank and the industrial powers led by the US, liberalization has now become the dominant ideology on the basis of which much of North–South economic interaction takes place.[5]

The African experience provides ample evidence that state intervention has, by and large, been both self-serving and inefficient. There are, however, some serious flaws in the diagnosis of the liberalization school and in its prescription that replacing the role of the state by the market (liberalization) would cure Africa's economic ills. First, while state intervention has, in most cases, aggravated the situation, neither recent empirical nor historical evidence provides a strong basis for the claim that intervention is the underlying cause of the prevailing economic crisis. Second, the liberalization school fails to distinguish the differences in the nature of the state and thus in the types of interventions, as it simply lumps them all together as harmful to economic development. Finally, even if the prevailing economic conditions were attributable to past policy failures, it does not provide any new solutions. It simply reverts to the old trickle-down theory.

This study proposes two general hypotheses. One is that state intervention is not the underlying cause of economic ills, although it is more likely than the market mechanism to lead to economic malperformance when the state is self-serving. The second hypothesis is that liberalization of the economy without more fundamental changes in the existing socio-economic relations is unlikely to lead to a workable market system, much less to Africa's socio-economic development. The chapter is organized into four parts. The first analyses why the African state is interventionist. The second attempts to explain why there are different types of interventions and why interventions have generally not succeeded in achieving the objectives of liberation. The third analyses why simply superimposing the market system over the existing socio-economic relations is unlikely to overcome Africa's economic crisis. The last part analyses why intervention is unavoidable and why a sustained and self-propelled socio-economic development in Africa requires partnership between a reformed state and a restructured market. This section argues that effort should be devoted to political reforms as well as to identifying the kind of division of labour between the market and the state that is most suitable for Africa.

Why the African state is interventionist

States in the developing world generally face more compelling reasons to intervene than do states in industrialized market economies. Among these reasons are: 1) the weak linkages between the large peasant sector and the small modern sector, which limit the domestic market and the benefits from external economies; 2) the inability of the private sector to generate sufficient capital to enter certain industries and public services that are regarded as essential to national development; 3) the more difficult international competition they face as newcomers to industrialization; 4) the domination of the modern private sector by foreign concerns, which is perceived as hampering economic independence; and 5) the high population growth that undermines their economies and threatens their political systems.[6] African states, as already pointed out, are generally more interventionist than other (non-socialist) states in the developing world. Africa's economic performance has also been generally poorer. However, it does not follow that intervention explains the poor performance of the economy. The suggestion by the liberalization school that it does so lacks empirical evidence.

An alternative hypothesis which is better grounded on historical evidence is that (all other factors being equal) the degree of state intervention depends on the level of economic diversification. In other words, the state tends to intervene more in societies where the subsistence peasant sector is predominant, the private sector is still weak, and the capitalist class has not established a hegemony over the rest of society. Data constraints do not allow rigorous tests of this hypothesis or the hypothesis of the liberalization school. Data are not available for many relevant indicators and when available the quality is very poor and often misleading, as Loutfi points out.[7]

There have been some empirical studies with results that support the hypothesis of the liberalization school.[8] Considering the poor quality of data, however, such results need to be approached with a great deal of caution. Furthermore, they are not replicable. Mengisteab and Logan compared the performances of three groups of African countries – highly interventionist, moderately interventionist and least interventionist – on agricultural performance and did not find Balassa's results replicable.[9] A study by the United Nations Economic Commission for Africa on the impacts of structural adjustment programmes,[10] which compares the performances of countries that have adjusted strongly, countries adjusting weakly and countries with no such programmes, also finds no significant differences between the three groups, although structural adjustment may require more time before its impacts can be realized fully.

A multivariate regression analysis of the relationship between intervention and economic performance in twenty African states also shows no significant relationship between the two. The countries included in the study, on the basis of data availability, are: Benin, Burkina Faso, Cameroon, Congo, Côte d'Ivoire, Ethiopia, Gabon, Ghana, Kenya, Malawi, Niger, Nigeria, Senegal, Sudan, Tanzania, Togo, Zaire, Zambia and Zimbabwe. The indicators for intervention include: 1) differences in nominal official and nominal black market exchange rates for 1980–83 (x_1); 2) general government consumption as a percentage of GDP for 1985–87 (x_2); and 3) average total government expenditures as a percentage of GNP for 1980–87 (x_3). Average annual GDP growth rates for 1980–87 (y_1), food self-sufficiency in percentages for 1980–85 (y_2), average annual growth of exports for 1980–87 (y_3), and average annual growth of gross domestic investments in percentages for 1980–87 (y_4) were selected as indicators for economic performance.[11] The results reveal no significant relationships (Table 8.1).

The alternative hypothesis that the level of state intervention depends on the level of economic diversification is also not supported by empirical evidence. This hypothesis was tested using the same indicators for intervention. Differences in nominal official and nominal black market exchange rates for 1980–83 (y_5), general government consumption as a percentage of GDP for 1985–87 (y_6), and average total government expenditures as a percentage of GNP for 1980–87 (y_7). The indicators for economic diversification are: 1) classification of countries on income levels into low-income and middle-income (x_5); 2) percentage of non-primary exports to total exports for 1985–87 (x_6); 3) the contribution of the manufacturing sector to GNP in percentages for 1987–85 (x_7); and 4) percentage of total population engaged in agriculture (x_8). None of the models shows significant relationship (see Table 8.2).

Thus, empirical evidence, perhaps due to the poor quality of the data, does not support either hypothesis. Historical evidence, however, favours the alternative hypothesis over that of the liberalization school. During colonial rule the development of an African bourgeoisie was impaired

TABLE 8.1

Results of the relationship between intervention and economic performance

Independent variables	B Coefficients	Dependent variables			
		Y_1	Y_2	Y_3	Y_4
X_1	B_1	-2.201	4.443	-0.973	0.929
X_2	B_2	7.192	-0.922	1.082	0.812
X_3	B_3	-4.391	1.320	-0.838	-1.145
F Value		0.082	0.438	0.776	0.941
Adjusted R^2		-0.169	-0.097	-0.037	-0.010
Intercept		2.421	96.198	2.948	-6.415

because Africans were deprived of access to resources such as credits. The fragile merchant and artisan classes were also destroyed by competition from large firms from the metropole states.[12] As Efange points out,[13] African entrepreneurs were also suppressed when regarded as a threat to the commercial interests of metropolitan enterprises. In Kenya, for example, Africans were forbidden to grow tea and other crops reserved for settlers. Iron smelting, as a traditional industry, was also prohibited for Nigerians.[14] By the advent of political independence in the 1960s, African economies were generally less diversified than those of other regions of the developing world. Manufacturing, for example, accounted for less than 6.8 per cent of gross domestic product for sub-Saharan Africa.[15] The capitalist class was only at an embryonic stage and the economy was dominated by the peasant sector. At the time of independence the market system was hardly operational. State intervention was thus filling a vacuum rather than displacing the market. In the 1960s, even the World Bank, and many development theorists, including some strong advocates of the market system such as W.W. Rostow, shared a consensus on the need for state-led industrialization in the new states.[16]

Another historical evidence that contradicts the hypothesis of the liberalization school is that between the early 1960s and the mid-1970s African economies, benefiting from relatively high commodity prices, grew modestly, despite active state intervention. Africa's industry, for instance, grew at an annual rate of 7.5 per cent.[17] Notable progress was also made in the development of infrastructure such as schools, hospitals

TABLE 8.2
Results of the relationship between economic diversification and intervention

Model independent variable	B Coefficients	Dependent variables		
		Y_5	Y_6	Y_7
X_5	B_5	-0.498	13.436	0.852
X_6	B_6	8.359	3.824	1.078
X_7	B_7	11.051	0.381	1.023
X_8	B_8	-0.354	0.857	74.369
F Value		2.491	2.651	1.740
Adjusted R^2		0.239	0.258	0.135
Intercept		2167.317	-0.048	15.928

and roads.[18] Since the middle of the 1970s, however, a number of factors such as the oil shocks, declining commodity prices, worsening terms of trade, escalating debt burden, droughts, continued fast rates of population growth and in many cases instability and conflict have undermined African economies.

Nevertheless, a quarter of a century after independence, some economic diversification and some growth of the indigenous capitalist class have taken place in Africa, although the level of these developments falls far short of expectations and varies from country to country. Côte d'Ivoire, Cameroon, Kenya, Zambia, Senegal and Zimbabwe are among the more successful. These developments have initiated a condition for liberalization, and some countries are already relatively less interventionist than others. Yet the development of the private sector and the diversification of the economy are still weak. The peasant sector, which is generally deprived of resources by the urban-biased development strategy, is still predominant.[19] Its links with the modern sector also remain weak.[20] Consequently, the modern sector has remained essentially an enclave relying heavily on the international market instead of expanding the domestic market. The capitalist class which normally champions the ideology of the market system is also by no means a dominant class that can impose its ideology over the rest of society in Africa. State intervention thus remains significant.

The failure of the state and different types of intervention

For the post-independence state to fulfil its expected goal of economic liberation, it needed the commitment and competence to change the disarticulated economic structures inherited from the colonial state by creating access to resources for the deprived general population. However, the state has, so far, largely failed to alleviate the dissociation of available resources from social need. Instead it has, in most cases, created its own privileged élite. This grand failure of the state has occurred, however, not because it intervened but because it lost its commitment to economic liberation of the masses.

In order to ensure the minimum state commitment necessary for achieving the goal of economic liberation, there needs to be a democratic political system which allows self-determination, expression and representation of interests, and freedom from exploitation, to all social entities. In most of Africa the leadership betrayed the goals of liberation and mostly substituted itself for the colonial administrators. The authoritarian colonial political system, the deprivation of the general population of access to resources, the gap between urban and rural areas, as well as the inequalities among ethnic groups and regions in many countries have remained unresolved and have caused chronic conflicts which aggravate the dissociation of resource use from social needs.

There have been a variety of arguments on the reasons for the failure of democracy in Africa, including the notion that democracy is incompatible with poverty and that Africa does not have a tradition of liberal democracy. The latter argument is theoretically as nonsensical as arguing that development in Africa has failed because Africa does not have a tradition of economic development. The first argument is also weak because, despite their poverty, many African villages operate democratic decision-making processes.[21] Village (consensus) democracy may not be suitable for a modern society and the liberal form of democracy was largely foreign to Africa before independence. Nevertheless, the substance of democracy and consensus democracy are not unknown to Africa. It is at the higher levels where unmitigated inequality prevails that democracy is non-existent.

In the absence of democracy, a hegemony of one class or an alliance of classes over the rest of society might be expected to bring about relative political stability. However, no hegemonic class capable of imposing its order has emerged in Africa. The development of the

African bourgeoisie as a class has been constrained by its inability to expand its productive capital and to develop a domestic market where it could ascertain its independence. Despite its relative dominance over the other classes in some countries, it has not yet succeeded in establishing a firm hegemony. The petty bourgeoisie has also been incapable of establishing a hegemony due to its class nature. This is a fluid class whose membership ranges from the owners of small enterprises to the intelligentsia and other professionals. This class has no common ideological affiliation and no common position on the restructuring of the African economy. The masses, on the other hand, are largely, as already pointed out, excluded from access to resources, including political decision making, and thus they are not in a position to form a hegemony. Even the legitimacy of the state has often come under serious threat as evident from the experiences of Chad, Liberia, Somalia, Ethiopia, Sudan, and many others. Due to the powerlessness of the general masses and the consequent wide inequality in power relations between the state and civil society, the state has in many cases degenerated into a self-serving institution.

However, in most African countries, the state does not truly represent any particular social class since no social class has established a viable hegemony. In some cases, the state represents a fragile coalition of the small bourgeoisie and certain segments of the petty bourgeoisie. In other cases, the state merely represents the interests of individuals or a particular social strata, such as the military who control the state and through state power obtain control of the means of production and essentially maintain the prevailing dependent structures. This type of state often resorts to brute force to maintain order. In some cases, the African state has attempted to legitimize itself or has maintained power by favouring some ethnic groups over others. However, unlike class hegemony, which gives a sense of inclusiveness through the possibility of social mobility of individuals, no matter how limited the possibility, ethnic hegemony is exclusive and essentially unstable. Thus, such states have also relied on repressive means for their existence.

The failure of this type of state intervention, however, does not necessitate the elimination of all types of intervention. Moreover, due to the absence of a hegemonic class and the consequent fluid nature of the state, the reasons for intervention and the types of intervention are diverse. There are also some differences in the results of intervention. Some states clearly intervene in order to advance the economic interests of the ruling élite or to create patronage with certain politically influential social groups or segments of the population. Ownership of enterprises generally provides such states with a means of strengthening their power by giving them direct control over resources. Price controls, especially those of agricultural producer prices, also give them a means of appeasing the politically more potent segments of society. The beneficiaries of such intervention have been the bureaucracy, the industrial sector, which with low food prices can keep wages low, and the urban consumers, who have a stronger political voice than the peasantry.[22] The benefits from interest rate controls and other subsidies have also been concentrated in the hands of the wealthier and politically more powerful segments of the population. No more than 5 per cent of African farmers are, for instance, estimated to have access to credit from formal financial institutions.[23]

This type of intervention thus diverts resources away from the masses and from the segments of society that would benefit from market allocation of resources towards the politically more dominant elements. While Zaire's 'kleptocratic' government under Mobutu is often regarded as the epitome of such intervention,[24] many African states fall within this self-serving type of intervention. Such distortive intervention has led many to argue that ending intervention in favour of the market would rectify the misallocation of resources. Blair, for example, argues that: 'If subsidized interest rates direct agricultural loans to the rich, then it should follow that raising those rates to market levels would cut off the differential access enjoyed by the wealthy.'[25] Decontrolling interest rates would certainly discontinue the benefits the rich and politically powerful obtain from controlled or subsidized rates. It would not, however, eliminate the differential access enjoyed by the wealthy, nor would it eliminate the deprivation of the poor. Unregulated and market determined interest rates would also be distributed in favour of the wealthier class, who would rely on their purchasing power.

Not all states intervene solely for advancing self-interest and for purposes of creating political patronage. Some intervene in order to bring about national development, although not necessarily always with the competence needed to achieve these goals. Some latecomers to industrialization, such as Japan, South Korea and Taiwan, have succeeded through interventionist strategies.[26] Some states control interest rates and subsidize agricultural credits in an attempt to encourage small farmers to adopt new technology and to increase productivity.[27] However, the benefits often go to the wealthier and more powerful farmers. One reason for this, according to Blair,[28] is that financial institutions, which find it less costly to loan larger sums of money to fewer people than small amounts to large numbers of people, undermine government policy.

Despite the controlled interest rates, the small farmers' access to credits from the formal financial institutions is therefore limited and they often have to do without or rely on non-formal lenders, who usually charge them higher than the market rates. Under these conditions, decontrolling interest rates can be beneficial since the formal institutions, benefiting from higher rates, may expand their operations, reach the small farmers and outcompete the informal creditors in the long run. However, it is not clear why the probability of this happening is any higher than the state, with the necessary political commitment, succeeding in correcting its policy errors and devising new means of reaching the small farmers.

Attempts by developing countries to modify their position in the international division of labour has also led to state intervention.[29] Many states, for instance, control interest rates, foreign exchange and imports as incentives to certain industries or sectors of the economy in an attempt to build a national industrial base. The strategy of import-substitution industrialization, for example, requires support for certain selected industries. States also participate in ownership of enterprises to provide products and services that the private sector is unable to provide. Industries that are necessary for national development due to their external economies and that require too large sums of capital for the private sector to enter are usually the prime candidates for state ownership.

As already noted, the political commitment that is essential for the type of intervention that mobilizes resources for national development has not been strong in Africa. Nevertheless there are cases, such as Zimbabwe and Botswana, that demonstrate that all intervention is not harmful. The government of Zimbabwe's intervention in agriculture through provision of favourable pricing, credits, marketing facilities, grain depots, health and educational services to small farmers has, for instance, led to an unusual agricultural success in Africa.[30] Botswana is another country that has paid serious attention to distributional problems such as protecting the victims of drought.[31] The difference between these two cases and other states is not in the degree of intervention but in the purpose for intervention and in the level of democratization.

To summarize this section, African interventions have mostly been self-serving. This type of intervention has clearly aggravated the distortions of African economies and hampered socio-economic development by diverting resources away from social needs as the liberalization school claims. However, not all interventions are self-serving and distortive. Some interventions, albeit few in number, have shown modest success in facilitating the alleviation of poverty and the transformation of the subsistence sector into a surplus-producing exchange economy.

The limitations of the market in Africa

As pointed out in the last section, the post-independence state has, by and large, failed to correct the distortions of African economies. However, the market also does not have mechanisms capable of rectifying them.[32] An essential function of the market is to relay to producers information on actual and expected effective demand on the basis of which they make decisions and formulate plans. The market also furnishes consumers with what they need provided that they can translate their needs into demand through their purchasing power. Purchasing power is thus the means by which members of a society individually satisfy their needs for goods and services and collectively, through their aggregate effective demand, influence economic decisions on the type and quantity of goods produced.

In the diversified and more advanced economies, where the purchasing power of even the relatively poor segments of society is significant enough to allow them to participate, the market performs these two functions reasonably well. However, in low-income undiversified economies such as those of Africa, where a large segment of the population is outside the exchange economy and the modern sector is largely an outward-looking enclave, the market does not perform these two essential functions properly. This failure, while compounded by factors such as inappropriate intervention, unfavourable international conditions and natural disasters, is not due simply to exogenous factors but also to the inherent forces of the market itself.[33]

One characteristic of the role of the market in the allocation of resources is that needs not accompanied by purchasing power, or goods and services whose production does not generate a certain profit rate to suppliers, are neglected. In most African states, the needs of the large subsistence segment of the peasantry are largely neglected due to the inability of this social group to translate its needs into demand via purchasing power. The subsistence peasantry's participation in the market is thus passive and limited. Some have argued, and case studies have confirmed, that African peasants are responsive to price changes.[34] Bates also argues that African peasants move out of the production of crops with declining prices into products with higher prices.[35] However, these studies treat the peasantry as a homogenous unit. They do not differentiate between the subsistence majority and the market-oriented above-subsistence minority. Thus such observations, by and large, over-represent the market-oriented segment of the farmers. Price changes due to both intervention and market forces explain the fluctuations of marketed output. They may also explain why some segments of the peasantry often refrain from participation in the market by withdrawing to subsistence production. However, market information hardly determines resource allocation in the subsistence sector.

The market has increasingly encroached on the traditional subsistence sector. Thus even this sector is not entirely outside the realm of the market. It is a source of cheap labour, sells limited quantities of food and livestock products, and buys farm inputs and a small group of basic consumer goods such as clothing, oil and sugar. Even in this limited exchange the peasantry faces unfavourable terms of trade for a variety of reasons, including lack of information, storage and other marketing facilities, as well as agricultural producer price controls.

The subsistence sector also trades within itself in the village or small town markets, which appear to be relatively less distorted as they tend to be characterized by freer competition among a large number of small producers. Yet the production of this overwhelming majority of the peasantry is essentially use-value oriented. Such markets are essentially mechanisms of simple exchange with limited allocative power, which makes them different from the market in a capitalist system. Unlike the market-oriented segment, the subsistence peasantry does not switch its production mix in reaction to price changes. Ghai and Smith,[36] for instance, express considerable doubt about the effect of price changes on food crops due to the tendency for self-sufficiency among African farm households and the large amount of produce that is not traded.

With improvements in productivity, such markets, of course, can be transformed to play an increasing role in resource allocation. The production of non-traditional products such as vegetables geared for the urban markets and for export may, for instance, facilitate the metamorphosis of the role of these markets. However, such a structural evolution requires the peasantry's access to productivity-raising extension services like credits, fertilizers and irrigation facilities in order to expand its production beyond the subsistence level. It also requires the coordination of the industrial sector with the rural sector to ensure that the needs of the peasantry are furnished. Presently, despite its size, the peasantry's influence on economic decisions at the national level is limited and major economic decisions are formulated with little regard to the needs and interests of this social class.

The marginalization of the peasantry deprives African economies of a domestic market. The most capable producers essentially bypass the peasantry's needs and rely on the international market. Consequently, the international market rather than internal social needs is the most important determinant of resource allocation and the source of dynamism of the modern sector of African economies. The emphasis that the export sector receives in the allocation of resources when domestic needs such as those for food remain largely deprived, and the amount of foreign exchange spent on food imports instead of on developing the productive capacity of the peasantry (see Table 8.3), are telling evidences of the continued distortion of African economies.[37]

Unlike in the economically more advanced societies, in Africa social need and market-guided allocation of resources therefore often fail to correspond with each other, and this is where market failure occurs, not simply in terms of efficiency. In other words, the distortions of African economies by past policies are not correctable by the market system alone. As long as large segments of the population are marginalized, allocation of resources via the market remains essentially élitist, serving the interests of the better-off minority and relegating the transformation of the subsistence sector to the trickle-down process. Contrary to the prescriptions of the liberalization school, the market mechanism is therefore unlikely to be a panacea for Africa's economic crisis.

Partnership between the state and the market

Under conditions where both the market and the state fail, the failure of the state might be more detrimental than that of the market. As we have already seen, the market's failure is primarily in terms of coordinating available resources with social needs. When state intervention fails, however, in addition to failing to coordinate resources with social needs, it also often fails in terms of efficiency. The private sector is certainly not a guarantee of superior efficiency. Generally, however, excessive centralization and incentive problems tend to make the public sector relatively less efficient than the private sector. Hence, expanding the domain of the market at the expense of that of the state may clearly be considered as the 'second best' choice since it is more likely to generate relatively faster growth than the interventionist state. It is also likely that the market's trickle is greater than that of the self-serving state. However, it takes a long time to alleviate poverty through trickles and African countries do not have time. The deprivation of large segments of their populations, the explosions of the growth rates of the population and its

TABLE 8.3
Deprivation of the food sector and expenditures on food imports

Country	Food imports as % of export earnings			Est. fertilizer use avg. 1979–81 (kg/ha)	
	1970	1980	1989	non-food	food sector
Ethiopia	13.8	25.0	47.6	28	3
Ghana	16.9	10.5	34.7	13	2
Kenya	16.3	15.4	15.6	34	20
Mozambique	–	40.6	–	126	2
Somalia	52.9	110.8	90.4	–	1
Sudan	21.9	71.8	27.3	96	3
Tanzania	12.9	32.3	39.5	31	2
Zaire	8.1	10.1	15.5	7	1
Angola	–	–	10.6	16	7
Cameroon	13.4	9.5	21.0	30	3
Ivory Coast	17.5	15.5	14.2	21	4
Nigeria	10.3	8.0	12.1	11	6
Senegal	46.8	53.4	25.1	53	1
Zambia	4.8	11.2	8.6	235	60

Source: FAO, *Atlas of African Agriculture* (Rome: 1986), for fertilizer data. Food imports are computed from World Bank and FAO figures.

expectations, and the consequent political instability are likely to undermine the trickle-down process and to pressure governments to intervene.

Furthermore, considering the increasingly difficult competition it faces in the international economic system and the weakness of the private sector to deal with this competition, intervention is unavoidable for the African state. Therefore, the priority task should be to reform African political systems to replace the existing self-serving intervention by a society-oriented one in order to alleviate poverty. Due to the deepening economic crisis, the African state is already under growing popular pressure for much wider social changes than liberalization. With such reforms, expansion of the market mechanism becomes easier, as Professor Mamdani's chapter in this volume suggests. Without them, however, even a meaningful liberalization is unlikely to take place.

One area where state activity is clearly needed and where state intervention does not hurt the operations of the market or the private sector is in industries that are essential for the development of the national economy and are presently beyond the financial reach of the private sector. As the private sector grows, however, its participation in such industries as shareholders with the state or as full owners and competitors should be open.

Infrastructure such as schools, hospitals, roads, railways, and telecommunication facilities is another area where state activity is clearly required. Investments in this area do not attract private capital as they do not render quick returns. They are, however, needless to say, essential for national development, creating external economies for all sectors of the economy.

Another area for intervention is support for the export sector to make it competitive on the international market and support for import-substituting industries to build a domestic industrial base. Intervention in this area is complicated by contradictions between the two objectives. Export promotion may require measures such as devaluation of national currencies, tax relief, and other export promotion subsidies. Support for import substitution, on the other hand, may require lowering import duties for selected industries and providing preferential access to foreign exchange to facilitate the importation of intermediate goods and other inputs. In an attempt to overcome such conflicts many countries use multiple exchange-rate systems and exchange-rate controls which often are additional administrative burdens on the economy. Despite these problems, African states have to experiment with different policy measures until they find a workable balance between the two objectives, because the problems associated with not intervening may also outweigh those of intervening due to the weakness of the private sector.

A more controversial and more complex area for state intervention is in the income redistribution area. As already noted, the lack of access to resources of large segments of the population has led not only to pervasive poverty and suffering but also to the failure of the market and political instability, which have threatened the process of nation-building. The state cannot avoid intervening to control these problems.

Revenue constraint limits the ability of African states to subsidize the basic needs of low-income consumers, and credits and inputs to low-income producers. Under this constraint, African states often intervene in the interest-rate and exchange-rate markets in an attempt to facilitate access for low-income producers. Such measures usually fail to ensure that the benefits go to the targeted groups. Price controls also compound the problem. Nevertheless, the state has to play an active role in this area, especially in transforming the peasantry into a surplus-producing exchange economy. Without such a transformation, the modern sector is likely to remain an enclave and the marginalization of African economies from the international economic system will continue. While they cannot refrain from intervening altogether, however, African states need to re-examine their policies to find ways to provide support to those with legitimate needs without stifling the operations of the market by over-intervening. Using macro-policies such as fiscal and monetary policies to allow cross-subsidization to those with legitimate needs might be better tools than direct intervention.

In conclusion, the deprivation of the general population of access to resources, including decision making, has led to the failures of the market and state intervention. The deprivation of the general population, dependency, and underdevelopment are perpetuated as a result of the failures of both devices of political economy. In other words, we have a vicious circle which is unlikely to be broken by simply changing the size of the relative spheres of the market and the state. The IMF/World Bank-sponsored structural adjustment programmes may thus be of little relevance or may even impede the development of the market system, since their protection of the needy through measures such as the Programme to Mitigate the Social Costs of Adjustment is grossly inadequate. Political and economic reforms that alleviate the deprivation of the general population through redistributive measures need to be implemented for the proper functioning of the market. Such changes are unlikely to materialize without the participation of the state.

Notes

1. World Bank, *Africa's Adjustment and Growth in the 1980s* (Washington, DC: World Bank and UNDP, 1989), 25.
2. Larry Diamond, 'Class Formation in the Swollen African State', *Journal of Modern African Studies* 25, no. 4 (1987): 573.
3. Bela Balassa, 'Adjustment Policies and Development Strategies in Sub-Saharan Africa', in Moshe Syrguin et al. (eds), *Economic Structure and Performance* (New York: Academic Press, 1984), 317–39; Ian Marceau, 'Privatization of Agriculture and Agribusiness', in Steve H. Hanke (ed.), *Privatization and Development* (San Francisco: International Center for Economic Growth, Institute for Contemporary Studies Press, 1987), 141–48; Keith Marsden and Therese Belot, *Private Enterprise in Africa: Creating a*

Better Environment, World Bank Discussion Paper no. 17 (Washington, DC: World Bank, 1987); Gray L. Cowan, *Privatization in the Developing World* (New York: Greenwood Press, 1990).

4. Balassa, 'Adjustment Policies and Development Strategies', 338.

5. Liberalization which has received added impetus from the recent collapse of communist regimes in Eastern Europe has also become a condition for the integration of these economies into the global economic system.

6. For details see James Caporaso, 'The State's Role in Third World Economic Growth', *The Annals AAPSS* 459 (January 1982): 103–11; and Cowan, *Privatization in the Developing World*.

7. Martha F. Loutfi, 'Development Issues and State Policies in Sub-Saharan Africa', *International Labour Review* 128, no. 2 (1987): 137–54.

8. Balassa, 'Adjustment Policies and Development Strategies'; Daniel Landau, 'Government and Economic Growth in Less Developed Countries', in *Report of the President's Task Force on International Private Enterprise: Selected Papers* (Washington, DC: Government Printing Office, 1984), 17–41.

9. Kidane Mengisteab and Bernard Logan, 'Implications of Liberalization for Agricultural Development in Sub-Saharan Africa', *Comparative Political Studies* 22, no. 4 (January 1990): 437–57.

10. United Nations Economic Commission for Africa, *African Alternative Framework to Structural Adjustment Programmes for Socio-Economic Recovery and Transformation* (Addis Ababa: E/ECA/CM.15/6/Rev 3, 1989).

11. A comprehensive list of indicators for intervention would include the proportion of publicly owned assets to GNP, and government controls of prices and interest rates. There are, however, no reliable data on these variables. Despite this limitation, the proportions of government expenditures and consumption to total expenditure and consumption respectively can reflect the degree of intervention. The difference between official and black-market rates of foreign exchange are also good indicators of government control of exchange rates. The indicators for economic performance are standard.

12. Immanuel Wallerstein, *Africa and the Modern World* (Trenton, NJ: Africa World Press, Inc. 1986); Claude Ake, *A Political Economy of Africa* (New York: Longman, 1981).

13. Peter Efange, 'An Overview of Public and Private Enterprises in Africa: Role, Status, Scope, Performance and Challenges for Implementing the Lagos Plan of Action', in *Public Enterprises Performance and the Privatization Debate*, African Association for Public Administration and Management (ed.), (New Delhi: Vikas Publishing House, 1987), 3–27.

14. Efange, 'An Overview of Public and Private Enterprises in Africa', 16–17. This is not to argue that there were no Africans who benefited from incorporation to the international economic system under colonialism. Cash-crop exporters who emerged in different countries, such as the cocoa exporters of Ghana, for example, were among the benefactors. However, the sector of the economy and the segment of the population that significantly

benefited from incorporation remained narrow.

15. Thandika Mkandawire, 'The Road to Crisis, Adjustment and De-Industrialisation: The African Case', *African Development* 13, no. 1 (1988): 11–12.

16. Jennifer Seymour Whitaker, *How Can Africa Survive?* (New York: Council on Foreign Relations, 1988), 46–47.

17. Mkandawire, 'The Road to Crisis, Adjustment and De-Industrialisation', 13.

18. Whitaker, *How Can Africa Survive?*, 31.

19. Goran Hyden, 'The Resilience of the Peasant Mode of Production: The Case of Tanzania', in Robert Bates and M.F. Lofchie (eds), *Agricultural Development in Africa* (New York: Praeger, 1980), 218.

20. There have been intensive debates on the nature and causes of the weak linkage between the modern and peasant sectors. Modernization theorists attribute it to the recalcitrance of the traditional peasant sector and describe African economies as dual economies. Radical scholars view the capitalist international division of labour as marginalizing the peasantry and preventing its transformation. The liberalization school also attributes it to the reverse income redistribution impacts and inefficiencies of state intervention. Despite the disagreements on the causes, there is little dispute that the modern sector has essentially been an enclave.

21. Asmarom Legesse, *Gada: Three Approaches to the Study of African Society* (New York: Free Press, 1973).

22. For detailed accounts of this see Robert Bates, *Markets and States in Tropical Africa* (Berkeley: University of California Press, 1981), 11–44; and D. Ghai and L. Smith, 'Food Price Policy and Equity', in John Mellor, C.L. Delgado, and M.J. Blackie (eds), *Accelerating Food Production in Sub-Saharan Africa* (Baltimore: Johns Hopkins University Press, 1987), 280.

23. Claudio Gonzalez-Vega, 'Cheap Agricultural Credit: Redistribution in Reverse', in Dale W. Adams, Douglas H. Graham and J.D. von Pischke (eds), *Undermining Rural Development with Cheap Credit* (Boulder, CO: Westview Press, 1984), 120–21.

24. Whitaker, *How Can Africa Survive?*, 46.

25. W. Harry Blair, 'Agricultural Credit, Political Economy, and Patronage', in Adams, Graham and von Pischke, *Undermining Rural Development with Cheap Credit*, 184.

26. Amartya Sen, 'Development, Which Way Now?', in Charles K. Wilber (ed.), *The Political Economy of Development and Underdevelopment*, 4th edn (New York: Random House, 1988); James L. Dietz, 'Overcoming Underdevelopment: What Has Been Learned from the East Asian and Latin American Experiences?', *Journal of Economic Issues* 26, no. 2 (June 1992): 373–83.

27. J. Edward Kane, 'Political Economy of Subsidizing Agricultural Credit in Developing Countries', in Adams, Graham, and von Pischke, *Undermining Rural Development with Cheap Credit*, 166.

28. Blair, 'Agricultural Credit, Political Economy, and Patronage', 183–93.

29. Paul Burkett, 'Financial "Repression" and "Liberalization" in the Third World: A Contribution to the Critique of Neoclassical Development Theory', *Review of Radical Political Economies* 19, no. 1 (1987): 1–21.

30. A. Giovanni Cornia and Frances Stewart, 'Country Experience with Adjustment', in G.A. Cornia, R. Jolly, and Frances Stewart (eds), *Adjustment with a Human Face*, vol. 1 (Oxford: Clarendon, 1987), 123.

31. Cornia and Stewart, 'Country Experience with Adjustment', 123.

32. The market is broadly defined in this text to mean a social arrangement of exchange of goods and services.

33. The market exchange system which is based on competition is not strong in alleviating inequality when initial endowments are distributed unequally. For details see Charles Edward Lindblom, *Politics and Markets: The World's Political Economic Systems* (New York: Basic Books, 1977).

34. J.K. Maitha, 'A Supply Function for Kenya Coffee', *Eastern Africa Economic Review* 1, no. 1 (1969): 63–72; Hossein Askarai and John T. Cummings, *Agricultural Supply Response: A Survey of Econometric Evidence* (New York: Praeger, 1976).

35. Bates, *Markets and States in Tropical Africa*, 83.

36. D. Ghai and L. Smith, *Agricultural Prices, Policy and Equity in Sub-Saharan Africa* (Boulder: Lynne Rienner Publishers, 1987), 60–67.

37. Liberalization scholars argue that exchange-rate controls limit the role the international market plays in the resource allocation process since they distort allocation against the internationally traded products. The export sector is, however, favoured in resource allocation despite exchange-rate controls (see Table 8.3).

9

Democracy in Africa:
Constraints and Prospects

Abdoulaye S.M. Saine

The 1960s are generally regarded as Africa's 'Age of Glamour'.[1] It was the decade in which many African nations gained political independence. Independence, it was hoped, would improve not only the living conditions of the masses, but would also engender genuine participatory democracy. Today, three decades after the 'age of glamour', conditions on the continent are sobering rather than euphoric and development seems a desperate struggle rather than an exhilarating challenge.[2]

To speak of development in most sub-Saharan African economies today is to speak of the past, not the present or the foreseeable future. The world's poorest region is rapidly becoming poorer – in a number of these economies, real resource availability measured in physical gross domestic product adjusted for terms of trade is lower than in 1970. In extreme cases, such as Ghana, Uganda and Zaire, it is probably lower than in the early 1960s. The current outlook in many cases is for 'more of the same'.[3]

'Continent in Crisis' has indeed become an apt and often-used description of Africa's condition. Yet the crisis is not merely an economic crisis reflected in massive unemployment, underemployment, a growing debt burden, deteriorating terms of trade and declining industrial and agricultural productivity in most countries. It is also manifest in social and political problems that include among others internal wars, growing abuse of human rights, and internal military intervention.[4]

Yet three years have elapsed since the process of popular protest and political reform in many African countries started. The twin ideals of democracy and freedom have provided the justification for challenges to authoritarian governments throughout the continent.[5] During 1990 in particular, citizens took to the streets of capital cities in some fourteen African countries to express discontent with economic hardships and political repression, and to demand political reform.[6] During the same period at least twenty-one governments launched seemingly significant reform efforts to permit greater pluralism, accountability, and competition within the polity.[7]

While three years is a short period in any country's transition to democracy, it is important to assess the democratization efforts in various countries. Clearly, the embryonic and uncertain nature of democratization vitiates against definitive answers. Yet an assessment that focuses on the limits, prospects, and the paradox of reform is imperative. Thus Nigeria and South Africa will be used as examples. General Ibrahim Babangida's scheme for a perfect democracy is in shambles after he cancelled the election results of June 1993 in which Chief Moshood K.O. Abiola of the Left-Centre Social Democratic Party is believed to have won. While at the time of writing (1993) Babangida is still in power, he relinquishes the throne on 25 August, to a handpicked interim civilian regime amidst the loud protestation of trade unions, students, and human-rights groups.[8]

A new government in Zambia, though one of the continent's most stable, resorted to the time-honoured tool of martial law to protect itself against coup plotters earlier in 1993. Opposition leaders have come to power in Congo and Niger, only to be pummelled by violence and military rebellions. Former dictators were recently returned to power in widely boycotted elections in Burkina Faso, Djibouti, Gabon, Mauratania and Cameroon. Togo represents the latest example: opposition leaders boycotted the elections of 25 August 1993 because of pre-election irregularities.[9] And even in countries where the opposition has participated, voting often has been marred by allegations of fraud. Kenya's president, Daniel Arap Moi, coasted to victory last December in Kenya's first multi-party elections in twenty-five years. Moi, however, is believed to have rigged the elections. Now as Kenya sinks even deeper into economic crisis, Moi's commitment to democracy remains questionable.

Before 1990, only five (Gambia, Senegal, Botswana, Namibia and Mauritius) were democratic. Today, twenty-six countries, or more than half the continent, have at least nominal democracies. And fifteen more have promised, with varying degrees of sincerity, to hold free elections.[10] The situation in South Africa inches grudgingly towards elections in April of 1994 amidst much bloodshed. No less important is the setback to democracy in Angola where, after 'fair' and 'free' elections in 1992,

UNITA rebels continue to massacre innocent civilians in violation of the May 1991 accords.

The situation in Mozambique is not any more promising, given RENAMO's unending assault against government-held territory in clear violation of the Rome accords signed in 1993. Somalia has deteriorated and sunk into a state of anarchy and is run by the United Nations.[11] The national constitution conference in Benin in February 1990 turned into a devastating indictment of President Kkerekou's regime, which in turn precipitated the birth of a protest movement in Togo and the Central African Republic.[12] A ceasefire is currently in force between the warring factions in Liberia with elections slated for 1994. Today the Sudan finds itself caught in the mire of hunger, poverty, and war between the Muslim north and the Christian south. Thus it has been a remarkable three years in Africa, so remarkable that it has been dubbed the 'Second African Revolution'; yet political analysts at the Carter Emory Center of Emory University in Atlanta, which tracks emerging democracies in Africa, think the continent has backslid on the promise of democratization in the past year. African leaders are increasingly using their powers to destabilize, discredit, and where necessary, bludgeon the forces demanding democratic renewal.[13] What then are the limits and prospects for sustained democratization in Africa? What kind(s) of democracy would be relevant for Africa?

These questions are important because the democratization process is intrinsically paradoxical.[14] And regardless of whether these reforms towards democracy succeed or fail, but especially when they succeed, its most salient initial product will be suffering – injustice, inequity, even repression, perhaps the very thing that democratization intends forever to banish from society.[15]

Prudence dictates a careful assessment, tentative as it may be, of the limits and prospects for sustainable democracy in lieu of the current crisis in Africa. This is because the leadership's class character, its urban and external support base, could usher in a type of democracy that consolidates the power and financial interests of this class and its external supporters. After all, some of those in leadership positions of various country movements on the whole share similar political views and fundamental economic interests with those they wish to replace. This chapter is subdivided into three sections: the first section addresses the causes of the unrest in the continent, while the second outlines state and civil-society relations, i.e., how such relations impeded the development of democratic norms, institutions and traditions. In the third section, I focus on recent events in Nigeria and South Africa.

Causes of the movements towards democracy

The causes of the movements towards democracy in Africa are complex. Clearly, the economic crisis reflected in massive unemployment, underemployment, a crushing debt burden, deteriorating terms of trade and declining agricultural and industrial productivity features prominently. Yet the crisis goes beyond these economic factors to manifest itself in the abuse of human rights, internal wars, and military interventions. In Zaire, Zambia, Kenya and the Ivory Coast, the push for democracy derives in part from the failure of the single-party governments and more specifically the inability of both civilian and military regimes to mitigate the negative social effects of World Bank–IMF-sponsored economic reforms.

Perhaps the single most negative aspect of IMF and World Bank conditionalities is the fiscal anti-inflationary programme which requires the eliminating of government budget deficits, reduced spending, increases in taxes, and higher prices for public services. In particular, the reduction of subsidies in education, food, health and housing have had adverse effects on the rural and urban poor, with women and children bearing the brunt of these cuts. These policies have had the added negative effect of provoking riots in Ghana, Egypt, Liberia, Morocco and Zaire, to name a few.[16] In fact, Stein and Nafzinger contend that serious conflicts exist within the World Bank's programme and the provision of basic needs.[17]

The economic crisis and the bitter adjustment pill are thus a ubiquitous background to the current unrest; political protest signals the rejection by African populations of developmental dictatorships as a model of governance.[18] Yet economic hardships alone do not explain why countries that experienced severe economic problems, such as Guinea, Tanzania or Guinea-Bissau, saw little or no unrest during 1990, nor does it account for the failure of previous protests to destabilize or even question the legitimacy of incumbent governments. What is crucial to the more recent protest movements was the transformation of economic grievances into broad political demands.[19] The one-party system had essentially depoliticized African society. It allowed the leaders to dispense with the substance of democratic participation while retaining its formal aspects. The establishment of a one-party state entailed the use of coercion and the use of violence to force the population to acquiesce in the reduction of their political participation.[20] It follows, therefore, that the demands for democracy in Africa derive in part from the 'pathology of political decay' and are made more acute by endemic socio-economic problems. Thus corruption by state officials became a convenient rallying point used to arouse popular resentment which was then directed against these leaders. Multi-party democracy hence became the ideological, albeit loose, foundation for the various movements. The leaders of these movements include relatively privileged intellectuals, including university students, labour, and other groups prone to political agitation based on ethno-regional and religious proclivities. These groups, curiously, are among those whom the reforms are designed ultimately to benefit.[21] This suggests perhaps the greatest and most nettlesome dilemma confronting the reform leadership, because they would be among the principal beneficiaries of the reform upon its completion.

State and civil society relations

By focusing on the conception of the state[22] both as an instrument and as an arena for intra-class struggle between the civilian, military, commercial, and bureaucratic elements of the petty bourgeoisie, and between these elements and the masses, one begins to see this petty bourgeois class not as a homogeneous or monolithic entity, but as differentiated, with multiple loci of power. This is true despite their sometimes common interests and use of the state to appropriate societal resources. Indeed the very use of religion, ethnicity, or regional identification by members of the petty bourgeoisie to gain access to the state, generally keeps them divided. Yet, in the light of the tenuous relationship of this class to actual production, the state has become an indispensable instrument of capital accumulation.[23] International capital and various factions of the petty bourgeoisie therefore, at one time or another, benefit from neo-colonial ties and relations.

While the peripheral capitalist state is central to direct appropriation and accumulation of surplus, it also makes the state vulnerable to attacks from other petty bourgeoisie factions hurt by state regulations.[24] This is particularly true where such opposing factions have some base in the military forces. Furthermore, the growing contradictions within the petty bourgeoisie and between it and the mass of the population, coupled with serious economic conditions, make it virtually necessary for any faction of the petty bourgeoisie to use the strong repressive apparatus of the state to control opposition. Thus the class faction in power, civilian or military, would use the state to formulate or redirect policy to meet their factional or institutional interests. It follows therefore, that coups, counter-coups, repressive single-party states, and bloody struggles between civilian and military factions of the petty bourgeoisie in African or Third World countries arise in part from the contradictions inherent in intra-class relations and are made more acute by endemic socio-economic problems.[25]

As access to the state constitutes the principal instrument for private appropriation of capital, different factions of the petty bourgeoisie engage in struggles to control the state and utilize its allocative and distributive powers for their own private ends.[26]

Furthermore, as various factions of the dominant class struggle to capture state power, they pay little or no attention to the economic and social concerns of ordinary citizens. The neglect of their material needs and the instability generated alienates them from politics. Politics thus becomes the exclusive domain of the dominant classes.[27]

The lack of participatory democracy in African countries, therefore, is in part rooted in the process of international capitalist accumulation and factional class struggle. The link between internal class and international capital lies in the state's symbiotic relationship with multinational corporations, marked by partnerships at executive levels on the one hand, and the creation of certain market privileges for multinational subsidiaries on the other.[28] The military, depending on its factional, institutional interests and economic orientation, will maintain the civilian faction of the petty bourgeoisie and its external links or replace them. The power of the military faction to overcome civilian regimes means it is particularly well placed to divert resources for its own consumption.[29] It is this unique position that enables and encourages the military to intervene.

Similarly, the lack of democracy in Africa and other Third World countries cannot be disassociated from their dependence on the US and the former Soviet Union and their role as primary products/mineral producers or manufacturers of semi-industrial goods. This residual Cold War condition leaves them vulnerable to the vicissitudes of international capitalism reflected in these countries as a state of social and economic crisis epitomized by a general condition of coup fertility. Data showing that Third World nations are more prone to violence cannot be denied. But we must also entertain the hypothesis that part of the political violence is due to the permeability of Third World nations; that is, because of the increasing ability of core societies to influence the internal economic conditions of dependent states, the core state may be motivated to encourage a coup d'état that will maintain a more favourable state of affairs for their economic interests.[30]

In addition, the training and arming of African and Third World armies to repress dissidents, or the support given dissident groups fighting against democratically elected governments by imperial powers, clearly undermine the declarations and putative support for democracy and human rights in dependent states. Whatever the attitude of the US leadership towards freedom at home, systematic policies towards Third World countries make it evident that alleged commitment to democracy and human rights is mere rhetoric, directly contrary to direct policy. The operative policy has been and remains economic freedom – meaning freedom for US business to invest, sell, and repatriate profit. Since a favourable investment climate and stability often require repression, the US has often supplied the tools and training for interrogation and torture.[31] Thus, the push for democracy in Africa is supported by the US and her allies and the World Bank in order to institute more liberal political conditions to ease the flow of international capital, and make capitalist penetration of these countries and regions more efficient. This new 'liberal democracy', if achieved, would further incorporate these countries and regions into the global capitalist economy, while simultaneously undermining alternative forms of economic strategy and governance.

The ideology of the 'New World Order', is therefore based on two key concepts of 'complementarity' and 'interdependence', both convenient justifications for further domination of Africa. In the final analysis, the ideology rationalizes the neo-classical theory of international development and the contemporary international division of force and labour.[32] Ultimately, it is the major actor, the US, and her European community allies who will benefit from the 'new' global order. The 'New World Order' is a euphemism for the continuation of an inherently unequal and fundamentally exploitative economic and political arrangement. Thus the insidious and predatory nature of the state is reconstituted. Democracy derived from such conditions becomes an exercise in political window-dressing adopted by the victors simultaneously to please the 'West' and to protect and aggrandize its power and privilege. In the process nothing changes fundamentally. We must therefore recognize the extraordinary obstacles and constraints to democracy in Africa. The euphoria that greeted various democracy movements, while warranted, must be tempered because of the high human cost and possible political subterfuge it could encompass. Many observers tend generally to support reform and democratization in particular, focusing so expectantly on the benefits and becoming impatient with, even exasperated by, what we consider slow and inadequate progress. The inevitability of suffering in Africa during this phase of democratization will be felt most in the economic sphere, where the intended positive effects of economic reform are yet to be realized.[33] The additional paradox of democratization is that it could promote or intensify social conflict and inequality, precisely the results the reform process was designed initially to mitigate.

Obstacles to democracy in Africa

Let me state the obvious, perhaps unspeakable. African countries in general are deeply divided along ethnic, religious, regional, class and clan lines. Such factionalism, when coupled with historical mistrust and hostility, is a deadly potion for democracy. The Nigerian election of June 1993 is a case in point. The various efforts by certain commercial and military leaders to maintain their hold of the state and society led to the annulment of the election results and the imposition of a court-ordered injunction against its release. Nigeria's attempt at establishing a democratic government to culminate in the transfer of power to a civilian government has been dealt a serious blow. The landslide victory of Abiola, a millionaire businessman, seemed a perfect compromise for Nigeria's ethnically fractured electorate. The predominantly Muslim north has controlled the country since independence. Although Abiola is a Yoruba from the south, he also is a Muslim. And many saw him as a conciliator for Nigeria's over one hundred million people who are divided into two hundred and fifty ethnic groups and speak nearly four hundred languages.

That Babangida would dissolve all democratic institutions set up last year – the senate and national assembly – and replace them with an interim civilian administration to be sworn on 25 August 1993, is yet another manoeuvre by Babangida to hold on to power. Although he is strongly nationalistic, Babangida's actions cast doubt on his putative commitment to democracy. Unfortunately, military rule in Nigeria as in other parts of Africa generally provide a repressive 'solution' to the internal crisis of development and external indebtedness. Babangida's rule serves merely as a distributive mechanism of spoils to various interests in the army and the commercial class, and his repressive regime provides the setting in which these special interests remain largely unaltered.[34] Repression by his regime, he thinks, can blunt the movement towards democracy.[35] Nigeria has become a clear example of what happens when the forces of democratization confront a ruler's shaky commitment to democracy. The wanton killing of civilians by the military and the banning of newspapers critical of his regime and policies attest to the lengths Babangida will go to hold on to power.[36] Even if Abiola were to assume the presidency in Nigeria, the military would almost invariably intervene under the pretext of salvaging a decaying political economy.

South Africa is also entering the zone of highest risk in its transition to independence and democracy. More than 130 killings have been attributed to political factional violence in the four-day period between 2 July and 7 July 1993, since elections were set for 27 April 1994. It has been the bloodiest four days of the year. Clearly, the scheduling of the elections for 27 April 1994 ignited more political violence between competing political parties. The African National Congress and Zulu-based Inkatha Freedom Party accuse each other of political recruiting at the point of a gun. South Africa has never had a democratic experience, leaving the democratization process open to high abuse of human rights. Unfortunately, democracy in an independent South Africa will be greatly challenged because people have been long accustomed, by force of circumstances, to mistrust each other as a function of state policy, and groups, homelands and leaders fear or loathe one another.[37] The poverty and economic underdevelopment among Africans in particular will have the likely effect of further aggravating decades of violence, mistrust and fear. South Africa's transitory phase to independence is entirely inhospitable to democracy. Nor are the transitions in other African countries smooth. Many democracy movements still battle against powerful, corrupt and entrenched leaders along with domestic economic downturns. It seems the transitions have been easiest in the smaller countries of Cape Verde, São Tomé and Príncipe, and the tiny republics of Benin and Burundi.[38]

In addition to these political impediments are its economic counterparts. The vast majority of African states currently undergoing democratization face severe economic and social problems. These problems must be expected, considering that the economic crisis is most often an important factor behind the ousting of earlier authoritarian rulers. When authoritarian governments leave office, they also leave behind acute economic problems to be addressed by the new 'democratic' government.[39] The inevitability of suffering, injustice and inequality during transitions to democracy is apparent in economic terms as well. These include major social and economic dislocations. In fact, most African countries are worse off today than they were at independence in the late 1950s and early 1960s. War and famine are primarily to blame. Although it has only 14 per cent of the world's population, Africa has had one-third of the armed conflicts and produced half the world's refugees.[40] Under such a state of affairs, 'economic democracy' could in turn make the 'freedoms' accompanying multi-party politics a farce.

Africa's current economic crisis renders democratization difficult to sustain. Democracy is unlikely to flourish in many African societies where most people are plainly and painfully poor. The mass of Africans, precisely because of these adverse economic circumstances, are not concerned, nor can they be expected to be, with democratic rights and freedoms, especially those of others, but only with survival needs.[41] Extreme levels of poverty effectively bar the marginalized from meaningful participation in society. Thus economic democracy is not likely to be easy to attain in most African countries, nor is the triumph of liberal democracy inevitable.

Similarly, transitions towards democracy do not guarantee rapid economic development and an improved human rights situation. Even the relatively stable democracies in Africa, Gambia, Botswana, and Senegal, seem to hold out few promises for a process of economic development that would benefit the large groups of poor people.[42] Paradoxically, economic development does not necessarily yield democracy, nor is democracy necessarily compatible with development. Economic development, at least in its early stages, is anti-democratic because it promotes social inequality.[43]

The promise of democracy is therefore not that of automatic improvement. It is the creation of a window of opportunity, a political framework where groups struggling for development and human rights have better possibilities than before for organizing and expressing their demands.[44] Similarly, normative prescriptions notwithstanding, the rights citizens enjoy are contingent. When the state is chaotic or absent, as in Somalia, political rights and freedom evaporate. And more important, these rights can hardly exist if the state is on the verge of economic collapse.[45] This does not, however, justify the abuse of human rights by governments under the excuse of poverty.

Prospects for democracy in Africa

Africa's prospects for democracy are indeed bleak but not hopeless, and by no means assured. It is unrealistic to think that such countries can suddenly reverse course and institutionalize stable democratic government simply by changing leaders, constitutions, and/or public mentalities. If progress is made towards developing democratic government, it is likely to be gradual, messy, fitful and slow, with many imperfections along the way.[46] Pauline Baker notes pointedly that people tend to think you can just flick a switch and hold an election – and then everyone can go home and not worry. But Africa has been so burdened, and the odds stacked against it for so many years, that it would be naïve to assume that the transition can occur quickly or smoothly.[47]

On the economic front, Africa continues to depend on commodities for foreign currency earnings, but it has little leverage to affect the continuing decline in international prices or to influence the outcome of the Uruguay round of GATT talks. So its current strategy, which consists of increasing the level of production of export commodities in order to offset the decline in prices, is a never-ending pursuit with distorting effects on Africa's balance of payments.[48]

Yet earlier judgements of Africa are unjust and ill-informed. They do great disservice to a growing number of ordinary Africans, intellectuals, workers, journalists, etc., who struggle against great odds to reverse the continent's perilous cycle of dictatorships and economic decline.[49] While situations in Somalia, Zaire and South Africa have been the victims of aid and media fatigue,[50] scorn and stereotyping that appear to have overtaken Western concern for development in Africa, the years since 1990 in fact bring seeds of hope. Africans are an immensely resilient and resourceful people; witness the street vendors of Lagos or Accra or the uninhibited dynamism of the informal sector of most African economies.

In the long run, however, Africa's sustained economic growth will hinge not so much on easy grants but, as elsewhere, on the ability to raise and repay loans in international money markets and the capacity to draw direct foreign investments.[51] The post-Cold War period could provide Africa with an historic opportunity to build a sound economic foundation in giving priorities to reforms and investments in health, education, housing, production, etc. The political, economic and social reforms to establish a healthy environment for investments and growth are well underway in many countries.[52]

In addressing South Africa's prospects for economic change and democracy, much of the debate on constitutional change centres on whether there is to be a free enterprise system or some form of socialism. While the ANC's National Executive Committee maintains that the inordinate concentration of wealth in the hands of a small minority of whites needs to be broken up, it recognizes that most economic systems are mixed and that some forms of private entrepreneurship can make positive contributions. The ANC continues to leave its options open on nationalization and talks about the importance of economic growth as the means to deliver a more equitable share of the country's resources to the black majority.[53]

Domestic political changes will undoubtedly have an effect beyond

South Africa's boundaries. The smooth transition to independence for Namibia and prospects both for a resolution of the Angolan conflict and for a more stable Mozambique could usher in the beginning of a new regional economic and political configuration. The 1990s present different options, possibilities and strategies. Increases in trade and investment and an end to regional violence could point the way to a Southern African Economic Common Market,[54] with positive linkage effects with the rest of Africa.

What happens in Nigeria is going to be fundamentally important for the future of democratization in Africa. If Nigeria gets away with the rape of the democratic process, it will lead other African authoritarian regimes to think they can get away with perversions of the democratic process, so long as they make some gesture in the way of multi-party competition.[55]

With the end of the Cold War, Western donor interest has shifted to Eastern Europe and whatever political chips Africa may once have had are lost. Africans must now take the initiative and see the world as it is, not as it ought to be; only then do Africans stand a chance of changing the world according to their vision(s). Africans will also accept, if grudgingly, domestic and international market fluctuations as have others in the Third World, though Africa's debt cancellation by Western governments and banks could go a long way in sustaining and consolidating what would otherwise be shaky democracies.[56]

Africa is on the edge of an abyss. The advent of real democracy in Africa might bring more noisiness and combativeness, but fundamentally it would be a better avenue for bringing about more legitimate political order and preventing the descent of these countries.[57] Democracy, with its provisions for protecting individuals and group rights, is the continent's only hope.[58] If we don't accept democracy, what else do we have?[59]

Conclusion

The issue of democracy in Africa, and the Third World, has a powerful intellectual and ideological fascination. It raises a range of important questions about the nature and relationship between competing (intra/ inter) class interests and the use of the state to protect them. The struggle within the petty bourgeoisie and between it and the masses, and the extent to which these struggles are conditioned by (and in turn condition) the crisis in the economy, must be at the root of any explanation of 'democracy' or the lack thereof in Africa and the Third World. The struggle between various factions of the petty bourgeoisie and the lack of consensus over the rules of the game further creates instability. Thus the close link of the military or repressive civilian regimes to imperialism, their (anti-democratic, anti-communist, and anti-people) willingness to use force to maintain 'law and order', sometimes makes them particularly attractive to imperialism. These types of regimes have often arisen to mediate the economic, political and social crisis set off by the contradictions of peripheral capitalism, and in particular World Bank and IMF conditionalities.

Yet it is also conceivable that intra-class conflict or disunity could force new alliances between factions of the petty bourgeoisie and the people and thus engender reform. Clearly, under such political conditions democratization could provide new opportunities for alliance formation between the people and progressive elements of the petty bourgeoisie. These reforms in the form of more people's rights (i.e., food, shelter, education, primary health care and participation), would constitute important and tangible improvements in the lives of the poor.

Students on the left have generally insisted on the limitations the economic structure sets on political structure and have at times denied any independence to the latter. On the one hand, it is argued, and somewhat contradictorily, that through political action a hegemonic class and economic structure can be overthrown, though little can be done by means of reforms. Many therefore maintain that, in a sense, nothing is possible except everything. The prevalence of authoritarian regimes particularly in Kenya, Malawi and Cameroon, where the leaderships resist the call for democracy or a national conference, encourages such a belief. Yet if the democracy movement in Africa were people-based, it could generate a momentum which has the potential of rising to meet the demands of the people and their progressive petty bourgeois allies.

The conference on 'Popular Participation in Development', held in Arusha, Tanzania in 1990, called upon African peoples themselves to press for democracy and to establish independent peoples' organizations that are genuinely grass-roots, democratically administered, and self-reliant.[60] Adebayo Adedeji, the former head of the United Nations Economic Commission for Africa, summed it up succinctly when he said, 'Popular participation is not a mere slogan. It is a matter of life and death'.[61] The neglect of these issues within the current democracy movement in Africa, coupled with its weak links to the countryside and its failure to articulate alternatives to the models of 'governance' and 'development' sponsored by the World Bank in particular, make the democracy movement suspiciously reminiscent of the 1960s independence movement.

The need for 'real democracy' that provides economic and political rights as opposed to formal democracy (multi-partyism and elections) can hardly be overstated. Yet this is not to suggest a monolithic set of norms and institutions for all countries. Each country, according to its own traditions, socio-economic and political values, must collectively or through struggle create those institutions that serve it optimally. Historically, democracy has evolved through modification both in theory and in practice throughout many parts of the world.

Clearly, economic democracy must be central in Africa's effort to democratize. Individuals, groups and collectives in society must be guaranteed a minimum level of economic security, to empower them to become full and active participants in political and economic decision making. Otherwise, extreme levels of poverty would effectively bar the most vulnerable – women, children and minority ethnic groups – from shaping their destinies. Thus economic rights and social justice – especially equality for women – must be rooted in collective responsibility, otherwise democracy will be severely compromised and weakened. Any effort by Western donor countries or the IMF and the World Bank to impose rigid political conditionality to encourage democratization in Africa will result in mere window-dressing.

Economic democratization would undoubtedly pose the gravest challenge to Africa's reform process. Perhaps for the larger and more prosperous countries like Nigeria and South Africa, prospects for formal and economic democracy are much better, but they are not assured. The task would be especially daunting, however, for those countries unable to arrest economic decline and still run by unstable military or one-party governments. In the final analysis, economic and political change will succeed only if it is a home-grown, indigenous process initiated by Africans themselves.

Notes

1. Jo Sullivan, *Africa: Global Edition Series* (Guilford: Dushkin Publishing Group, 1989), 1.
2. Ibid.
3. Julius E. Nyang'oro, *The State and Capitalist Development in Africa: Declining Political Economies* (New York: Praeger, 1989), 1.
4. Bade Onimode, *A Political Economy of the African Crisis* (London: Zed Books, 1988), 1.

5.   This period in African political history is dubbed the 'Second Revolution'.
6.   M. Bratton and N. Van de Walle, 'Towards Governance in Africa: Popular Demands and State Responses', in G. Hyden and M. Bratton (eds), *Governance and Politics in Africa* (Boulder: Lynne Rienner, 1992), 27.
7.   Ibid.
8.   On hearing the announcement of new elections and barring the old contenders, 'ignore the latest threat by the outgoing military present', Abiola said in a statement. See '11 Nigerians Dead as Dictator Battles Protest', *Denver Post*, 7 July 1993, 2A.
9.   S. Kraft, 'Africa Moves Fitfully Toward Democracy', *Los Angeles Times*, 27 July 1993, 3.
10. Ibid.
11. In Somalia the combined efforts of three movements – the Somalia National Movement (SNM), the Somalia Patriotic Movement, and the United Somalia Congress (USC) – led to the fall and flight from Somalia of former president Siad Barre in January 1991.
12. Kraft, 'Africa Moves Fitfully Toward Democracy', 3.
13. Ibid.
14. T. Tsurutani, 'Paradox of Reform', *International Review of Administrative Sciences* 57 (1991): 101.
15. Ibid.
16. E. Ezeani, 'An Appraisal of the African Debt Burden', *Africa and the World* 1, no. 2 (January 1988): 30.
17. H. Stein and E. Nafzinger, 'Structural Adjustment, Human Needs and the World Bank Agenda', *Journal of Modern African Studies* 29, no. 2 (1991): 177.
18. Bratton and Van de Walle, 'Towards Governance in Africa', 41.
19. Ibid.
20. C. Ake, quoted from Robert Fatton, Jr., *The Making of a Liberal Democracy, Senegal's Passive Revolution 1975–1985* (Boulder, CO: Lynne Rienner, 1987), 26.
21. Tsurutani, 'Paradox of Reform', 103.
22. This class is generally described in the literature as a monolith. This conceptualization is misleading, as many objective divisions do exist. For various conceptions of the state, see Hamza Alavi (ed.), *Introduction to the Sociology of 'Developing Societies'* (New York: Monthly Review Press, 1982); Larry Diamond, 'Class Formation in the Swollen African State', *Journal of Modern African Studies* 25, no. 4 (1987): 567–96; Howard Stein, 'Theories of the State in Tanzania: A Critical Assessment', *Journal of Modern African Studies* 23, no. 1 (1985): 105–23.
23. This class generally does not owe its origin in production or control of the means of production. Its power resides in its control of the state apparatus.
24. Steven Langdon, 'Multinational Corporations and the State in Africa', in Jose J. Villamil (ed.), *Transnational Capitalism and National Development* (New Jersey: Humanities Press, 1979), 227.

25. Robin Luckham, 'Militarism and International Dependence: A Framework for Analysis', in Jose J. Villamil (ed.), *Transnational Capitalism and National Development* (New Jersey: Humanities Press, 1979), 155.

26. Pita O. Agbese, 'The Impending Demise of Nigeria's Forthcoming Third Republic', *Africa Today* 37, no. 3 (1990): 27.

27. Ibid.

28. Langdon, 'Multinational Corporations and the State in Africa', 227.

29. Ibid.

30. Herold Kerbo, 'Foreign Investment in the Pre-conditions for Political Violence', *Journal of Conflict Resolution* 22 (September 1978): 365.

31. Noam Chomsky and Edward Herman, *The Washington Connection and Third World Fascism: The Political Economy of Human Rights*, vol. 1 (Boston: South End Press, 1979), 12.

32. Guy Martin, 'Africa and the Ideology of Eurafrica: Neo-Colonialism or Pan-Africanism', *Journal of Modern African Studies* 20, no. 2 (1982): 238.

33. Tsurutani, 'Paradox of Reform', 101.

34. Babangida orchestrated the elections, choosing both candidates and writing their platforms, and then claimed the elections were rigged and barred the initial contenders from running in July 1993.

35. Kraft, 'Africa Moves Fitfully Toward Democracy', 3.

36. Critics say it was another play in a series of Babangida's manoeuvres to hold on to power. He has scrapped timetables for a return to civilian rule several times since coming to power in 1985.

37. Tsurutani, 'Paradox of Reform,' 109.

38. Kraft, 'Africa Moves Fitfully Toward Democracy', 3.

39. Tsurutani, 'Paradox of Reform,' 108.

40. Kraft, 'Africa Moves Fitfully Toward Democracy', 3.

41. For a critical analysis of the prospects for democracy see Samuel Decalo's 'The Process, Prospects and Constraints of Democratization in Africa', *African Affairs* 91 (1992): 7–35.

42. G. Sorensen, *Democracy and Democratization* (Boulder, CO: Westview, 1993), 89.

43. For a critical analysis of the incompatibility between development and democracy, see C. Douglas Lummis, 'Development Against Democracy', *Alternatives* 16, no. 1 (1991).

44. Sorensen, *Democracy and Democratization*, 89.

45. Perhaps the gravest challenge to Africa's democratization process is to meet the economic expectations of its people.

46. Kraft, 'Africa Moves Fitfully Toward Democracy', 3.

47. Ibid.

48. S. Mbaye, 'Rebuilding the Continent', *West Africa*, 11–17 May 1992, 798.

49. While Africa can boast of many successes, the continent's woes are not insurmountable nor is its future so gloomy as depicted in the Western media.

50. Somalia is a casualty of the Cold War. The pro-West interests in making Somalia a bulwark against pro-Soviet influence of Ethiopia resulted in a

flood of weapons from the US and the then USSR. After the Cold War Somalia was left to fend for itself. See S.J. Hamric, 'How Somalia Was Left in the Cold', *New York Times*, 6 February 1993.

51. Mbaye, 'Rebuilding the Continent', 798.
52. Ibid.
53. P. O'Meara and B.N. Winchester, 'Political Change in South Africa', *The Fletcher Forum* (Winter 1991): 41.
54. Ibid.
55. Kraft, 'Africa Moves Fitfully Toward Democracy', 3.
56. Mbaye, 'Rebuilding the Continent', 798.
57. Kraft, 'Africa Moves Fitfully Toward Democracy', 3.
58. Ibid.
59. Ibid.
60. Jeffress F. Ramsay, *Africa: Global Studies* (Guilford, Connecticut: Dushkin Publishing Group, 1981), 178.
61. Ibid.

10

Empowering the African State: Economic Adjustment Strategies in Kenya and Zimbabwe

Howard P. Lehman

A central debate in the literature on the state has focused on its relative strength and weakness in relation to society.[1] While this debate initially examined developed states and, more recently, semi-industrialized states in Latin America, increasing attention has shifted to African states.[2] It is here that a paradox has emerged which has generated further questions about state power and state–society relations. Africa is plagued with political instability, coup d'états, deteriorating economic conditions and ineffective policy implementation.[3] The current difficulties in meeting scheduled debt repayment deadlines and the pressure to make significant economic adjustments further illustrate the precarious financial status of African states. Yet African societies are well known for their heavily centralized bureaucratic apparatus, which consumes a substantial portion of expenditures and capital investments. Scholars, whether conceptualizing this influential social group as an 'organizational bourgeoisie' or a 'managerial bourgeoisie', consider African state bureaucracies with their own power capabilities and defined interests.[4] Another indicator of state influence is the steady growth of parastatals in African countries. As they have expanded in number and in function, state power over these firms has also grown. And, in response to rapidly deteriorating economic conditions, many African states have enacted wide-scale debt management controls on foreign investment, public borrowing and public sector investment.

This chapter attempts to explain the apparent paradox in the simultaneous existence of both strong and weak components in African states. Krasner presented an early formulation of state power in terms of the state's power to resist private pressure, change private behaviour and change the social structure.[5] The state is considered strong when its governing apparatus generates a set of interests, objectives and capabilities that is separate or autonomous from societal interests. A weak state, then, is considered as consumed by social interests, domestic or foreign, which further weakens the effectiveness of state policy. Since African states appear to be strong and weak at the same time, Krasner's conception of state power needs to be altered to explain African state-society relations. What is required is an alternative framework which considers the dual occurrence in countries with weak state power and weak societal interests, yet within a highly centralized state apparatus which imposes economic controls and affects policy change in certain areas.

The thesis of this chapter is that a continuum of strong–weak states is not suited to the special characteristics found in Africa today. Neither state nor societal interests are dominant in most African countries. The two sets of interests have shown the ability at times to merge their objectives into the governing apparatus, at other times, to conflict with each other as two autonomous agents, and at still other times to cooperate in order to advance their distinct interests. All of these possibilities occur in the current environment of profound economic stress and political instability. The relationship between state and society and the level of autonomy accorded to the state require a more specific examination of policy choices, specifically of the role of public and private investment capital.

Economic adjustment strategies open a Pandora's Box from which conflicting domestic and foreign interests carve out their bargaining positions. They react to the substantial costs of liberalization (such as de-industrialization, unemployment, trade deficits, political instability and foreign exchange gaps) which threaten state autonomy and state legitimacy with these groups. Adjustment, though demanded by most international creditors and some domestic groups, imposes sufficient costs as to require the state to control the direction and timing of economic policy. Thus adjustment has the unintended effect of empowering the state specifically in the areas of foreign investment, public borrowing and public sector investment.

Kenya and Zimbabwe are selected for this study since both have adopted a mixture of orthodox and heterodox adjustment strategies. These middle-income African states in many ways exemplify the attempt to balance these economic development models. Over the years both have sought a policy mix that would attract foreign capital while controlling the effects of foreign investment in society and the economy. Furthermore, Kenya and Zimbabwe's colonial heritage, common official language, and relatively sophisticated economic and financial structures provide a strong case for comparative research.[6]

The chapter first considers the apparent paradox of state power in Africa. It then examines the state's investment policies in Kenya and Zimbabwe.

The paradox of state power in Africa

In a recent article, Almond criticized recent research efforts that attempt to 'bring the state back in' by arguing that the state had never left the political arena.[7] In a similar fashion, the state in Africa has been a consistent social force at least since the colonial period. In African societies, the colonial experience contributed towards the formation of a centralized state bureaucracy that continues to intervene in nearly all facets of economic, social and political life.[8]

The African state can be interpreted as being 'strong' in the sense that it has become partially independent of societal interests. The relative weakness of domestic economic groups allows more extensive state activity. In the absence of a vigorous private sector, the public sector has had to participate more forcefully in the production, distribution and consumption of capital and goods. The state seeks to consolidate its power and authority out of an environment of dispersed power. As Rothchild writes, by the way the African state has created marketing boards, immigration controls, the Africanization of the public and private sectors, and parastatal monopolies, the state displays 'a limited but real capacity to affect the activities of domestic and international actors and to enlarge its own sphere of enterprise'.[9] It thus develops an institutional capacity as a means to manage and protect its own interests. Rothchild further suggests that 'the state's ability to distance itself from these domestic (or international) class and ethnic interests gives public officials room to overpower or ignore some of the less pressing interest group demands and to expand their administrative functions and powers'.[10]

While growth in state institutional capacity reflects a more active state, the absence of effective power and legitimacy reveals a weakening and, perhaps, decaying state. Callaghy's term for this paradox, 'lame Leviathan', juxtaposes the centralized bureaucratic component of the state and the weak efforts of the state to dominate society.[11] In place of widely perceived legitimacy, the state attempts to use the blunt force of its coercive power to impose its narrow interests on society. Yet the failure of central state authorities to carve out and protect their own autonomous interests facilitates the take-over, as it were, by any hegemonic interests, domestic or foreign, that exist in society. State capacity, according to this perspective, thus does not reflect its own autonomous set of interests nor the entire interests of society, but only mirrors the élite interests that have 'captured' the state.[12]

The weakness of the state is often considered in terms of African states' negotiation, acceptance and implementation cf adjustment strategies. Most African governments are unable to respond to their investment crisis without negotiating with the international financial community. This places the state in a position of obligation to international financial institutions, especially to the IMF. Not only must these countries accept IMF conditionality, the implementation of adjustment policies generally imposes hardships on various social and economic groups in society. The end result for many countries is a pattern of ineffective policy implementation. The state, it has been suggested, is unable or unwilling to mobilize societal interests behind a required adjustment agreement.[13] It lacks the political will and strength to force the necessary support for policy implementation.

In the context of severe indebtedness, the 'political will' argument fails to explain the rise of significant state controls over the diverse aspects of foreign investment, capital borrowing and public-sector investment. Contrary to the argument that African states are weak in implementing policy reforms, this chapter argues that developing states have shown considerable will in exerting control over their deteriorating economic conditions.[14] Rather than focus on the state's inability to adjust to the debt crisis, this chapter questions the end to which the state imposes economic controls and which groups benefit from such controls. In a critical way, the debt crisis has become an important variable in the 'hardening' of the state. The state has responded to indebtedness by providing incentives for export growth, regulating the allocation of foreign exchange, controlling additional foreign borrowing, and overseeing parastatal activities.

Kenya

Since its independence Kenya has been one of the most ardent followers of African capitalism. In the last ten years, the government has pursued a strong agricultural export strategy, promoted both foreign and domestic investment, and sought to maintain political order throughout society. By adhering to this long-term strategy, Kenya created and maintained an image of an active supporter of conservative economic policy. This conservative strategy has sought to increase the level of exports and control domestic demand through liberalizing all facets of the national economy and eliminating the government deficit through expenditure control and encouraging foreign investment.[15]

As with most former colonies, the new regime constructed its economic base on institutional features inherited from the colonial administration.[16] The leadership, first under Kenyatta and sustained under Moi, supported an open international strategy as a means to maintain access to foreign capital, technology and markets. Given the leadership's emphasis on export growth and international trade, the state provided institutional safeguards and incentives for foreign investors.[17] The state has undertaken steps to liberalize certain components of its economy in order to attract additional foreign capital and to expand its export base, while centralizing other components as a means to protect its credit standing among the international financial community. Although Kenya is not entirely willing to implement controls that go against free trade and the uninterrupted flow of foreign capital, the costs of liberalization have forced it to impose temporary controls. These are not intended to discontinue foreign borrowing or to discourage foreign investment, but to bring the economy back into a balance which would enhance the state's international credit standing.

DIRECT FOREIGN INVESTMENT

Over the years, Kenya has worked to project itself as a haven for foreign investment. A major plank of the national development plan addresses the lack of investment capital in Kenya and calls for a heavy reliance on foreign capital. Increasingly, Kenya has turned towards international financial institutions for its investment requirements. Indeed, external capital inflows accounting for Kenya's gross investment grew from nearly 17 per cent in 1966 to 43 per cent in 1979.[18]

The government has implemented several policies that encourage and protect foreign capital investment. According to the Minister of Industry in 1988, Kenya provides the conditions for protecting foreign investment, generating profits for foreign firms, and repatriating capital gains.[19] The Foreign Investment Protection Act of 1964 became the foundation for this supportive policy. In August 1983, the Central Bank introduced an incentive policy that allowed the remittance of foreign investors' dividends and profit payments for the previous year. Then, in June 1984, the Central Bank lowered the withholding taxes on royalties and dividend remittances. The 1986 budget included a revision of the Foreign Investment Act to encourage increased inflows of foreign capital directed toward technological investments. The Minister of Finance, in the 1987 Budget Speech, made it clear that 'Kenya has always welcomed foreign investors, whose capital, technology, management, and worldwide marketing skills can add enormously to our own productive capacity and especially our ability to export'.[20] More recently, the government has favoured foreign investors with other concessions. In 1988, the government widened the tax exemptions on private capital investment and promulgated the revised Foreign Investment Protection Act, which makes foreign exchange losses on hard currency investments tax deductible. The government also promised to permit the outflow of unremitted dividends, which have accumulated to $5.6 million since 1986.[21] The remittance policy was liberalized again in 1988 by allowing the immediate repatriation of the initial foreign exchange invested while depositing any capital gains from this investment in a government account for five years. In the intervening five years, the foreign investors' gains must be invested in government securities that attract market rates of interest.[22] As another means to attract foreign investment, Kenya has recently signed the Multilateral Investment Guarantee Agency of the World Bank, which guarantees against non-commercial risks to enterprises that invest in signatory countries.

However, the government's public rhetoric in support of foreign capital investment has been offset by the actual regulation of foreign exchange allocation. Kenya still maintains blocked funds from which foreign exchange is made available through petition. Tension is most evident between foreign investors in the export agricultural sector and those in the domestic, import-substituting industry market. Since the export-oriented agricultural firms hold a competitive edge over state-protected, costly manufacturing interests, their representatives favoured increasing foreign currency allocation to those firms and downplayed the use of controls as reasonable and merely regulatory.[23] Yet the government continues to protect and, thus, establish investment incentives favouring the domestic market and local firms. Indigenous industrialists and manufacturers tend to support the government's restrictions on foreign exchange to the extent that more capital is then available for local investment. These controls, they argue, are a 'necessary evil' during this 'stage of development'.[24] They provided several reasons for the continued implementation of controls. First, many respondents recognized the current generous remittance policy for foreign dividends and profits.

While a central tenet of orthodox economic adjustment holds that the flow of foreign investment should be unhindered, economic and political realities in Kenya dictate that foreign capital should be directed, on a temporary basis, towards the achievement of state investment objectives.[25] Foreign capital interests have gravitated towards the domestic market, especially towards local manufacturing industries, with the support of the government which encourages commercial banks to lend to import-substituting industries. Any significant liberalization of foreign currency controls would risk the immediate outflow of scarce capital, thus leading to a more serious foreign currency crisis. A second reason concerns the economic competition between the Asian and African communities. Since Asians dominate the commercial market and control a large share of the industrial sector, most Africans assume that Asians would export their profits out of Kenya. Given the perceived likelihood of massive capital flight among the Asian community, the 'risk [from liberalization] is too great and the potential abuse too likely'.[26] Capital flight is indeed a genuine problem. A 1989 report estimated that official plus illegal net transfers amounted to between $500 million and $650 million in 1988; or equivalent to between 6.7 and 8.7 per cent of GDP.[27] State regulation over this outflow, in addition to the large (nearly $1 billion) foreign bank deposits amassed by Kenyan residents and state enterprises, would strengthen the economy and increase the confidence of foreign companies investing in Kenya.[28]

Given this mixture of state controls over foreign investment and partial liberalization, it is not surprising to witness mixed economic results during the mid-1980s. Liberalization, by opening up the economy to competitive foreign capital interests, jeopardized Kenya's international trade position. The trade deficit jumped 150 per cent between 1986 and 1987 and is expected to expand another 35 per cent by 1991. The growth in the deficit is attributed to a rapid rise in imports of about 10 per cent per year from 1986 to 1990, while exports actually fell by nearly 2 per cent annually in the same period.[29] In its attempt to contain the balance of payments deficit, the government drew heavily from the reserves, which cut the import cover to less than one-half of a month in 1992.[30]

The political ramifications of economic liberalization have also taken their toll on government policy. A serious dispute broke out in the mid-1980s between two ethnic groups (Kikuyu and Kalenjin) and erupted into a major financial scandal in 1988. According to a financial adviser involved in Kenya's economic strategy, President Moi (a Kalenjin) precipitated the crisis in 1986 by having the Ministry of Finance and state companies withdraw their funds from three banks owned by Kikuyus.

Then, in the summer of 1990, in response to growing dissent and mobilized opposition to Moi by Kikuyus, the government unleashed the police and army resulting in at least twenty casualties.

In the light of the overall deterioration in the investment climate, which had caused the number of American subsidiaries to fall from 140 to 115 since 1982, the government in 1990 began a new campaign to attract foreign capital, especially in the export sector.[31] The government is struggling with a transition to an export-oriented economy as the means to attract capital while still clinging to the protective measures of import substitution. The state is caught directly in the cross-fire between international financial interests pressing for an open investment regime and domestic manufacturing interests seeking continued protection of ISI firms.

As part of this endeavour, devaluation has been an important and frequently used state tool. Devaluation of the Kenyan shilling has not only garnered support from the IMF, international banks, and industrialized governments, but has also received strong backing from agricultural exporters and domestic bankers.[32] Between 1981 and 1985, the currency depreciated by 82 per cent in dollar terms followed by a more stable rate through 1988. During the following year, the Kenyan shilling again depreciated in relation to the dollar by 16 per cent. Another round of depreciation between 1989 and 1991 is expected to drop the shilling by 24 per cent.[33] Such massive shifts have resulted in an income redistribution from non-tradeables to tradeables, especially for agricultural exports. Since foreign investments are significant in the agricultural sector, the state's devaluation policy has benefited foreign firms and large domestic agricultural interests.

In addition to devaluation as a means to attract foreign investment, the government has introduced a centralized system of export incentives. Since the agricultural sector supplies over three-quarters of Kenya's export earnings, it is not surprising that the government has created additional incentives for coffee, tea and meat production. The government also established an export compensation plan by which the state pays exporters 10 per cent of their exports.[34] Another incentive offered by the state is direct export finance and insurance. The government recognizes the attitude of local and foreign bankers who are unlikely to lend money to exporters without government guarantees covering the expected return from the transaction. A third support set up by the state is an institutional system coordinating the export-promoting activities, such as the Kenya External Trade Authority and the Investment Promotion Centre. The latter is the key agency in the government's plans to attract foreign business. Set up in 1983, its objective is to formulate investment packages according to the government's development priorities. In its first seven years, the centre only processed thirty investment applications worth more than $70 million. Between 1987 and 1991, 229 projects valued at $371 million were processed by the IPC, of which eighty-five are operational.[35] The centre is also responsible for the Export Processing Zone. Based on similar zones in the newly industrializing countries in Asia, it is hoped to attract large-scale foreign investments with a ten-year tax holiday, 100 per cent investment allowance, and duty-free and tax-free incentives.[36]

There are some early indications that Kenya's latest attempt to use state controls as a means to attract foreign capital has been successful. A 1990 bank study forecasts that the annual change in gross fixed capital investment will increase to over 6 per cent between 1990 and 1991. A more direct indicator is that of annual net equity investment which is expected to more than double from the 1984–89 period to the 1990–91 period.[37]

STATE CAPACITY TO REGULATE THE FOREIGN DEBT

Throughout the 1970s and into the early 1980s, Kenya instituted few controls over its foreign borrowing. Parastatals had been allowed (in fact, the state never provided instructions) to enter into contract negotiations directly with international financial institutions. The state thus had no veto power over the agencies' borrowing decisions. The absence of meaningful controls also meant incomplete information on the amount, structure and terms of Kenya's foreign debt. In fact, no one in the government kept tabs on debt service ratios until 1984, when an American adviser was asked to put together an external debt database.[38]

Although Kenya hesitated during the 1970s to embark on heavy foreign borrowing, the sudden unravelling of its debt capacity by the early 1980s took state officials by surprise. A shift in the state's role as a central figure in debt management occurred as the debt burden expanded, combined with weakening terms of trade and deterioration of the export market. The state borrowing apparatus moved in quickly to manage the external debt. By 1982, the organizational responsibilities for debt reporting were clarified though not implemented. In the following few years, an External Debt Unit was established in the Ministry of Finance and prepared an external borrowing plan.[39] Specific measures were taken, including a limit on public-sector borrowing of 6 per cent of the budget deficit and a requirement that all parastatal borrowing be incorporated into the Forward Budget and approved by the Ministry of Finance. Government ministries must now submit their list of priorities for Treasury approval.[40] In his 1990 Budget Speech, the Minister of Finance further stated that in the future, the debts of parastatal firms, even those guaranteed by the government, would not be honoured 'without a thorough investigation of the circumstances behind the payment default'.[41]

What is important about the state's capacity to regulate foreign borrowing is its objective of sustaining a high level of cooperation with the IMF and donor governments. Kenya's borrowing measures are in near total agreement with IMF debt management guidelines and they represent the state's efforts to remain in the IMF fold. An IMF official said that Kenya and the IMF see 'eye to eye' and are in total agreement with such measures as price decontrols, import liberalization, and a user charge for education and health.[42] Kenya has been a prolonged user of IMF funds with a series of standby arrangements running from 1975 to 1986, during which it drew the equivalent of $640 million. Following a two-year interlude, Kenya obtained in 1988 both a standby loan and a Structural Adjustment Facility. These agreements again were followed in 1989 by a $240 million Enhanced Structural Adjustment Facility, the second tranche of which was released in April 1990. Although Kenya has experienced difficulty in implementing some IMF-directed policies, at least one banker has suggested that it was due more to external economic factors than unwillingness by Kenya's leaders to undertake such policies.[43] Another economic source concludes that:

> donors have accepted that if the government's commitment to some of their desired measures (including not only maize control but also parastatal reform and trade liberalization) is lukewarm, its commitment to the fundamental principles of market determined exchange rates, interest rates and agricultural prices is total, and there is now a tacit agreement to condone the former in recognition of the latter.[44]

This claim has been confirmed by recent action on the part of official bilateral creditors who have made Kenya the prime beneficiary of their debt cancellation programmes. In a three-year period (1988–90), Canada, Britain, the Netherlands, Germany, France and the United States cancelled over $900 million of official debt.[45]

PUBLIC-SECTOR INVESTMENT

Kenya's adjustment strategy contains a long-term objective of establishing a base for liberal economic development. The most recent national development plan reaffirms this strategy, in which the state is expected to shift investment resources from the public to the private sector.

Government development statements stress the importance of the private sector and the need to eliminate state firms.[46] Yet, as Kenya continues to grapple with insufficient resources, political instability and lingering budget deficits, the government remains an active agent in redirecting scarce resources to public-sector firms, especially those in the agricultural sector that promote export-oriented growth.

The government's relationship with state-owned enterprises is indicative of Kenya's investment dilemma. During the 1980s, the government made an effort in the redirection, but not the elimination, of public investments to parastatals. Yet the state continues to intervene in favour of parastatals that are considered integral to national security (airlines, railroad), infrastructural development (steel, construction), and exports (marketing boards). Furthermore, the government has centralized the decision-making process of guaranteeing foreign loans made to these parastatal firms. The government's strong financial and political support for parastatals has brought adverse reaction by official creditors and weakens the government's claim that it is pursuing a strategy of liberalization.

As early as 1982, a major government statement on parastatals recommended the gradual shifting of investments from the public to the private sector. The study reported that 'some parastatals have exceeded their original mandates and have made investments in commercial and industrial activities that should be left entirely to the private sector'.[47] The report argued that state firms had become inefficient largely because of the intrusion of domestic political interests in the commercial decision-making process. These vested interests are generally of two kinds: domestic economic groups in the manufacturing sector, and certain Africans benefiting from the anti-Asian stance of the government. Several commercial bankers and IMF officials have agreed that one of the most serious problems is the friction between manufacturers close to the government and international institutions pressing for economic liberalization.[48]

A government report issued in 1986 made specific recommendations towards the restructuring of state-owned enterprises. As a major component of a budget rationalization programme, parastatals were recognized to cause considerable strain on scarce resources. The statement issued a number of objectives that, in theory, would eliminate parastatals which were inefficient and whose projects could be equally achieved through the private sector. The remaining state firms must improve their productivity and become self-financing in the activities that can be operated on a commercial basis. The government also established administrative control over the firms' budgets in order to have them stay within their budget and, in particular, to stabilize parastatal borrowing of foreign capital.[49]

Yet, rather than dissolve or sell parastatals to private interests, the government has sought only to reform the existing state controls over parastatal behaviour. In the late 1980s, the government restructured the National Cereals and Produce Board and the Kenya Meat Commission. Moreover, in 1989 the state expanded the public sector by creating new parastatals, including the Nyayo Tea Zone and Nyayo Bus company. By far, the most critical controls have been imposed on parastatal borrowing. Several respondents would agree with a remark made by a Kenyan representative of an American bank in Nairobi that 'the government is the first and last guarantor of bank loans made to state-owned enterprises'.[50] The state currently controls parastatal borrowing through a set of criteria reviewed by the Treasury. Through state guarantees, the government seeks to redirect scarce foreign resources to state agricultural export firms, national security parastatals, and national developmental agencies. By centralizing borrowing practices, the central government can obtain foreign currency directly from parastatals and, through currency conversion, it can transfer the loans to the Treasury in exchange for domestic currency. Parastatals receive Kenyan shillings while the Treasury obtains foreign currency which it passes on for debt repayment or investment in the export sector.

The government also has assumed central borrowing control for such important national firms as Kenya Airways, the national railway system, the Post and Telecommunications agency, and major electrification projects. State guarantees not only permit the state to oversee parastatal borrowing procedures, but they also facilitate state control over parastatal economic performance. The state additionally regulates the finances and activities of industrial and manufacturing parastatals, through agencies like the Industrial and Commercial Development Corporation (ICDC).

Zimbabwe

Since independence in 1980, the government's relationship with foreign capital interests has often been labelled as contradictory and conflictual. The oft-remarked incongruence between early calls for a socialist transformation of the economy and the use and expansion of inherited market capitalism is seen as the basis for the inconsistent approach towards foreign capital.[51] In part, this contradictory pattern can be explained by the inability of the governing élites to consolidate and solidify their power bases into a united ideological force. Ethnic, racial and political divisions remain as powerful obstacles to a coherent development strategy. The conflict between stated development objectives and actual policy implementation during the 1980s became more dramatic in the late 1980s, as the government embarked on a policy of economic liberalization. Yet the one objective that has remained a thread throughout has been the effort by the state to exert control over the direction and timing of economic policy. By using regulations over foreign investments, the borrowing process and public-sector investment, the state remains committed to maintaining control over its development strategy.

The establishment of a centralized regulatory system in Zimbabwe has roots in the historical evolution of the state reinforced by an ideological leadership that fought against the Rhodesian whites for many years. To speak of the role of the state in the economy, we first must recognize the highly centralized and sophisticated state apparatus already intact at the time of independence.[52] The current regime inherited from the period of the Unilateral Declaration of Independence (1965–79) the traditions of state controls and an inward-looking economic strategy. The Rhodesian government, by necessity of international isolation, developed a relatively sophisticated import-substitution industry with strong financial links to South Africa. The absence of foreign exchange required the regime to impose tight controls over the use of foreign currency and redirected those resources towards internal productive sectors. The UDI government responded to the country's structural rigidities by choosing a heterodox policy of increasing domestic supply.

The development of this kind of state structure had several implications for the post-independence government.[53] First, a foreign exchange allocation system was already in place with years of experience and acceptance when independence occurred in 1980. Second, the powers of the Reserve Bank and the Ministry of Finance increased as government policy controlled the use of foreign exchange and held down import levels.[54] Third, the issue of South African ownership of Rhodesian assets became an influential factor in the current government's aversion to foreign investment. Fourth, in reaction to the former regime's emphasis on public investment in productive sectors, the new government shifted its investments towards improving the quality of life for the majority of the population in basic goods and social service sectors. Finally, the government borrowed heavily from commercial sources in the early 1980s, but rigourously kept to the repayment schedule. By maintaining punctual repayment of its loans, Zimbabwe was able to avoid IMF conditionality and the costs of rescheduling while using the capital for development purposes.

The government's policy orientation towards foreign capital derives from the interaction of two ideological groups found in the society. Most of the respondents who have been active in economic decision making described the conflict as a struggle for power and influence between ideological 'radicals' and 'pragmatists'.

The heterodox model contains an implicit pessimism against a liberalized development strategy. The radical group argues that a free-market system incorporating an open and integrated economy would fail to overcome structural rigidities and bottlenecks. Indeed, a complete liberalization of the economy would increase the economy's vulnerability to external forces, impinge on domestic economic firms and, as one respondent claims, would entail the surrender of Zimbabwe's sovereignty to market forces.[55] Liberalization, they argue, poses a threat to the state as it could lead to firm closures in the manufacturing sector, rising unemployment, and a major reduction in foreign exchange availability. Moreover, the policy was too closely aligned with the austerity measures pushed by the IMF and the World Bank.[56] Instead, the radicals favour the tools of direct state economic management (such as dividend and remittance controls, import controls, and wage and price controls) in an attempt to balance economic growth with redistribution. The state thus seeks to redistribute income in a way that will increase the proportion of domestic content in manufactured goods, and to redistribute productive assets (as in land) to protect those people who fail to be absorbed into the employment structure.[57]

While the radical group was most vocal, the pragmatic group was able to offset implementation of radical economic policy. The IMF and World Bank have given strong support to this latter group for their objectives of reducing the government deficit, increasing export performance, shifting incentives away from the protected domestic industries and towards agricultural and mining sectors, and greater cooperation between the state and the private sector.[58]

DIRECT FOREIGN INVESTMENT

Upon independence, the new government's economic strategy was restricted by the massive presence of foreign capital invested in the productive sectors of the economy and the perceived need to generate domestic support and ratification of the government's adjustment strategy. A former Secretary of Finance said in an interview that the government was 'suspicious of foreign investment since it could become a permanent edifice in the economy's foundation'.[59] If direct foreign investment expanded into vital economic sectors, not only would profits from the investments leave Zimbabwe, the country would become increasingly dependent and vulnerable on foreign (and South African) sources of investment capital. According to an economist of the Zimbabwe National Chamber of Commerce, 'why should the government pay repatriation for investments which the government could have done as well?'[60] Government policies on direct foreign investment have intended to establish national control over capital investments in order to allocate resources to social and economic priorities.

In considering government policy towards foreign capital, one must first distinguish existing foreign investment from new investment in Zimbabwe. Despite the anti-foreign capital rhetoric espoused by many government officials (including Mugabe),[61] the government only implemented partial restrictions on the foreign capital invested in the country at the time of independence. From the perspective of foreign investors, the greatest barrier was the regulation over dividend and remittance repatriation. At first, the government allowed foreign investors to repatriate 50 per cent of their after-tax profits. In March 1984, the government suspended all remittances of dividends, branch and partnership profits made prior to September 1979. Zimbabwe further suspended income remittances from blocked funds, with a provision for the eventual release of the blocked capital.[62] The Minister of Finance stated in a 1986 Reserve Bank report that the removal of restrictions on the use of blocked funds would burden the already overstretched foreign exchange capacity with additional foreign currency demands for capital and raw materials requirements.[63] In reaction to the continued outflow of capital amounting to Z$150 million in 1986, the government, in May 1987, halved the dividend remittances from 50 to 25 per cent of after-tax profits. Foreign firms have the option of divesting from Zimbabwe, but the process is complex. Capital could be repatriated either through the purchase of long-term interest-bearing bonds or immediate repatriation, but for a heavy discount of 70 per cent.

Restrictions were also imposed on foreign investments that occurred after independence. One regulation concerned the definition of 'foreign' investment. By equating 15 per cent foreign involvement with foreign ownership, the government sought to minimize foreign domination in the economy as well as to maximize its control over the purposes of investment. A second restriction focused on the bureaucratic process by which foreign investment projects had to be submitted to obtain necessary government approval. A three-stage process, centred around the Foreign

Investment Committee (FIC), lengthened the approval period by up to two or three years. The government also refused to sign bilateral guarantees such as the Overseas Private Investment Corporation (OPIC), claiming such an action represented an infringement on the country's sovereignty. OPIC is designed to improve the investment climate in the developing world by protecting foreign firms against the political risks and possible disruption of flows of remittances and dividends. The government claimed that the country's constitution (and a 1982 investment policy statement) sufficiently protected private investment.

However, by 1987, the government was faced with a number of economic constraints that emerged from the previous strategy of restricting foreign investment. Over the previous year, gross fixed capital fell by about 7 per cent per year between 1984 and 1987 and, since 1987, has grown by less than 3 per cent per year.[64]

Faced with a declining investment rate, burgeoning population growth, rising domestic discontent in industry and manufacturing over the inadequate access to foreign exchange needed for imports, and with divestment running at an annual rate of US$75 million in 1988, the government began to incorporate some incentives favourable to foreign investors.[65] In 1989, the government instituted a more liberal foreign investment code and, in 1990, signed an international agreement guaranteeing foreign investments, both of which have been demanded by foreign investors as measures of the government's approval of foreign investment. The new investment code sought to reassure investors of government protection of their investments and the unlikelihood of a decline in the remittability of investment income. The investment code also liberalized the use of blocked funds, amounting to US$460 million, by allowing foreigners to reinvest those funds in approved projects. Foreign investors now can buy local currency with foreign exchange, at a discounted price, and invest it in new projects. The Reserve Bank is to issue non-negotiable certificates of deposit for subscription by nonresident-controlled firms, with the Zimbabwe Development Bank and the Small Enterprises Development Corporation acting as intermediaries. The state decision affecting the allocation of these blocked funds depends on whether the new investment will: 1) generate net export earnings or net import savings; 2) generate net employment; 3) result in adaptable technology transfer using local inputs; or 4) result in the decentralization of industry from urban to rural areas.[66] The new investment guidelines also broadened and relaxed the definition of 'foreign' investment by increasing the percentage from 15 to 25 per cent of capital owned by non-residents. Finally, the government eliminated the bureaucratic Foreign

Investment Committee and created an investment centre to streamline procedures for investment approval.[67] It has recently been provided with a permanent staff and legal status in making decisions. Decisions are meant to be reached within ninety days instead of the two to three years under the FIC.

The Economic Policy Statement issued in July 1990 clearly reflects government concern over the lack of foreign investment needed for major infrastructural overhaul. The investment guidelines were therefore implemented specifically to increase the investment rate from around 14 per cent of GDP to at least 20 per cent.[68] A year after the establishment of the Investment Centre, the total value of investment projects approved is over Z$500 million, with additional projects worth Z$20 million submitted each week.[69] Multilateral financial organizations, which had been holding back funds for Zimbabwe, suddenly reopened negotiations for large loans and grants. During spring 1990, negotiations were held with the International Finance Corporation and the African Development Bank for medium-term export finance of US$130 million each to be invested exclusively in the private sector. The World Bank is also anticipated to provide US$420 million over the next five years.[70]

Although the state has liberalized its foreign investment policy, it has done so in order to attract investment while remaining firmly in control of these projects. Although these reforms created the perception among foreign investors that Zimbabwe is becoming more open, the state has reserved for itself control over investment.[71] The government seeks to attract foreign investment and to be in a position to direct it towards development projects determined by the state. The new investment guidelines specifically exclude foreign investment from commercial farming and services while providing incentives for investments in the agricultural, manufacturing and mining sectors.[72] Moreover, the large pool of blocked funds continues to exist from which the government can draw needed funds. Despite the ongoing liberalization process, then, the state continues to play a significant role in influencing the pattern of foreign investment. The nature of state controls has shifted from purely negative (i.e., preventing firms from undertaking certain actions) to somewhat positive (i.e., providing incentives for firms to invest in state-determined economic and development sectors).

STATE CAPACITY TO REGULATE THE FOREIGN DEBT

Soon after achieving independence, the new regime negotiated a number of loans from international sources. There are a number of reasons for Zimbabwe's initial reliance on this form of foreign capital. According to a senior official in the Ministry of Finance, the government operated without any firm borrowing guidelines. 'The market', he said, 'was awash with money . . . and the government used any money, no matter the expected use, for short-term uses.'[73] The government immediately identified several priorities which required borrowed capital. It came under mounting pressure from the high expectations held by the public for the immediate establishment of viable social welfare, education, health and job-generating programmes. The new government also invested this capital to finance capital development projects, such as the Hwange Thermo plant, dams, electrification and road construction.[74] Along with these major long-term bank loans, the government contracted for short-term balance of payments financing loans. Foreign borrowing also was sought to finance the demobilization of the guerrilla armies and a resolution to the conflict with the Ndebele in southern Zimbabwe. The government also turned to international creditors, in part, as a reaction to the slow and disappointing level of disbursement of ZIMCORD funds.

The government began to realize in 1983 that its borrowing policies had led to serious debt-servicing problems and a depletion of foreign exchange.[75] It enacted several strict measures over the loan agreements with international creditors. First, the government required Reserve Bank approval for any foreign loan over Z$2.5 million, whether the loan was projected for use by the private or public sector.[76] Second, only short-term, standby loans would be accepted, provided they bridged the balance of payments gap, or generated exports and foreign exchange. Third, after projecting the debt burden, the government further decided to accept non-standby loans only with a maturity of more than five years. Fourth, the terms of the loans had to be 'most acceptable and concessionary'.[77] Indeed, a former senior official in the Ministry of Finance recalled in an interview that, between 1983 and 1984, the government turned down Z$100 million in foreign bank loans since they would have jeopardized Zimbabwe's repayment capacity.[78]

Through the imposition of these borrowing controls, by 1989, Zimbabwe had become credit-worthy in the eyes of many international creditors and ready to embark on another round of commercial borrowing.[79] The liberalization programme is expected to cost the country US$2.7 billion in foreign exchange over the next five years, of which half is projected to come from international loans.[80] The government recognizes that foreign borrowing must increase to facilitate investment capital inflows. Still, increased foreign borrowings will be subject to government approval by the External Loans Coordinating Committee for individual private sector projects of by the state-controlled Zimbabwe Development Bank.[81]

PUBLIC-SECTOR INVESTMENT

A government with self-proclaimed socialist intentions that inherits an economy with capitalist features must undoubtedly face a significant dilemma in its relationship with the private sector. Radicals in government (many of whom fought during the civil war) pushed for sweeping nationalization of the financial, mining and manufacturing sectors. To do so, according to the pragmatic faction, would have had several adverse implications. First, nationalization (without compensation) would have broken the Lancaster House Constitution which led to Zimbabwe's independence and, if compensated, the action would have cost the government around $2.5 billion.[82] Second, leaders of the pragmatist group (such as Finance Minister Chidzero) realized that nationalization would have incurred the anger and likely punishment of the West. Any move towards taking over the private sector during the early years would have jeopardized the ZIMCORD aid negotiations. Moreover, since the majority of foreign firms operating in Zimbabwe at the time of independence were South African, many government leaders feared economic reprisal and/or attempts to destabilize the new regime.

Despite what might be called structural constraints on government policies, the new government embarked upon both an indirect and direct approach towards regulating private capital interests. The state's main agent is the Reserve Bank, working in close partnership with the Ministry of Finance. The Reserve Bank administers a complex network of exchange control regulations and governs the allocation of foreign exchange to the private sector. According to an early study, the private sector received a 36 per cent increase in foreign exchange allocations in 1979 over the previous year, which jumped by another 47 per cent in 1980, followed, however, by only a 20 per cent rise in the following year.[83] The restrictive policy towards the private sector continued, since between 1982 and 1985, that sector's foreign exchange allocation dropped by 30 per cent. Given the government's ideological predisposition towards the peasant class and the export strength of the white agricultural class, foreign exchange allocations have benefited the agricultural sector to the detriment of industrial and manufacturing interests. Foreign exchange allocation was slashed during the first six months of 1987 to industrial and commercial sectors by 40 per cent and 55 per cent, respectively.[84]

Implicit in the government's controls of private-sector investment is a government effort to regulate foreign (mainly South African) firms embedded in the private sector. The government has established a number of parastatals in an attempt to assert control over key economic sectors. Among the most important are the Industrial Development Corporation, the Zimbabwe Development Bank, and the Minerals Marketing Corporation. The government uses its power to extend subsidies to parastatals as a direct tool of influence. Between 1981 and 1985, public subsidies amounted to an average 42 per cent of the budget deficit.[85] By 1987, that figure had jumped to 60 per cent.[86] The policy reforms since 1988 have helped to lower the percentage to around 40 per cent of the 1991–92 budget deficit.[87] Still, the bulk of these subsidies are allocated to inefficient parastatals which have consistently lost money. The largest requirement for subsidies by a single parastatal is from the National Railways of Zimbabwe, which amounts to almost 40 per cent of total subsidies. Agricultural marketing boards consume another 30 per cent, followed by ZISCO (the state-owned steel company) with 14 per cent of total subsidies.[88]

Though the government has not conducted a policy of sweeping nationalization, it has consistently intervened in the economy in its pursuit of the 'Zimbabwenization' of the productive capital stock. Through direct investment, sometimes on a joint-venture basis, or through indirect investment, using the state-owned Industrial Development Corporation, the government has used its authority to control the economic structure of the country.[89] For example, in 1983 the government acquired a 40 per cent equity interest in the Hwange colliery, and in 1984 it purchased all the shares of Lancashire Steel. A 1985 study also found that the government's investment in the private sector covers a wide spectrum, including holdings in newspapers, banks and manufacturing industries.[90] A senior economist in a Zimbabwe bank suggested in an interview that 'through these bureaucratic regulations, the government has all of the power with nationalization, but none of the initial costs of responsibility'.[91] A 1989 study noted that 'paradoxically, the government is encouraging new foreign investment while at times expanding its control over the private sector which it considers to be dominated by the foreign ownership'.[92] The policy reforms, introduced in 1990, are intended to eliminate subsidies and inefficient parastatals by 1994. Given the conflictual domestic environment, in which trade unionists and industrialists have not shown strong support of these reforms, it seems likely that the government will only gradually and not entirely effectively implement the new policy of public-sector reform.

Conclusion

State power is a misleading concept when both state and social forces in Africa are weak. The state, at times, can be a powerful restructuring force in society, but, in Africa, a categorization by state strength and weakness tends to reify the state structure by separating state interests from societal interests. This chapter suggests that a more precise examination of policies and actors, both state and society, provides an important explanatory alternative. Economic adjustment is clearly a process that unleashes a wide range of domestic and foreign interests, some of which seek to weaken the state while others attempt to align themselves with it. The state responds to these societal pressures on the basis of the particular mix of economic orthodoxy and heterodoxy present at that time. Thus it is not surprising that many of the policy moves in Kenya are also found in Zimbabwe. Kenya, widely perceived as a conservative regime, has often used its state power to manipulate international creditors and to award narrowly defined domestic interests. Zimbabwe, though viewed as a more radical regime following heterodox policies, is also using liberalization as a means to maintain state control over investment objectives.

An assumption of Kenya's orthodox strategy is an emphasis on opening the national economy to private and foreign sources of capital which, according to liberal economic theory, would facilitate economic growth. However, as Kenya felt the effects of economic imbalance during the mid-1980s, the government consolidated old controls and established new ones. Foreign investment, borrowing, and public-sector investment controls are not considered as long-term instruments of monetary and fiscal policy, but as temporary controls that are a 'necessary evil'. Instead of using these controls as weapons against foreign investors, the state regards them as institutional incentives that should promote investments. Rather than using controls as a means to block repatriated profits as in Zimbabwe, the Kenyan government seeks to manage indebtedness in order to attract additional foreign capital. The state is using its enhanced power to broaden its ties to foreign and domestic export-oriented, agricultural, and foreign exchange-generating firms.

Zimbabwe's extended use of economic controls can be understood as an attempt to obtain foreign capital that offers the least resistance to Zimbabwe's development objectives. Until the late 1980s, the government relied more on its authoritative powers of allocating foreign exchange and restricting outflow of capital than on a market system of allocation. The objective was to obtain foreign funds that did not impinge on either state behaviour or the state investment of those funds.[93] Unlike Kenya, it purposively (until 1992) avoided financial reliance on the IMF, while studiously keeping out of debt arrears with international financial institutions. While seeking to avoid the internal political ramifications of accepting IMF conditions, the government failed to attract sufficient foreign capital to serve the interests of the crucial private sector and, by depleting foreign reserves to finance a growing government deficit, the government is faced with serious economic dilemmas. Recently, the government has backed away from a clear anti-foreign capital stance as it realigns its strategy to fit the reality of insufficient amounts of foreign investment. However, any incentives promoting such investment are countered by a highly regulatory state policy.

Kenya and Zimbabwe can be considered, to a great extent, as representatives of other middle-income level countries in the developing world. In Africa, in particular, there are a number of countries which have a relatively sophisticated economic structure and a defined political system which provide a setting for diverse groups and interests in both state and society. The state for these countries is not withering away as a result of economic and political instability. Although foreign indebtedness has affected state economic capacity by limiting growth performance, state political and institutional powers, in some instances, have become strengthened and centralized under government authorities. The paradox of state power is revealed when state investment policies are examined as direct responses to the debt crisis. Examination of these policies and the reasons for their imposition indicate the state's willingness and capacity to assert its autonomy over domestic and foreign interests.

However, the analysis presented in this chapter should not imply that the 'hardening' of the state is the long-term trend. Indeed, in the light of worsening economic conditions placed in the context of instability, ideological conflicts and regressive patron–client relations, the African state remains in a precarious position. In Kenya's case, state intervention in foreign and domestic investment may be a last-gasp effort by a desperate government to forestall collapse. It is not clear at this point if Zimbabwe's move towards economic liberalization portends a general transition to more integrated and liberal economic relations with the international economy and, if so, whether it will be successful. The African state may be expanding its powers over its debt position, but it has declining influence over such structural and external concerns as its terms of trade, growing international protectionism and IMF conditionality.

Notes

1.   Theda Skoçpol, *States and Social Revolutions: A Comparative Analysis of France, Russia, and China* (Cambridge: Cambridge University Press, 1979); Eric Nordlinger, *On the Autonomy of the Democratic State* (Cambridge: Harvard University Press, 1981) and 'Taking the State Seriously', in Myron Weiner and Samuel P. Huntington (eds) *Understanding Political*

Development (Boston: Little, Brown, 1987); Peter Evans, Dietrich Reuschemeyer, and Theda Skoçpol, eds, *Bringing the State Back In* (Cambridge: Cambridge University Press, 1985); and Martin Carnoy, *The State and Political Theory* (Princeton: Princeton University Press, 1984).

2. Chapter 1 in Nora Hamilton's book, *The Limits of State Autonomy: Post-Revolutionary Mexico* (Princeton: Princeton University Press, 1982) presents an excellent description of major issues in the state autonomy literature with particular emphasis on Latin America. Two edited books contain several relevant essays on state-society relations in Africa. See Zaki Ergas (ed.), *The African State in Transition* (New York: St. Martin's Press, 1987); and Donald Rothchild and Naomi Chazan (eds), *The Precarious Balance: State and Society in Africa* (Boulder, CO: Westview Press, 1988). Joshua B. Forrest examines the components of state 'hardness' in 'The Quest for State "Hardness"' in Africa', *Comparative Politics* 20, no. 4 (July 1988).

3. For a description of Africa's economic crisis, see Richard Sandbrook, *The Politics of Africa's Economic Stagnation* (London: Cambridge University Press, 1985).

4. Irving Leonard Markowitz, *Power and Class in Africa* (Englewood, NJ: Prentice-Hall, 1977); Richard Sklar, 'The Nature of Class Domination in Africa', *Journal of Modern African Studies* 17, no. 4 (1979).

5. Stephen Krasner, *Defending the National Interest: Raw Materials Investments and U.S. Foreign Policy* (Princeton, NJ: Princeton University Press, 1978), 57; and 'Approaches to the State: Alternative Conceptions and Historical Dynamics', *Comparative Politics* 16, no. 2 (January 1984).

6. Michael Bratton, 'Structural Transformation in Zimbabwe: Comparative Notes from the Neo-Colonization of Kenya', *Journal of Modern African Studies* 15, no. 4 (1977).

7. Gabriel H. Almond, 'The Return to the State', *American Political Science Review* 82, no. 3 (September 1988).

8. Two recent books that pay close attention to the economic development of the colonial state are Ralph Austen, *Africa in Economic History* (London: James Currey, 1987); and D. K. Fieldhouse, *Black Africa, 1945–1980: Economic Decolonization and Arrested Development* (London: Allen and Unwin, 1986).

9. Donald Rothchild, 'Hegemony and State Softness: Some Variations in Elite Responses', in Zaki Ergas (ed.), *The African State in Transition* (New York: St. Martin's Press, 1987), 120.

10. Rothchild, 'Hegemony and State Softness', 121.

11. Thomas Callaghy, 'The State as Lame Leviathan: The Patrimonial Administrative State in Africa', in Zaki Ergas (ed.), *The African State in Transition* (New York: St. Martin's Press, 1987).

12. For a diverse reading of Marxist literature on this point, see Ralph Miliband, *The State in Capitalist Society* (London: Camelot Press, 1969); Nico Poulantzas, *State, Power, Socialism* (London: New Left Books, 1978); and Bob Jessop, *State Theory: Putting the Capitalist State in its Place*

(Cambridge: Polity Press, 1990).

13. Stephen Haggard, 'The Politics of Adjustment: Lessons from the IMF's Extended Fund Facility', in Miles Kahler (ed.), *The Politics of International Debt* (Ithaca: Cornell University Press, 1986); and Joan M. Nelson, 'The Politics of Stabilization', in R.E. Feinberg and V. Kallab (eds), *Adjustment Crisis in the Third World* (Washington, DC: Overseas Development Council, 1984).

14. Forrest, 'The Quest for State "Hardness" in Africa'.

15. R. Van der Hoeven and J. Vandemoortele, *Kenya: Stabilization and Adjustment Policies and Programmes* (Helsinki: World Institute for Development Economic Research, 1987); N. Calika, 'Kenya's Economic Difficulties Are Worsened by Drop in Coffee Prices', *IMF Survey* 16, no. 10 (May 1987); M. Godfrey, 'Stabilization and Structural Adjustment of the Kenyan Economy, 1975-85: An Assessment of Performance', *Development and Change* 18, no. 4 (1987); Paul Mosley, 'Kenya', in Paul Mosley, Jane Harrigan, and John Toye, *Aid and Power: The World Bank and Policy-based Lending*, vol. 2 (London: Routledge, 1991).

16. E. A. Brett, *Colonialism and Underdevelopment in East Africa* (London: NOK, 1973); Nicola Swainson, *The Development of Corporate Capitalism in Kenya, 1918-77* (Berkeley: University of California Press, 1980); and Colin Leys, *Underdevelopment in Kenya: The Political Economy of Neo-Colonialism* (Berkeley: University of California Press, 1974).

17. Republic of Kenya, *Development Plan, 1984-1988* (Nairobi: Government Printer, 1983); *Budget Rationalization Programme* (Nairobi: Government Printer, 1986); and *Sessional Paper* (Nairobi: Government Printer, 1986).

18. Republic of Kenya, *Development Plan, 1984-1988*, 43.

19. Chamber of British Industry, *Kenya: The Opportunities for Investment* (London, 1988), 10-13.

20. Republic of Kenya, *Budget Speech, 1987-88* (Nairobi: Government Printer, 1987), 8.

21. 'Kenya', *African Economic Digest* (September 1988): 1.

22. Chamber of British Industry, *Kenya*, 13.

23. Managing Director of an export centre, Executive Director of a regional trade group, February 1985.

24. Managing Director of a Kenyan bank; executive officer of the Industrial and Commercial Development Corporation, February 1985; senior officer of Barclays Bank in Kenya; senior official of the Developmental Finance Corporation of Kenya, March 1985.

25. Banker with Kenya National Capital Corporation, March 1985.

26. An official with Barclays Bank in Kenya, March 1985.

27. 'Kenya Survey', *African Business* 132 (August 1989): 42.

28. 'Kenya Survey', 42.

29. Institute of International Finance, *Kenya* (London: IIF, 1990).

30. Institute of International Finance, *Kenya* (London: IIF, 1992).

31. Economist Intelligence Unit, *Kenya: Country Report*, 3 (London: EIU,

1990), 13.

32. A report on the 1987 government budget noted that the domestic business sector is pleased with the government focus on export and import liberalization rather than on any restrictions on foreign currency outflows ('Kenya: Budget, 1987–88', *African Research Bulletin* 24 (31 July 1987): 8745.

33. Institute of International Finance, *Kenya*, 1990.

34. Senior official, Kenya Association of Manufacturers, Nairobi, 1985.

35. Economist Intelligence Unit, *Kenya: Country Profile, 1991–92* (London: EIU, 1991), 12.

36. 'Kenya', *African Economic Digest* (September 1990): 11.

37. Institute of International Finance, *Kenya*, 1990.

38. IMF economist, June 1988.

39. Republic of Kenya, *Budget Speech, 1984–85* (Nairobi: Government Printer, 1984), 10.

40. Republic of Kenya, *Budget Rationalization Programme* (Nairobi: Government Printer, 1986), 5-6.

41. Economist Intelligence Unit, *Kenya*, 10.

42. IMF economist, June 1988.

43. Lloyds Bank economist, London, 1984.

44. Economist Intelligence Unit, *Kenya*, 12.

45. 'Five Year Economic Reform Program', *African Research Bulletin* 28 (16 February 1991).

46. Republic of Kenya, *Development Plan, 1984–1988* (Nairobi: Government Printer, 1983), 39; Republic of Kenya, *Budget Speech, 1987–88*, 6.

47. P. Ndegwa, *Report and Recommendations of the Working Party* (Nairobi: Government Printer, 1982), 40.

48. IMF economist, Standard Chartered economist, June 1988; Bankers Trust banker, Barclays bank economist, July 1988.

49. Republic of Kenya, *Sessional Paper*, 41.

50. Vice president, Citibank, Nairobi, 1985.

51. Colin Stoneman and Lionel Cliffe, *Zimbabwe: Politics, Economics, and Society* (London: Pinter, 1989).

52. Martin Meredith, *The Past Is Another Country: Rhodesia, 1890–1979* (London: A. Deutsch, 1979).

53. Several analyses have been published recently on Zimbabwe's economic policy. See R.H. Green and X. Kadhani, 'Zimbabwe: Transition to Economic Crises, 1981–1983', *Report to the Group of 24* (New York: UNDP/UNCTAD, 1985); I. Mandaza (ed.), *The Political Economy of Transition, 1980–86* (Dakar: CODESRIA, 1986); World Bank, *Zimbabwe: A Strategy for Sustained Growth* (Washington, DC: World Bank, 1987); O.I. Nyawata, 'Macroeconomic Management, Adjustment and Stabilisation', in Colin Stoneman (ed.), *Zimbabwe's Prospects* (London: Macmillan, 1988); and Peter Robinson, 'Trade and Financing Strategies for the New NICs: The Zimbabwe Case Study', Working Paper no. 23 (London: Overseas

Development Institute, July 1987).

54. Green and Kadhani, 'Zimbabwe', 5.

55. Official from the Zimbabwe Mission to the United Nations, 1988.

56. Tony Hawking, 'Time to Grasp the Nettle of Reform', *African Economic Digest Special Report* (April 1989): 2.

57. Peter Robinson, 'Relaxing the Constraints', in Stoneman, *Zimbabwe's Prospects*, 349.

58. IMF economist, September 1984; World Bank economists, November 1987, June 1988.

59. April 1985.

60. April 1985.

61. Robert Mugabe said in a July 1987 speech to Parliament that further investment is unnecessary when foreign investors already own many of the country's resources. 'The more we have them', he said, 'the more dividends we shall be remitting abroad and the more the indebtedness' (Economist Intelligence Unit, *Zimbabwe: Country Report*, 4 (London: EIU, 1987), 13–14.

62. Blocked funds are monies due and payable to non-residents which are blocked in local banks by exchange controls.

63. Reserve Bank of Zimbabwe, *Quarterly Economic and Statistical Review* (Harare: Government Printer, 1986), 23.

64. Institute of International Finance, *Zimbabwe* (London: IIF, 1990).

65. One financial analyst estimated that for Zimbabwe's economy to grow at the development plan target rate of 5 per cent per year, the economy needs to invest 25 per cent of GDP and, on 1989 figures, a shift of the order of Z$1 billion into investment is necessary. Michael Holman, 'Zimbabwe: Financial Times Survey', *Financial Times* (21 August 1989): ii.

66. 'Chidzero Gives Nod to Blocked-funds Trading', *African Business* 132 (August 1989): 47.

67. Republic of Zimbabwe, *The Promotion of Investment: Policy and Regulations* (Harare: Government Printer, 1989), 5.

68. Republic of Zimbabwe, *Economic Policy Statement*, 17.

69. Economist Intelligence Unit, *Zimbabwe: Country Report*, 3 (London: EIU, 1990), 15.

70. Jan Raath, 'We'll Do It Our Way', *The Banker* 140 (May 1990): 76.

71. According to a recent World Bank report on investment in Zimbabwe, the main concern for investors should not be the rate of profitability arising from remittance controls. The report argues that Zimbabwe's allowed figure is in line with most other countries' policies. The real and troubling concern is the uncertainty with the government's policy direction towards foreign investment. Mansoor Dailami and Michael Walton, 'Private Investment, Government Policy, and Foreign Capital in Zimbabwe', Working Paper no. 248, Policy, Planning, and Research (Washington, DC: World Bank, August 1989), 62.

72. Republic of Zimbabwe, *The Promotion of Investment*, 4.

73. April 1985.

74. April 1985.

75. Zimbabwe's total external debt had jumped in just three years (1981–84) by almost 60 per cent while official reserves fell by about 75 per cent. The country's debt service as a percentage of exports also had increased quickly from 14.5 to 30.5 per cent in the same period. Institute of International Finance, *Zimbabwe*, 1990.

76. Economist, Reserve Bank, Harare, 1985.

77. April 1985.

78. Former official, Ministry of Finance, Harare, 1985.

79. Several financial indicators are suggestive of the country's credit standing. Despite the absolute growth in total debt service, the debt service ratio (to exports) has dropped from 34.5 per cent in 1987 to a forecast of 27.9 per cent in 1991. Moreover, total external debt as a percentage of exports has also fallen from 197.0 per cent in 1985 to 140.9 per cent in 1991. Institute of International Finance, *Zimbabwe*, 1990. The government's historical adherence to debt repayment has also strengthened its case for additional loans.

80. 'Harare Concessions', *African Economic Digest* 11, no. 37 (24 September 1990): 21.

81. Dailami and Watson, 'Private Investment', 50.

82. Herbst, *State Politics in Zimbabwe*, 116.

83. Whitsun Foundation, *Money and Finance in Zimbabwe* (Harare: Whitsun Foundation, 1983), 120.

84. 'Special Report: Zimbabwe', *African Economic Digest* (April 1987): 1.

85. A. Hawkins, *Public Policy and the Zimbabwe Economy"* (Harare: USAID, 1985).

86. 'Special Report: Zimbabwe', 2.

87. Institute of International Finance, *Zimbabwe* (London: IIF, 1991), 6.

88. Republic of Zimbabwe, *1990 Budget Statement* (Harare: Government Printer, 1990), 31.

89. Republic of Zimbabwe, *First Five-Year National Development Plan, 1986–1990* (Harare: Government Printer, 1986), 10.

90. Hawkins, 'Public Policy', 27.

91. Harare, 1985.

92. Institute of International Finance, *Zimbabwe*, 1989.

93. Some observers have claimed that Zimbabwe has been searching for an intermediate stance that has been called 'semi-autarchic'. Robinson, 'Relaxing the Constraints'.

11

Economic Progress:
What Africa Needs[*]

Adebayo Adedeji

Reviewing the development challenges of the 1980s, one cannot but sadly surmise that for Africa it has been a decade of lost opportunities and diminished achievements.

Throughout the 1980s Africa experienced a vicious and unremitting socio-economic crisis. All the major indicators point to significant and sometimes precipitous retrogression to the extent that Africans are worse off today than they were ten years ago. Output and income growth, capital formation and export growth have declined. Deficits in the balance of payments and inflation rates have accelerated, while the debt and debt-servicing burdens have reached unmanageable levels. The productive and infrastructural facilities have crumbled, while the basic social services – especially education, health and housing – have been rapidly deteriorating. Piling on top of the recurrent drought and chronic food deficit phenomena, these problems have contributed to uninterrupted economic decline and falling standards of living of the African people.

Throughout the decade, per capita income also declined unabated in Africa – the only continent where such a development took place. Average per capita income, already abysmally low, fell from $752 in 1980 to $545 in 1988, declining by 2.6 per cent annually. Whereas investment as a proportion of the GDP was 25.2 per cent at the end of the 1970s, it decelerated to 15.8 per cent in 1988, an amount insufficient in many cases to maintain even the existing capital stock. In 1978 export

[*]Reprinted with permission from *TransAfrica Forum* 7 (2), Summer 1990.

and import growth rates were 11.2 and 1.9 per cent respectively; ten years later, they had fallen to 3.8 and 0.3 per cent respectively. The balance of payments deficits, which amounted to $3.9 billion in 1980, stood at $20.3 billion in 1988. Inflation escalated from 15.1 per cent in 1980 to 21.3 per cent in 1988. With regard to the debt problem, Africa owed $48.3 billion in 1978. This figure multiplied by more than five times to $257 billion in 1989, with debt-servicing obligations accounting for 40 per cent of export earnings on average and going beyond 100 per cent for many countries.

This economic decline has had a devastating impact on the well-being of millions of Africans. Since 1980, per capita private consumption has fallen by one-fifth. Total gainful employment has declined by over 16 per cent. Unemployment has reached crisis proportions: the unemployed in the formal wage sector are estimated to number over 30 million (over 13 per cent of the labour force) and another 95 million are underemployed; real wages have declined by a quarter; and almost three-quarters of Africans are afflicted by poverty. The illiterate population increased to 162 million in 1985 from 124 million in 1960. The average share of health and education in public expenditure dropped from over 26 per cent at the beginning of the 1980s to 19 per cent in 1988; and over 26 per cent of the African population is now undernourished or suffers from malnutrition, while endemic diseases – which had actually been brought under control by the 1970s – have re-emerged on the continent. Some 10,000 children die in Africa every day of causes linked to malnutrition and to the non-availability of rudimentary health care.

It is no wonder then that the number of African countries officially classified as least developed countries (LDCs) – the wretched of the earth – increased from seventeen countries in 1978 to twenty-eight countries in 1988, a total of 56 per cent of all African countries. And more are knocking at the door. Thus the 1980s were indeed a lost decade for Africa in every sense.

It cannot be overemphasized that Africa cannot afford to have a repeat performance in the 1990s – a decade which promises to bring even greater challenges, not least of which is a literal population explosion. It is imperative, therefore, that one must pause to consider why, in spite of all efforts, the economic performance has been so disappointing.

Why has this happened in spite of the fervent search by Africans for solutions and the adoption by Africa of innovative programmes such as the Lagos Plan of Action (LPA) and Final Act of Lagos (FAL) in 1980, Africa's Priority Programme for African Economic Recovery (AAPER), 1986–90, and the UN Programme Action for African Economic Recovery and Development (UN-PAAERD), 1986–90? Why has it happened in spite of the stabilization and SAPs launched by the World Bank and IMF in over thirty countries in Africa during the decade? Admittedly, these questions are easier asked than answered. Nevertheless, some basic explanations are necessary.

A careful and reasoned analysis of the African economic problematique can only lead to the conclusion that its underlying causes are the lack of structural transformation and the pervasive low levels of productivity, aggravated by a host of endogenous and exogenous factors. The endogenous factors include the structural imbalances evident in the great disparities in urban and rural development and in income distribution, rapid population growth, the inadequacy and/or misdirection of human and financial resources, poor economic management, inappropriate economic policies, political instability, and the prevalence of social values, attitudes and practices detrimental to development. Among the more serious exogenous factors are the formidable constraints posed by the intertwined problems of the heavy debt burden, diminished export earnings and declining real resource flows.

Therefore, left to itself, the African economy has a built-in tendency to generate crises from within and to assimilate others from abroad. Unless these fundamental structural problems and bottlenecks are dealt with, the African economy cannot right itself and break away from the vicious cycle of underdevelopment. This phenomenon has significant implications for the strategies, policies and programmes directed towards revitalizing the African economy.

While the LPA and FAL did correctly aim at the restructuring and transformation of the African economies and the realization of the long-term objectives of self-reliant and self-sustained development, these objectives regrettably were not put into practice. This was due to the refusal of the donor community, particularly the Bretton Woods institutions, to accept and support Africans' perception of their development objectives and strategies. Instead, the institutions proposed their own strategies for the development path that they thought would be good for Africa. This lack of international support, coupled with the intensification of the drought and the economic crisis in the early 1980s, led to the abandonment of the LPA. The main preoccupation of most African policy makers became crisis management for economic survival. The focus of economic policies shifted to short-term concerns, resulting mainly from external shocks. Long-term development objectives were put on hold. In their place were devised SAPs, by the Bretton Woods institutions, which these countries were required to adopt if they were to qualify for external support and, in particular, have access to the desperately needed foreign exchange.

The reality that the badly needed external financial resources could be forthcoming only within the framework of SAPs has literally shackled African countries to these programmes. They have thus been pressurized into accepting solutions that may, at best, cope with the symptoms of the crisis and not with its root causes. Even when APPER and UN-PAAERD were adopted in 1985 and 1986 respectively, and it was thought that a new consensus had emerged on Africa's medium-term development objectives, they were quickly ignored by the Bretton Woods institutions which continued with business as usual – adoption of orthodox SAPs with their overriding concern with fiscal and financial balances and external equilibrium. It should be evident by now that policy reforms aimed merely at improvements in financial balances and price structures are unlikely to succeed in bringing about socio-economic transformation and sustained development.

Over the past years, numerous assessments have been conducted to determine whether SAPs have led to a sustainable basis for development. Beyond these assessments, the ECA has also had the benefit of personal contact with Africans from all walks of life, be they entrepreneurs, traders or ministers.

Despite the view of the Bretton Woods institutions – that countries which have imposed structural adjustments perform better economically than those without such programmes – there is increasing evidence that economic performance has not rebounded in any sustainable fashion as a result of these programmes. Studies by ECA as well as by the World Bank itself show that main economic indicators have actually worsened following the adoption of SAPs. Indeed, one authoritative review after another has demonstrated the inadequacy of SAPs.

Much worse, SAPs have afflicted the African people and societies in ways that threaten their very future. The Khartoum Declaration is illuminating. It was adopted by the ECA-sponsored International Conference on the Human Dimension of Africa's Economic Recovery and Development. The gathering included over 200 African ministers, high-ranking officials, and senior experts from government, UN agencies, representatives of international and regional development and financial organizations, donor agencies and NGOs, African and non-African scholars, and the mass media who met in Khartoum in March 1988. The Declaration states that:

The severity of the African crisis is such that country after country has been putting in place structural adjustment programmes in their effort to halt their economic degradation and achieve a turn-around. Unfortunately, far too many of these programmes – whether nationally conceived or in collaboration with the World Bank, the International Monetary Fund and the donor community – are rending the fabric of the African society.[1]

This assertion of The Khartoum Declaration is echoed by similar findings of the ECA, UNICEF, ILO, UNESCO, and other UN agencies as well as an overwhelming number of independent studies.

In his report to the UN General Assembly on the mid-term review of UN-PAAERD, the Secretary-General drew attention to the fact that:

The implementation of structural adjustment programmes has given rise to general concerns. The limited objectives and short-term perspectives of those programmes are sometimes viewed, by African countries and others, as being at variance with the objectives of more balanced long-term development. Their human and social costs have often been seen as out of proportion with their real or intended benefits. The most vulnerable population groups, in particular women, youth, the disabled and the aged, have been severely and adversely affected, directly and indirectly, by such measures as the withdrawal of subsidies on staple food items, the imposition of limits on wage increases at or below the inflation rate, the retrenchment of civil servants and private sector personnel frequently belonging to the lowest salary categories, and the cutting of expenditures on social services, including health and education, and on basic infrastructure. Access to food has become more difficult for large segments of the population, with the result that malnutrition has increased, particularly among children, infants and pregnant women. As a result of these concerns, African Governments and donors are now more keenly aware of the need to address the social impact of reform programmes. Moreover, some of the main ingredients of the programmes, such as re-alignments of exchange rates and rises in producer prices, are not generating the full expected benefits because of the structural rigidities that characterize the current stage of development of most African countries. Structural adjustment programmes need to be designed as an integral part of a long-term development strategy and the human dimension needs to be made a central concern of both the shorter-term adjustment programmes and the longer-term development strategy.[2]

The UN General Assembly itself concluded at the mid-term review of the implementation of the UN-PAAERD that:

The implementation of structural adjustment programmes has given rise to general concerns, such as human, social and political consequences, as well as long-term financing needs for Africa's economic recovery and development efforts. . . . Structural adjustment programmes should be designed in such a way as to mitigate their adverse socio-economic effects, ensure that the human dimension is integrated in them, further improve the well-being of the poor and disadvantaged in African societies, notably through redirecting social and developmental expenditure, and make short-term structural adjustment measures compatible with and built into long-term structural transformation.[3]

The findings and conclusions of the report, entitled *Structural Adjustment in Africa: Insights From the Experiences of Ghana and Senegal*, which was submitted by the staff of the Subcommittee on Africa of the Committee on Foreign Affairs of the US House of Representatives, were equally critical:

The available evidence strongly suggests that, despite rising per capita growth, structural adjustment has produced little enduring poverty-alleviation, and certain policies have worked against the poor.

In rural Ghana, adjustment has benefitted the minority of cocoa farmers, but these gains appear to have mainly gone to a relatively small and privileged group. Real per capita income of the overwhelming majority of food farmers has stagnated, with especially unfavourable consequences for women and children. Certain adjustment policies, such as dramatic devaluations and tight credit have had negative impacts on the poor. Mainly, structural adjustment has ignored the key constraints to equitable development in the rural food economy.

Efforts in both countries to address equity problems, including Ghana's Programme to Mitigate the Costs of Adjustment, Senegal's Employment Plan, and various donor projects, appear inadequate and have not affected other adjustment policies that are hurting the poor.

In both Ghana and Senegal, a weak equity performance and rising political expectations have generated threats to the sustainability of adjustment and to overall political stability.

The report concluded:

The international donors and recipients could modify structural adjustment to fully incorporate poverty-alleviation objectives. Reductions in external and internal deficits could be carried out more gradually. 'Supply-side' policies could give greater priority to stimulating the production and income of the poor, while 'demand-side' policies could better sustain their standard of living. Social sector spending could be directed more efficiently to serve the poor. In addition, foreign decision-makers could be less insulated from national realities and the poor could be given more effective representation in economic policy-making.[4]

Adjustment and transformation: a better solution

For over a decade, crisis management has replaced sustained growth and development policies in Africa and SAPs have been substituted for genuine structural change and transformation. To permit a second generation of SAPs to dominate the 1990s would be to reduce Africa to an abyss so deep it might never emerge again.

As we stand at the doorsteps of the 1990s, there is an imperative need for African countries to move away from SAPs and to embrace and genuinely implement economic policies that would attack the root of the problem of underdevelopment and achieve steady and sustained growth and development. This would, at the same time, deal with the short-term problems that arise along the developmental path, i.e. a policy of adjustment with transformation.

In this regard, it is important to stress that Africa has to adjust. The problems – of balance of payments disequilibria, fiscal imbalances, inflation, and others – cannot just be wished away. But what needs to be emphasized is that in adjusting, transforming the structures that fundamentally serve to precipitate and aggravate the African socio-economic crisis must constitute the focus of attention, hence the need for adjustment with transformation.

'Adjustments with transformation' is indeed the whole essence of the African Alternative Framework to Structural Adjustment Programmes for Socio-economic Recovery and Transformation (AAF-SAP). The Framework was adopted by the African ministers of finance and of economic planning and development in Addis Ababa on 10 April 1989, and endorsed by the African heads of state and government in May 1989, as an alternative to the current stabilization and adjustment programmes in Africa. In doing that the African States literally took up the challenge of the UN General Assembly at the mid-term review of UN-PAAERD when it urged that the 'African countries should increase their efforts in the search for a viable conceptual and practical framework for economic structural adjustment programmes in keeping with the long-term development objectives and strategies at the national, subregional and regional levels'.[5]

Unlike conventional adjustment programmes, which on the whole prescribe a set of policy measures that all African governments are supposed to follow, AAF-SAP is a broad and flexible framework within which governments can design their own individual national adjustment with transformation programmes. It is pertinent in this regard to remind ourselves that programmes for economic recovery and development can only be successful if governments, drawing on the broad support and democratic participation of their people, actually assume the prime responsibility for determining their country's programmes and direct responsibility for preparing them.

It has been most gratifying to observe the build-up in international support for AAF-SAP after it was launched in July 1989. The Summit Meeting of Non-Aligned countries, which took place in Belgrade, Yugoslavia, gave it its endorsement. And in November 1989 the General Assembly of the United Nations adopted it as a basis for constructive dialogue by a vote of 137 in favour and one against. It was very much regretted that the only country which voted against AAF-SAP was the United States.

Let me also stress that no matter how faithfully African countries would implement AAF-SAP, such programmes cannot succeed without the creation of the necessary conditions by both bilateral partners and the multilateral donors. If the World Bank and IMF were to insist on the dogged pursuit of SAPs, and if the major Western powers were to continue backing them in spite of the mounting evidence against the efficacy of such programmes, then AAF-SAP would be cut off from a vital life-line, as was the case with LPA and UN-PAAERD. A genuine opportunity to reverse economic decline on the continent and engineer human-focused sustained growth and development would thus be lost. And at the end of the 1990s the donors will again have little to show in terms of sustained progress and human welfare in Africa for the resources they would have pumped into the continent. Persistence in supporting the flawed strategy implicit in orthodox SAPs will end up in frustration for both donors and recipients.

With the publication of its recent long-term perspective study *Sub-Saharan Africa: From Crisis to Sustainable Growth*, the World Bank has moved closer to the concerns of AAF-SAP. It accepts, if only implicitly, that conventional SAPs are not working and that what Africa needs is adjustment with transformation. The study recognizes that despite orthodox SAPS, Africa's economic crisis has continued to deepen; that these programmes have failed to address the issue of poverty alleviation and equity; and that they have ignored the human dimension of development. It has correctly addressed these issues and many others such as human resources development, capacity building, creation of an enabling environment conducive to initiative and enterprise; the education, health, and welfare of the people who are to bring about and foster the development process on a sustained and sustainable basis; environmental degradation; and the all-important issue of fostering regional cooperation and integration in Africa. But having done this, the World Bank has yet to translate the LTPS into reality and admit to its implications for current SAPS.

Personally, I have often stated my sincere hope that a broad consensus would be built around AAF-SAP to achieve the necessary turnaround in Africa. As already indicated, the UN General Assembly – in the resolution in which it welcomed AAF-SAP by 137 votes to one and no abstentions – invited the international community, including the multilateral financial and development institutions, to consider the Framework as a basis for constructive dialogue.[6] The United States Congress, guided by influential committees and individual members who are true friends of Africa, could greatly help in bringing this change around. Such American support would set in motion the implementation of programmes concerned not only with adjustment but also with genuine development.

African responsibilities

Another basic question remains regarding who should be the lead actors ensuring that by the beginning of the twenty-first century we do not have yet another disastrous decade to deplore. In answering this question, let me quote from a statement I made at the opening of the International Conference on Popular Participation in the Recovery and Development Process in Africa in Arusha, Tanzania on 12 February 1990:

> It will continue to ring hollow every time we say that people are Africa's greatest resource if we cannot create the environment that will enable them to unleash their energies and creativity, and if we persistently fail to mobilize them in the task of economic and social reconstruction. The democratization of the development process – by which we mean the empowerment of the people, their involvement in decision-making, in implementation and monitoring processes – is a *conditio sine qua non* for socio-economic recovery and transformation.[7]

I maintain that Africa has an immense potential of resourceful people who are able to unlock the riches the continent holds. But unfortunately, after three to four decades of political independence, the issue today is to reset the stage for their total involvement in the development process – from the conceptualization of policies and strategies to the formulation, implementation and monitoring of programmes and projects. The marginalization of the people in the recovery process is the major obstacle. Is it any wonder that all these externally designed and imposed programmes have not led to socio-economic recovery on a sustainable basis?

In this connection, the international community must critically examine its own record. For example, is technical assistance, as currently practised, truly oriented towards establishing sustainable structures determined by the interests of the African people? The 600 delegates from NGOs, grass-roots groups, institutions and governments assembled in Arusha clearly spelled out their expectations *vis-à-vis* the international community in the African Charter for Popular Participation in Development and Transformation by stating:

> We call on the international community to examine its own record on popular participation, and hereafter to support indigenous efforts which promote the emergence of a democratic environment and facilitate the people's effective participation and empowerment in the political life of their countries.[8]

The external environment

The adverse external economic environment with which Africa has had to contend – as mainly manifested in the interlinked problems of declining export earnings, mounting debt and debt-servicing obligations, and inadequate and stagnating external real resource flows – has played a major role in aggravating Africa's economic crisis and could certainly compromise any efforts to achieve meaningful growth and development in the future. Indeed, the report of the Secretary-General of the United Nations to the General Assembly on the mid-term review of the implementation of UN-PAAERD concluded that:

> Efforts by the African countries to pursue and deepen the reform process cannot be sustained indefinitely in the face of an adverse external environment and without increased support from the international community. Low export earnings and the severe debt-servicing burden combined with insufficient concessional finance are constraining growth and hampering recovery and development programmes.[9]

The Secretary-General further added:

> The experience of the first two years of the Programme demonstrates that Africa's efforts at economic restructuring and policy reforms are severely limited by the external constraints posed by the closely intertwined problems of debt, commodities and capital resource flows. These constraints will continue to hinder recovery and growth unless concerted actions are taken

by the international community to provide lasting solutions. They have to be tackled in an integrated manner in order to ensure that net resource transfers to Africa are sufficient to meet the region's development requirements.[10]

Most African countries are highly dependent for their foreign exchange earnings on the export of one or two primary commodities. This overdependence and high concentration makes the African economies exceptionally vulnerable to undesirable changes in the world market prices of those commodities. During the 1980s, these prices fell continuously. The ECA commodity price index shows that in 1988 wholesale prices for Africa's key exports (including oil) stood at a mere 54.2 per cent of their 1980 levels. In the past three years alone, Africa has lost close to $50 billion through the crash in the prices of some of its major exports such as coffee, cocoa and cotton. Non-oil primary commodity prices for Africa are at their lowest levels since the Great Depression. Due to deteriorating transport facilities, insufficient inputs and other factors, export volumes have also declined, further reducing Africa's export earnings. With exports as the major source of foreign exchange and investment, the negative impact of these decreases in export volume and prices on growth prospects is grave.

The resulting scarcity of foreign exchange has forced African countries to incur foreign debts beyond their capacities to pay. High interest rates, arrears, and fluctuations in the value of the dollar have further increased the collective debt burden to $257 billion in 1989. Compared to the debt of the Third World's heavily-indebted countries, Africa's total debt may appear to be less menacing. However, by other measures – such as the growth of the stock debt, the debt and debt-servicing ratios, the capacity of African countries to service it and the implications of its growth for recovery and development prospects in the region – the problem is quite serious.

Africa's outstanding external debt amounted in 1988 to over 81 per cent of the region's GDP and over 314 per cent of the exports of goods and services. For Africa, these two indicators are significantly higher than those of the heavily-indebted countries, at about 50 and 270 per cent respectively. Africa's scheduled debt-service to exports ratio of 40 per cent in 1988, compared to a similar ratio for the heavily-indebted countries of about 25 per cent, is also indicative of a heavier debt burden.

The fact that the rising debt and debt-servicing obligations have coincided with an eroded capacity to service debts has resulted in mounting arrears. These arrears, especially to the IMF and World Bank, have led to blockage of new commitments and disbursement of already approved credits and also to frequent reschedulings by the London and

Paris Clubs. The reschedulings averaged about eight agreements per year during 1980–85 and up to twelve agreements per year in 1986 and 1987, involving twenty-six African countries. The magnitude of the debt burden can be further exemplified by the fact that no less than thirty-one sub-Saharan African countries are officially classified by the World Bank as 'debt-distressed' countries.

The external resource flow situation has further been made worse through inadequate resource flows, which in 1988 were below their 1985 level in real terms. Ironically, the deterioration in resource flows has been further compounded by a net transfer of resources, close to $1 billion each in 1986 and 1987, $1.2 billion in 1988 and $1.5 billion in 1989, from Africa to the IMF and World Bank. Indeed, when account is taken of the escalating debt-service burden, the decline in export earnings and capital flight, net resources outflows from Africa are estimated to have reached $5.8 billion in 1988 and $5.5 billion in 1989.

In the 1980s the World Bank and IMF played important roles in the attempt to ease the debt and foreign exchange crunch of African countries. This was done by instituting programmes of their own and by mobilizing the support of the international community. While these initiatives deserve commendation, a critical assessment of their impact as they have evolved over the years demonstrates that they need to be rectified in many ways.

In their efforts to mobilize the support of the international community in favour of Africa, both the Bank and IMF have tended to promote the need for such support to be given within the conditionality of SAPs. Increasingly, there has been a practice on the part of the donor community to tie enhanced or new levels of resource flows to the adherence by the recipient African countries to SAPs. This conditionality has now extended to agreements such as Lomé IV.

Likewise, debt relief is increasingly being made conditional upon the adoption of SAPs. The cancellation of Official Development Assistance (ODA) debt, and the implementation of the initiative of the Toronto Summit of the G7 on debt (through the Paris Club) are both linked to SAPs. This condition has eliminated many debt-burdened African countries who otherwise would have qualified for debt relief. It has also denied many foreign exchange-starved countries the benefits of additional resource flows.

While there is certainly a need to ensure that additional resource flows and debt relief are utilized within the context of credible reform programmes, more damage would be done if assistance were to be tied to the implementation of orthodox SAPs. I am for full accountability. But 'accountability' should not be confused with 'SAPs conditionality'. The pretext of 'SAPs conditionality' should not be used to tie African countries more tightly to programmes that have lost their credibility. Therefore, an important agenda item for the 1990s is the delinking of resource flows and debt-relief measures from the conditionality of SAPs. Donors and African countries should agree to mutually acceptable alternative modalities and criteria for performance by both sides. The criteria might include the extent to which the process of sustainable recovery and development is advancing; the success of the countries and donors in helping the economies to move steadily and consistently along the path of socio-economic transformation with necessary adjustment along the way; and the extent of the democratization. In this connection, the criteria contained in the African Charter for Popular Participation in Development are worth examining.

The World Bank's concessional lending to sub-Saharan African countries has been increasing over the years. Disbursements through the International Development Association (IDA) and the Special Facility for the poorest countries of sub-Saharan Africa (SFA) reached $1.3 billion in fiscal year 1986 and $1.8 billion in 1987. The proportion of IDA funds going to sub-Saharan Africa has increased from 27 per cent in 1981 to 35 per cent in 1987 and 50 per cent recently in the eighth replenishment of IDA resources (IDA-8). This principal source of concessional assistance has helped to provide resources that are badly needed by the poorest countries of Africa.

Important as they are, IDA resources and the SFA fall far short of African needs. Indeed, the resources made available to Africa under IDA-8 barely maintained the level of lending in real terms of IDA-7 and SFA combined. It is vital, therefore, that no effort be spared during 1990, the last year of IDA-8, to ensure that Africa actually receives the full 50 per cent of IDA-8 resources that have been allocated to it.

The negotiations of the ninth replenishment of IDA resources (IDA-9) have entered their final phases. In view of the importance of these resources for Africa, it is vital that the US support this replenishment. Further, it is critical that these negotiations be concluded as rapidly as possible, to avoid any interruption in the Association's operations; that the replenishment be higher in real terms than IDA-8; and that African countries receive over 50 per cent of IDA-9 resources.

The share of the World Bank and the IMF in the total debt of the region now stands at about 24 per cent, while they receive 40 per cent of debt-service payments on non-concessional debt. As mentioned earlier, more worrying is the fact that there has been a reverse flow of resources from Africa to the IMF at about $1 billion a year since 1986. The fact that the debt owed to the multilateral institutions has neither been rescheduled not written off has meant that there has been no relief from this large and growing burden. Many low-income and middle-income African countries have run into difficulty servicing their debts to those institutions. As of April 1989, eleven countries were over six months in arrears to the IMF and eight to the World Bank.

The IMF created the Structural Adjustment Facility (SAF) in 1986 and later supplemented it with the Enhanced Structural Adjustment Facility (ESAF). However, the resources provided under SAF and ESAF have not been adequate. Moreover, arrangements for utilizing these two facilities have been extremely slow. As of the end of June 1989 only SDR 1.6 billion had been committed to sub-Saharan African countries, of which only SDR 662 million was disbursed. Another drawback is that these funds are restricted to only low-income IDA eligible countries.

While the World Bank launched a Special Programme of Assistance (SPA) in December 1987 to ease the problems of low-income debt-distressed countries, no significant measures have been undertaken by the Bank to deal directly with its multilateral debt owned by Africa. The same is true for the IMF's ESAF initiative. Both facilities are designed to support adjustment programmes and alleviate balance of payments constraints, and will not lead directly to debt relief.

Imaginative solutions to the problem of multilateral debt need to be found. The UN Secretary-General's High Level Advisory Group on Financial Flows to Africa (the Wass Group) recommended that new funds should be made available directly to African countries to enable them to refinance their debt to the World Bank and IMF. While this proposal merits support, efforts should go beyond the mere refinancing of debt to a significant reduction in the stock of this debt. Measures could include rescheduling, conversion, and repayment in local currency. Furthermore, such initiatives should not be restricted to special categories of low-income countries. Other low-income countries and many middle-income African countries are heavily indebted to the Bank and the IMF. Their debt and debt-service burdens are excessive and threaten growth and development prospects.

Net additional inflows to refinance current and reduce further debt service, at highly concessional terms, can be provided through new special facilities solely created for this purpose. It has been suggested however, that such inflows be introduced through ESAF, IDA and World Bank loans. This would entail complex changes such as faster disbursement of these; extending and expanding ESAF; softening terms on the IMF's Extended Fund Facility; and making middle-income countries eligible. Net additional inflows can be made available without cost to governments through selling part of the IMF gold reserves and using 100 per cent of IDA reflows.

It has been recognized that current financial difficulties of African countries are largely due to unforeseen external factors over which African countries have no control. In 1963 the IMF established a Compensatory Financing Facility (CFF) to finance temporary shortfalls in overall export earnings. In 1981 it was expanded to meet sudden surges in cereal import costs. Commendable and welcome as the Facility is, it does have several drawbacks:

1. In 1983 the IMF limited access to the CFF, making it another window of standard adjustment financing.

2. Furthermore, quota limits have been unduly restrictive. Each country's access to the CFF for export shortfalls or cereal imports excesses is presently limited to 83 per cent of its IMF quota, and a combined ceiling of 105 per cent quota.

3. The repayments are made on a fixed schedule, three to five years after drawing on the Facility, while keeping in mind the contingent nature of the financing and the likely continuation of the conditions that prompted the use of the Facility.

4. The interest charges imposed by the Fund for the use of the CFF are high and are the same as for the standard credit tranche drawings. It is thus unreasonable for low-income countries which are granted highly concessional terms for IDA, SAF and ESAF loans to have to pay near commercial rates for loans required to meet unforeseen developments beyond their control.

The Wass Group, which studied the operations of the CFF, observed that in 1980 and each year since 1984 African countries together have repaid to the IMF Facility more than the amount they have received. The annual net outflow for the years 1985, 1986 and 1987 amounted to over $150 million dollars.

It is obvious that the Facility has not served the purpose for which it was intended, i.e., to provide bridging finance to countries facing temporary self-reversing short-falls in foreign exchange earnings thus ensuring that their development efforts and import programmes are not adversely affected by the short-term problem. As a result, the Wass Group recommended the following:

1. The Compensatory Financing Facility of the IMF should be returned to its earlier role as a low-conditionality, relatively automatic and quickly available source of funds for short-term contingency needs. It should also be expanded to cover additional contingencies and the amount of resources it is able to provide should not be unduly restricted by current quota-based formulas. If the CFF is to be of use to African and other low-income countries, it should have a concessional window. The cost of such a concession should be met either by direct contributions or by a new gold sale by the IMF.

2. If the conditions that require a country to use the CFF do not improve as anticipated, the repayment period should be lengthened or a new loan issued to repay the outstanding one; if recovery is quicker than expected, repayment should be accelerated.

3. Pending completion of the Ninth Review of IMF Quotas, CFF access limits should be substantially enlarged.[11]

Recently, the CFF has been expanded into a Compensatory and Contingency Financing Facility (CCFF) to provide for contingency financing covering external variables, including interest rates, that affect the current account. The basic features of the compensatory financing, including the terms for charges and repayment, have been maintained. While a few African countries have drawn on the compensatory financing component, none have used the contingency financing. Indeed, many observers believe that it is highly unlikely that contingency financing, as currently implemented by the IMF, will attract the interest of African countries given its commercial rates of interest and balance-of-payments adjusted orientation of repayment conditions. A wise recommendation is to relate the contingency financing to disruptions in growth oriented development programmes caused by earnings shortfalls.

Conclusion

With the advent of the 1990s, Africa must achieve the transition from 'stabilization and adjustment' to 'adjustment with transformation'. A process of sustained and sustainable growth and development – human-centred, self-reliant, and participatory in nature – must be set in motion and must take hold in the coming years. The responsibility for bringing about this socio-economic revival rests, first and foremost, with the African governments and people themselves. However, unless the international economic environment is made receptive to the efforts of

Africa, the continent's socio-economic revival will remain forever elusive.

The international community has, therefore, the responsibility to create the external conditions that are both necessary and sufficient to enable Africa to realize its objectives. Over the years, the World Bank and IMF have come to wield tremendous – and certainly disproportionate – power over Africa's economic and social destiny, by literally dictating the orientation and pace of economic reforms in the majority of African countries through SAPs. Increasingly, these institutions successfully convinced Africa's bilateral partners of the efficacy of linking co-financing, bilateral aid, and debt-relief measures to the conditionality of SAPs.

A generation of SAPs has glaringly revealed the inadequacies of those programmes. To further tie all assistance and debt-relief initiatives that favour Africa to SAPs is to mortgage the economic future of the continent to failed policies.

Notes

1. 'The Khartoum Declaration', ECA 1988, 21.
2. General Assembly Document No. A/43/500 of 10 August 1988.
3. General Assembly Document A/RES/43/27, 13 and 16.
4. 'Structural Adjustment in Africa: Insights From the Experiences of Ghana and Senegal', Report of a Staff Study Mission to Great Britain, Ghana, Senegal, Côte d'Ivoire, France and Washington, 29 November–20 December 1988.
5. General Assembly Document No. A/RES/45/27, 68.
6. General Assembly resolution, A/44/L/20 Rev. 1, 14 November 1989.
7. 'Putting the People First', Opening Statement, Arusha 1990, 3.
8. African Charter for Popular Participation in Development, ECA, Addis Ababa, March 1990.
9. General Assembly Document, A/43/500, 4.
10. Ibid., 11.
11. 'Financing Africa Recovery', Report and Recommendations of the Advisory Group on Financial Flows for Africa, United Nations, New York 1988.

12

Structural Adjustment Programmes and Regional Integration: Compatible or Mutually Exclusive?

Cyril Daddieh

Structural adjustment in fact encourages many characteristics which have long been identified with persistent underdevelopment. Foremost among these is the reliance upon a few export crops or commodities as the primary source of economic growth. This locks individual African countries into a dependence upon declining markets in industrialized states, and holds them hostage to the wild swings which typify commodity price movements. Rather than instigating movement away from neo-colonial patterns of trade and exchange, those patterns are instead being reinforced . . . adjustment programs tend to work against many of the elements which favor sustainable development. These include regional economic integration and South–South trade internationally.[1]

Introduction

Since the attainment of formal political independence in the 1960s, African leaders have consistently reaffirmed their desire to forge mutually beneficial economic and political linkages in order to enhance the continent's development prospects and promote the well-being of their people. This desire to achieve greater cooperation has led to the creation of the single most extensive network of regional organizations anywhere in the world. The World Bank estimates that more than 200 integration schemes are in existence in Africa.[2] The vast majority of these organizations (some 160 of them) are intergovernmental organizations or IGOs, although the remaining non-governmental organizations or NGOs received various forms of government assistance.

These regional initiatives cover a catholic spread of issue areas from service, research, and professional activities to market or trade-related schemes. A number of purely technical and research-oriented initiatives have been created to complement the more familiar orthodox market integration schemes such as the West African Economic Community (CEAO), the Economic Community of West African States (ECOWAS), the Central African Customs and Economic Union (UDEAC), the Southern African Customs Union (SACU), and the Preferential Trade Area (PTA), or the more innovative experiment in development coordination known as the Southern African Development Coordination Conference (SADCC).[3]

The proliferation of regional schemes

The proliferation of regional integration (RI) schemes in Africa is a function of the confluence of several factors, namely the legacy and memories of history, contemporary African realities, global developments, and the theoretical premises and promises of regionalism. First, African leaders are conscious of the fact that regional economic ties are deeply embedded in the African past. Long-distance trade was well established before the advent of the Europeans. While colonialism undoubtedly disrupted and even altered some patterns of interaction, it did not completely destroy all such ties. Moreover, colonial powers even found ways to restructure some economic activities and institutions so as to give them a decidedly regional focus.

With this legacy serving as a backdrop, Kwame Nkrumah of Ghana embarked upon his quest for a redefinition of regional and continental integration as colonialism drew to a close. He campaigned with a rather crusading zeal for continental unity. In his words, 'Just as I was convinced that political freedom was the essential forerunner of our economic growth and that it must come, so I am equally convinced that African Union will come and provide that united, integrated base upon which our fullest development can be secured.'[4]

He combined his enormous charisma with the power of his ideas to stimulate debate about Africa's future. The core of this continuing debate revolved around the articulation of alternative futures for the continent based on either regionalism and gradualism or continentalism and structural transformation. A flurry of diplomatic activities developed around this issue and as various leaders staked their positions Africa's international relations experienced its own balance of power period in the early 1960s. As a result, three competing political groupings reflecting divergent assumptions and orientations were conceived: the radical Casablanca group, followed by its conservative antithesis, the Monrovia group, and the 'Franco-African' Brazzaville group. The radical camp staked its reputation on continental unity as the mechanism through which the necessary structural transformation of the African economy would be achieved. However, opposition from the combined nationalist and Euro-African factions proved too formidable. In the end, Nkrumah and his Casablanca colleagues had to settle for a half-full glass and accept major revisions to their original pan-African vision so that a continental interstate organization could be born in the form of the Organization of African Unity (OAU) in May 1963, which in turn provided a framework and legitimization for the explosion of functional organizations.

From these tentative beginnings, the search for new definitions and related organizations continued until it culminated in the adoption by the African heads of state of the historic Lagos Plan of Action (LPA) in 1980. The OAU pinned its hopes on the prescriptions or agenda for action enunciated in the LPA being able to 'lead to the creation at the national, sub-regional and regional levels, of a dynamic and inter-dependent African economy and will thereby pave the way for the eventual establishment of an African Common Market leading to an African Economic Community'.[5]

Looking back on the intellectual foundations of the LPA five years after it was signed, Negussay Ayele argued that Nkrumah deserved much of the credit because he had long espoused many of the ideas in the document,[6] especially the emphasis on integration, which 'the OAU is groping to help realize 20 years later'. Ayele contends that:

> Though he was a political animal par excellence, his approach was systematic and wholesome. He related economic matters with internal, political conditions and related international, theoretical notions with concrete reality. Thus, he did not perceive his campaigns for African unity in purely political terms. . . . Through facts and figures he showed the economic advantages of political unity. In other words, Nkrumah did not call for political unity as an end in itself but as a means to economic (in today's jargon – development) ends.[7]

In one sense, then, the contemporary experiments in cooperation must be viewed as attempts to revive earlier patterns of cooperation and interaction that had been disrupted, discontinued, or allowed to deteriorate. As such, they symbolize essential continuities in African historiography as well as reveal unresolved debates about how to repair the Garden of Eden.[8]

It must also be remembered that Africa came of political age at a time when regional economic cooperation was pretty much in vogue. Raul Prebisch and his ECLA associates were pressing Latin American states to embrace regionalism if they wished to overcome their problems of underdevelopment. Moreover, the launching of Europe's own experiment in regional cooperation through the signing of the Treaty of Rome in 1957 coincided with the terminal phase of Africa's struggles for political independence. Latin America's debates and Europe's experiment both had a profound influence on African thinking. In the end, it was Europe that provided the model and the inspiration for the market-oriented integration initiatives in Africa. There was a feeling that what was good for Europe had to be good for Africa. Regional integration was the new game in town at the time, just as structural adjustment is now the new, some would say the only, game in town.

More importantly, regional integration promised attractive tangible benefits, especially to the many land-locked African states with small markets and meagre resources. For instance, it offered the possibility of enlarged markets which would free up factors of production such as labour and capital so that industries could take advantage of new regional market opportunities and expand their scale of production. Labour mobility was expected to ease the burden of unemployment in some member states while allowing others to meet their manpower needs by tapping into a regional labour market. Labour-exporting states as well as families could also expect to enjoy benefits in the form of remittances from migrant labourers, while the economic growth of host states could be enhanced through unlimited access to skilled and unskilled labour. With the help of regional integration, member states would have the opportunity to pull scarce resources in order to finance applied research and investments in directly productive activities.

Finally, regionalism has been difficult to resist politically because there is a general recognition on the part of African leaders that they need to act in concert in order to enhance their bargaining position *vis-à-vis* foreign governments, multinational corporations (MNCs), and multilateral financial institutions. It is fairly well understood that continued fragmentation and extroversion (i.e., division into small states, weak economies, with a heavy dependence on a narrow range of export commodities, external markets, and sources of financing and handouts) would only exacerbate Africa's vulnerability to external pressures and cooptation.

To sum up, African leaders have been favourably disposed in general towards embracing regionalism as an economic and foreign policy tool because of the interactive mix of historical, economic, political, practical and idiosyncratic factors, as suggested above. It is true, however, that they have looked askance at Nkrumah's core conviction – continental political union – because they viewed it as an implicit invitation to commit political suicide by jettisoning hard-won political power or national sovereignty. It is fair to say that for most of these leaders, regionalism represents a kind of defensive reflex against continuing economic and political paralysis, rather than offering possibilities for developing a 'think Africa' ethos rooted in a shared commitment to the quest for Nkrumah's continental political and economic kingdom.[9] As Carol Lancaster has noted, membership in and attendance at annual meetings of such schemes became 'a form of defensive diplomacy – the avoidance of isolation and an expression of regional solidarity'.[10]

Meanwhile, the 1980s witnessed the emergence of a second preoccupation being superimposed over that of regional integration. It followed on the heels of a prolonged and deepening economic crisis in Africa characterized by spiralling budget and balance-of-payment deficits; falling international market shares; mounting external debt burden; hyper-inflation; crumbling transport and communications infrastructure; massive unemployment; under-utilization of plant capacity because of lack of foreign exchange to sustain imports of critical inputs, including spare parts; severe shortages of food and other consumer goods; collapsing health and educational systems for lack of equipment, supplies and personnel; falling per capita real incomes and overall deterioration in standards of living. The resultant struggle for survival by individuals and groups led to various forms of withdrawal from the state, including the widespread use of informal channels for trade and financial transactions, all of which rendered the state impotent or irrelevant. Domestic social and political unrest was played out in the form of a succession of military coups and personal rule. The continental crisis was ripe for resolution.

It was under these appalling circumstances that one by one virtually all African states turned to the Bretton Woods institutions for balance-of-payments and other support to jump-start their economies. In return for increased access to the financial resources controlled by the World Bank and the IMF, African governments had to agree to undertake painful policy reforms. These macro-economic reforms, which came under the ill-conceived title of structural adjustment programmes (SAPs), aimed at tightening up government expenditures in order to reduce or eliminate budget and balance of payments deficits. It is not surprising, therefore, that the main instruments of SAPs have been principally monetary and budgetary in nature and oriented towards addressing individual countries' problems. However, portions of the reform package have also been aimed at increasing productivity and restoring economic growth through liberalized trade and the creation of new incentive structures. The expectation is for liberalization to stimulate efficiency and Africa's international competitiveness.[11]

We have seen how two preoccupations, one dating back to the early years of African independence, the other propelled by the economic crisis of the 1980s and beyond, have been competing for the mind and soul of Africa. Together, they have become the most salient frameworks for policy analysis and praxis. Yet the relationship between these two has been largely neglected in the burgeoning literature on SAPs and on regional integration in Africa.

This chapter focuses on this essential relationship by asking the following questions: are SAPs compatible with regional integration or are these two competing preoccupations mutually exclusive? Will SAPs prove to be contributors to integration or will they frustrate efforts to create lasting regional integration? In addition to making a modest contribution by filling the lacunae in the literature, this chapter hopes to present a more nuanced and dispassionate analysis in order to move the commentary about the relationship beyond the dialogue of the deaf between the unabashed SAP-optimists and their equally unflappable detractors.

As important as the need to understand the relationship between these two policy frameworks is, the difficulties inherent in the analysis cannot be underestimated. These are of two kinds. First, as already indicated, there is a dearth of hard-nosed analyses focusing preferably on particular sectors and dyadic relationships between countries. The result is that we are left with highly questionable conjectures and inferences based primarily on how one feels about the social consequences of adjustment. The second difficulty stems from the recognition that SAPs are 'programmes in the making', notwithstanding their apparent stable menu of prescriptions. These adjustment programmes involve a continuous process, themselves requiring adjustments as new evidence about performance comes to light. They are, after all, only the latest response to the deepening economic malaise that has plagued Africa for two decades or more in some cases. As Reginald Green has remarked, 'poverty, vulnerability, inequality and threats to the social fabric in Africa are not a product of the 1970s or 1980s much less of the Fund and the Bank's proposed prescriptions for stabilisation and adjustment'.[12]

Prominent World Bank officials have also echoed this line of defence. As noted by the Regional Vice President for Africa at the Bank, Edward V.K. Jaycox:

Between 1980 and 1985, a period when relatively few African countries had adopted structural adjustment programs, the social indicators for 33 countries deteriorated. Per capita education expenditures fell; per capita health expenditures fell; daily per capita caloric intake dropped from 2,060 to 1,911. By the mid-1980s, therefore, it was clear that not only economies were being hurt by Africa's failure to adjust – so were people, and on a massive scale.[13]

He goes on to argue that 'Adjustment is very much a learning-by-doing process for all concerned, and it is different in every country – the specific measures taken, the phasing, funding and so on. Most African governments have adopted these programmes cautiously and nervously. Some have stopped, restarted and tried again.'[14]

Finally, it is worth noting that because SAPs have been quite controversial, to say the least, and some countries have had to adopt them under duress or else forfeit access to needed balance-of-payments and other supports such as debt rescheduling or new loan disbursements,[15] they have rarely been implemented without political struggles and official and unofficial attempts to subvert them on the ground.

The foregoing opening remarks should help to situate the debate about the impact of SAPs on the prospects of successful integration in Africa within its proper context. They suggest, for instance, that any final assessment will have to be conducted with specific temporal markers in mind. For it does make a difference whether one adopts a short-, medium- or long-term perspective. Bearing these caveats in mind, perhaps the more appropriate question to ask is whether the prospects for integration would be much improved in the absence of SAPs. Such a view reminds the analyst of the need to raise counter-factual arguments. If the answer to the above question, for instance, is in the negative, then one would want to know what other obstacles stand in the way of increased interdependence through regionalism. In addition, analysts may have to define the kinds of integration that are under discussion. After all, there are varieties of regionalism, as the experiences of SADCC and ECOWAS clearly demonstrate.[16]

While this chapter does not purport to provide answers to all these pertinent questions, it provides pathways to a more nuanced and fruitful approach to the subject. To begin with, it raises serious doubts about treating SAPs and RI as cause and effect. It suggests that it makes more sense to treat SAPs *not* as an independent variable that explains the success or failure of regionalism but rather as an intervening variable that can either facilitate or impede progress towards regionalism, however the latter may be defined. Additionally, it suggests that the issue of the impact of SAPs on RI cannot be addressed with any degree of certitude in the abstract. Rather, it must be related to concrete experiences, attitudes and behaviours of significant actors involved in the effort to build greater interdependence.

For RI to succeed in the long run, it needs clear and strong African ownership – a mixture of popular or grass-roots involvement and political leadership to provide vision, new definitions and financial sustenance. While external donors can nurture the process, as they seem to have successfully done in the case of SADC, they cannot be counted on to provide such support indefinitely. An African state has to step up to provide the necessary leadership. This is where the role of Côte d'Ivoire and, to a lesser extent Senegal, in CEAO has been significant. Abidjan used the *Fonds de Solidarité*, which was initially introduced in 1959 and which amounted to an Ivorian subsidy of the budgets of the other states, to increase the political cohesion of the Entente Council which Benin and Burkina Faso had agreed to join without much enthusiasm.

CEAO also used differential intra-union tariffs designated as 'transfer taxes' in order to compensate the poorer countries and concomitantly to alleviate the problem of unfair gains/losses which is a byproduct of unequal development.[17] According to one estimate,[18] by 1980, 410 industrial items, mostly originating from Côte d'Ivoire and Senegal, were registered under the *Taxe de Coopération Régionale* (TCR). TCR revenues were channelled into the *Fonds Communautaire de Développement* (FCD) and amounted to CFA 6,760 million by 1980. Two-thirds of that amount was redistributed as compensation for revenue losses incurred under trade liberalization and the remainder was allocated to development projects within the Community. Between 1976 and 1986 Abidjan and Dakar contributed 60.7 and 38.8 per cent respectively to the Community Development Fund (FCD).

African experiences with regional integration schemes

The phenomenal growth of RI schemes has already been acknowledged. It has been suggested that such proliferation vouchsafes African leaders' desire to translate continental aspirations into concrete plans of action.[19] In reality, however, it is symptomatic of deep-seated problems rather than of successful spillover.[20] The trade figures alone are painful reminders of the failure of these schemes to achieve their primary goal of promoting regional trade expansion. The World Bank estimates that official trade among sub-Saharan African countries amounts to a paltry $4 billion or only 6 per cent of a total African trade worth $65 billion.[21] The Bank hastens to add that African trade has stagnated or declined for most countries since the 1970s, a time when most of the market integration schemes were negotiated. The good news is that the potential for trade expansion exists. The Bank indicates that an additional $5 billion of imports from extra-continental sources could be supplied by African countries already exporting similar products to destinations outside the region.

Intra-regional trade in West Africa has been just as insignificant (less than 5 per cent) relative to the region's total trade volume. Regional trade is not only paltry, it continues to be characterized by intra-community trade imbalances with apparently no concerted and coordinated efforts being made to correct them.[22] Nigeria, Côte d'Ivoire and Senegal remain by far the dominant actors in the regional marketplace.[23] Together, they accounted for about 50 per cent of recorded intra-regional exports in the early 1970s and 75 per cent by the late 1970s.[24] Significantly, even officially-recorded trade is either the transit of non-African goods to land-locked states or the export of manufactured goods produced by branch plants of MNCs located in regional centres such as Abidjan, Dakar, Harare, Lagos and Nairobi.[25]

Meanwhile, even as official trade has stagnated or declined in real terms, and with it reduced confidence in formal blueprints for RI, people-to-people exchanges through informal commerce and other unofficial transactions that are subject to varying degrees of official interference and harassment continue unabated.[26] Such informal exchanges across Africa's permeable borders are partially re-establishing the extensive pre-independence network of trade in goods and associated migratory patterns. In the process they are promoting competition and sustaining entrepreneurial activities, in some cases containing prices and in other cases fuelling them and all the while providing employment opportunities and maintaining supplies across borders.[27]

Challenges to regionalism in Africa

It is no secret that a certain number of pre-SAP conditions have always plagued RI in Africa in general and West Africa in particular. Many of these pressures are internal to African states, but others are induced by Africa's increasingly difficult external environment. They are multidimensional, involving logistical, institutional, linguistic (West

Africa especially), political, as well as economic constraints and failures. These problems have been so well documented elsewhere that they will be given limited coverage here.

One recurrent view is that Africa lacks the complementarity between national economies necessary for successful trade-driven integration. The imbalances between the national economies impels the weakest states to protect themselves against their stronger neighbours.[28] However, even where complementarity exists, lack of information has become a serious barrier to increased trade. A case in point, according to the World Bank,[29] is that Cape Verde seems unaware that Cameroon could replace Portugal as a source of aluminium discs for making cooking utensils. This lack of information may also explain the popular perception that product specifications are more easily verifiable, and quality control and reliability of delivery are better, from suppliers outside Africa. Similarly, the products of a Nigerian bicycle manufacturer apparently became more acceptable to customers in neighbouring African countries when they were re-exported from the United Kingdom.

Also bedevilling African regionalism are the inefficient or non-existent transport and telecommunications services. Much of the infrastructure has been geared toward servicing the import and export trade with extra-continental rather than with African countries.[30] In West Africa, the problem of poor communications goes beyond postal and telephone links. Even surface transport for goods is often non-existent, unreliable, or simply too costly. Such problems are exacerbated by linguistic barriers in a region where there are fewer than forty professional translators and interpreters in the sixteen countries, according to a UN study.[31]

The agricultural trade sector has the potential to promote the region's basic needs and thereby imbue West Africans with the spirit and marketing policies pursued in some countries. However, market and price controls have undermined regional trade even in border areas where the transportation system might permit it. It would appear that trade expansion in agricultural products depends on a combination of continuing transport improvements and a progressive removal of price and market controls.[32]

Improvements in intra-African transport and communications must be coupled with a frontal assault on the dizzying assortment of regulatory, procedural and administrative hurdles that obstruct trade. The Bank cautions that large investments in infrastructure are unlikely to stimulate RI unless these other barriers are first eased or removed. It makes its case by observing that a bridge between Liberia and Sierra Leone, 'one of the few achievements of the Mano River Union', is hardly used because of restrictions on both sides of the border.[33]

> Border checks and unduly complex transit procedures cause long waiting periods that reduce intraregional trade and contribute to the high cost of doing business in Africa. Up to 70 administrative steps may be involved in moving goods legally across African borders. In Zaire there are 39 steps for exports and 30 for imports, including signatures, validations, licenses, and authorizations from innumerable administrators, with each official collecting a 'fee'. An open general license system for imports from regional partners is essential to increased trade and integration.[34]

And then there is the intractable problem of exchange-rate management, including convertibility, and money and banking facilities. With the exception of member states of the BCEAO, complex exchange control systems, overvalued currencies, slow and inefficient clearing arrangements, disparities in national customs procedures, not to mention poor staff performance resulting from a lack of proper training in some of the customs' bureaucracies, have all hampered increased trade and RI. As Knowles has argued:

> A customs union cannot be sustained without a considerable degree of harmonization of procedures, which requires staff with both the training and ability to operate these procedures. Quite inadequate attention was given to these points by the architects of ECOWAS, as well as to the time needed to achieve them.[35]

This raises a host of institutional/political problems that have yet to find adequate solutions. Most analysts have agreed that most of Africa's regional initiatives have been overly ambitious, requiring cumbersome centralized bureaucracies (something SADCC has consciously eschewed). Key administrative appointments have been highly politicized. Governments have shown more willingness to pay their dues when the secretary-general is from their state or important institutions are headquartered in their state, and vice versa. Furthermore, there has been a real reluctance on the part of African leaders to give meaningful power to the chief operating officers of these organizations. As Ambroise Foalem, the uncompromising secretary-general of UDEAC, bluntly reminded UDEAC member states, community institutions have been rendered 'inoperable' because the political leaders have gone to great lengths to ensure that no supranational decisions are taken. He also laments the weakness of community institutions, especially the absence of a Union Court of Appeals capable of adjudicating disputes arising from the implementation of treaty provisions and making binding judgements.[36]

There is a broad consensus that the running of a common market requires high standards of administrative skills and supporting services, as well as communications. There is a dearth of such services in West Africa at the moment. Moreover, even the working conditions at the secretariat in Lagos are said to verge on the impossible: cramped office space, housing shortage, high cost of living, poor security, poor or non-existent post and telephone communications to other ECOWAS countries; recurrent power failures paralyse all electric office equipment, including typewriters, interpretation booths and air conditioning. Predictably, these conditions have undermined recruitment efforts, particularly for francophone staff, 'in a situation where a system of national quotas already limits the scope for recruiting from the relatively limited number of qualified bilingual candidates available'.[37] The resultant shortage of experienced staff has stretched and strained senior staff at the secretariat. Their difficulties have been compounded by the system of rotating ECOWAS meetings between different capitals.[38]

For their part, Ali Mansoor and Andras Inotai[39] have argued that attempts at economic integration in the Third World have generally failed because of: 1) the costs associated with failure to allow free trade for products produced in more than one member country; 2) the emphases on regional import substitution behind high barriers; and 3) the attempt at industrial planning to ensure an equitable distribution of benefits among participating countries. They imply that national ISI strategies and equity concerns, in a context where effective compensatory regimes are difficult to fashion for trade losses especially after commodity prices collapsed and debt burdens grew in the early 1980s, have led to either stagnation or setbacks.

There is a constant refrain in the debate that suggests that most of the challenges are surmountable if only African leaders would summon the necessary political will to stay the course. The test of this political will is seen in the grand failure of African states to implement agreements they have signed amidst pomp and fanfare and, above all, in their reluctance to pay the arrears on their membership subscriptions.[40] This widely-held view has been given additional credibility by none other than the unflappable and crusading champion of regionalism, Adebayo Adedeji, whose view is that:

> The real constraint to the realization of African multinational enterprises is the lack of political goodwill. Total commitment to the cause of African economic integration is still more of an ideal than a practice; too often individual African leaders regard economic cooperation as a threat to their political sovereignty.[41]

While the notion of political will is popular, it puts the spotlight on the wrong issues. I have already indicated that I view political leadership as much more salient. This leadership deficit, coupled with the failure to organize, nurture and involve civil society in the articulation and implementation of policies for regional organizations, perhaps best explains the poor record of implementation of RI schemes in Africa. Part of the problem, as a long-time Africa watcher has confided, is the curious belief that passing a resolution or signing a document actually achieves something. Unfortunately, this orientation is likely to persist as long as there is little pressure from public opinion, and what little pressure there is remains parochial. Under these circumstances, one can expect RI schemes to suffer the same fate of benign neglect as the LPA.[42]

Moreover, the emphasis on political will fails to acknowledge the real economic motivations that lie at the heart of all the regional efforts. To be sure, where RI schemes were able to produce tangible economic and not just psychic gains, African leaders would find the necessary will to persevere. Political will becomes a scarce commodity where the costs of regionalism outweigh the benefits or become too onerous. The basic problem, as Carol Lancaster has argued so persuasively,[43] is that the economic costs of participation for member states are often immediate and concrete, while the economic benefits are long-term and uncertain and are often unevenly distributed among member states.

Understandably, in the face of mounting budgetary and balance-of-payments deficits, leaders seek to avoid the immediate costs of RI. These costs include tariff and related government revenue reductions. Such reductions could impose a substantial burden on states that rely on tariffs to generate significant government revenues. Additional costs may be imposed by the collapse of local firms that find themselves unable to compete with firms in other member countries, resulting in a loss of national income, production and employment. Hence, 'political leaders in Africa, like political leaders elsewhere in the world, are unwilling to sustain the immediate costs of integration for uncertain benefits available – if at all – only in the long run'.[44]

Finally, from a radical perspective, the continuing challenge of RI is how African leaders can avoid being distracted by the continent's linkages with the north in general and the former metropoles in particular. It has been argued that to the extent that north–south linkages, institutionalized in such high-profile diplomatic pageantry as Franco-African and Commonwealth summits and various Lomé Conventions, etc., remain salient and can produce some tangible benefits for government officials, if not for their peoples, African leaders are likely to maintain the dense network of Euro-African relationships while giving rhetorical support to increased RI. In sum, the radical view does not expect high levels of integration as long as Africa remains enmeshed in global networks, as the opening citation also makes clear. The effects of vertical integration with Europe are viewed with alarm in part because even where complementarity has existed between industrial productions within Africa, the foreign or made-in-Europe label has been preferred. In short, the psychology of dependence rather than the lack of information may explain the enduring north–south trade patterns.

Notwithstanding the above shortcomings, there is a continuing affirmation of RI as evidenced by attendance at annual meetings which, in turn, suggests that African heads of state derive some benefits from it. The benefits are of two kinds: First, there is the exposure heads of state receive in their own media and in the media of other West African states when they participate in a meeting with a large number of other heads of state. As Carol Lancaster contends,[45] ECOWAS summits are media events that are at times even featured in the world press. Second, they provide opportunities for the leaders to deal with critical regional issues that could not be effectively handled within the much larger annual meetings of the OAU or at the bilateral level.

At the 1988 ECOWAS summit in Togo, for instance, the Ghanaian head of state, Flt. Lt. Jerry Rawlings and President Eyadema of Togo had an opportunity to repair the strained relations between them. The following year, the heads of state of Senegal and Mauritania met under ECOWAS auspices for their first face-to-face meeting since the expulsion of each other's citizens and were reconciled. This mediation function was officially recognized at the 1990 ECOWAS heads of state meeting when a Nigerian proposal to create a Standing Mediation Committee was adopted.[46] This regional diplomatic or political function of ECOWAS can be enormously helpful on a continent where cordial interpersonal relations count for a great deal, partly because foreign policy decision making is highly personalized.[47] But however useful this function is, will it be sufficient to sustain ECOWAS even in the face of its failure to realize its formal goals of economic integration?

In this connection, it must be noted that it is entirely possible that bureaucratic self-interest may be keeping these schemes alive. Regional organizations have to be staffed by diplomats. And even if we recall that some staff posts carry with them more hardship than glamour in Africa, most treat their personnel as international civil servants. Hence, persistence may be explained by the fact that African bureaucrats have developed some stake in their existence and they therefore have an interest in perpetuating and expanding regional initiatives. Finally, RI is increasingly becoming the only international game in town as far as access to external financial resources is concerned.

The changing context of regionalism

The emergence of regionalism rather than global interdependence as the new international diplomatic game is clearly reflected in the strong endorsement given by the EC to regional cooperation and integration under Article 7 of its Lomé IV Convention with the ACP countries.[48] Indeed, European officials have been encouraging Africans to get ready for 1992. In late 1989, Jacques Pelletier, the French minister of cooperation and development, is quoted as urging African officials to build up their own regional cooperation efforts:

> The changes in Europe, are to my mind, a model. Without a regional market, sub-Saharan Africa will not be organised on a sufficient scale to become an arena of economic growth. Without political co-ordination in all areas – fiscal, social and legal – it will remain too weak in the face of the large groupings which are being established everywhere in the world.[49]

African leaders cannot be oblivious to the fact that in such an inhospitable climate the sympathies of European governments and international aid agencies are likely to flow to those states that follow their advice or policy prescriptions.

The contemporary African and global political imperatives are remarkably different from what they were when most of Africa's integration schemes were first launched in the 1960s and 1970s. The continent has experienced a deep and prolonged economic crisis, with twenty-nine of the forty-five sub-Saharan African countries currently sharing the dubious distinction of belonging to the club of the world's least developed countries, the poorest of the poor. Deteriorating living and social conditions have fuelled social unrest; internal strife and civil wars and attendant refugee problems have added to the economic and political woes of African states. An already stressful situation has been aggravated by the growing debt burden caused in part by previous attempts to suffer-manage through a combination of borrowing and cutbacks.[50]

By the end of the 1980s, virtually all sub-Saharan African countries were implementing one form or another of IMF- and World Bank-mandated SAPs, whose major preoccupations were to ensure that 'African countries would, first of all, reduce the deficits on external accounts and, second, achieve a balanced government budget'.[51] The central tenets of this macro-economic adjustment package included elimination of subsidies, dismantling of price controls, and implementation of cost recovery; 'rationalization' of the state sector through privatization, firings, wage cuts and closures; liberalization of the economy, guided by 'market forces' domestically and 'comparative advantage' internationally; promotion of commodity exports and foreign investment; currency devaluation and interest rate increases.[52]

Meanwhile, the pair of policy initiatives – *glasnost* and *perestroika* – introduced by Mikhail Gorbachov in Moscow in 1985 triggered unprecedented changes at home and abroad and transformed Africa's external arena in fundamental ways. The whirlwind of changes in Eastern Europe and in the former Soviet Union, which included the dismantling of the Soviet empire, democratization, German reunification and economic liberalization, began to be felt almost instantaneously. Gabon's President Omar Bongo, whose regime was among the earliest to be seriously affected by the new global realities, summarized his chagrin by serving up this evocative African idiom: 'The wind from the east is shaking the coconut trees.'[53] African leaders have been alarmed not only by the apparent cosiness of the superpowers and their disengagement from the continent (witness their apparent disinterest in the troika of struggles for Liberia, Ethiopia and Somalia) but also by both the economic opening to the East and the continuing preparations for 1992 and the establishment of a Single European Market (SEM).

There is genuine apprehension that the changes in Eastern Europe will be perceived to offer far more exciting new possibilities for more lucrative private investment as well as for secure official lending, so that aid and capital flows to Africa will further diminish. Thus the period of superpower withdrawal has coincided with the 'growing division of the world into trading blocs'[54] and a concomitant European disinterest in Africa. As a result, sub-Saharan Africa's access to the SEM, for both its peoples and goods, is bound to be severely curtailed.[55]

Africa's changed external environment has become an unavoidable frame of reference for the recent flurry of diplomatic activities designed to concentrate the continent's collective leadership mind on the imperative of greater cooperation through integration. The Secretary-General of the OAU, Salim A. Salim, was quoted as saying recently that he was hopeful that in the longer-term changes in Eastern Europe, European integration and a general European recovery will bode well for Africa. But he also confessed that Africa has reason to be concerned that the preoccupation with Eastern Europe is being sustained at its expense. There is an official African perception that the OECD countries have made a conscious political decision to bolster Eastern European recovery and reconstruction. Salim has drawn attention to Europe's lukewarm attitude towards Africa's problems and warned that Africa will have to adjust to a less charitable Europe. Given Europe's diminishing interest in Africa's well-being, Salim insists that Africa's challenge is to begin on the road towards self-reliance, individually as countries and collectively.[56]

Abbas Bundu underscored the challenges of this changing environment in his own review of ECOWAS developments during 1989–90:

> Europe's current pre-occupation is with the reunification of West and East Germany, a conspicuous example of the warm embrace that Eastern Europe's democratisation process has earned it from Western Europe and the rest of the industrialized world. By the end of 1989, there were already almost 3,500 joint ventures between the East and the West, compared with only 165 ventures at the beginning of 1988. Indeed, the East/West detente is further finding eloquent expression in the significant diversion of development resources from Africa to Eastern Europe, thus worsening Africa's marginalisation on the agenda of the industrialized world.[57]

African economic realities and extra-continental developments loomed large as African leaders met in Kampala in May 1991. The former Nigerian leader, General Olusegun Obasanjo, did not mince words: 'While the world is grouping into blocs to strengthen national economies, Africa remains fragmented and drifting, and is therefore in danger of being completely marginalized'.[58] At the subsequent OAU summit in June, a treaty for the establishment of an African Economic Community by the year 2025, complete with an Africa-wide monetary union, was signed.[59]

Quite clearly, the threat of further marginalization is pushing African leaders towards more sober assessment of their economic and political futures. By all accounts they seem to have become more convinced than before that Africa has no choice but to pursue collective self-reliance and economic integration if it is to transcend its current unenviable status on the periphery of the global economy. As Dr Bundu again noted in his annual report, the prevailing hostile international environment and the state of health of West African economies had led the secretariat to 'the inescapable conclusion that the only viable way out of the development crisis facing the sub-region is the redoubling of efforts towards early and effective sub-regional integration'.[60]

SAPs and regional integration

Debates about structural adjustment have generally focused on the social consequences of the programmes, creating two antagonistic camps in the process. In the camp of SAP-advocates one can find officials of the Bretton Woods institutions, other donor agencies and officials in critical African ministries responsible for programme implementation and a smattering of independent scholars. These representatives are generally more optimistic about the long-term impact of their reforms. The opposing camp of SAP-detractors is generally much less sanguine about the future, influenced, no doubt, by its focus on the pain and suffering of societies undergoing adjustment. It is difficult to characterize this camp precisely, although it is fair to include in it the ECA and its former Executive Secretary, Adebayo Adedeji, a variety of organizations in civil society (teachers, students, trade unions, women's groups, etc.) and many scholars of different ideological stripes.

Again, while this line-up developed in relation to SAPs *per se*, similar reactions have been transposed onto the relationship between SAPs and RI. The official view at the Bank and Fund is that SAPs are compatible with successful RI. Indeed, both are seen as 'imperatives'.[61] The general feeling of SAP-advocates is that trade liberalization, exchange-rate rationalization or devaluations, and competitive costs are all measures that will resuscitate national economies and promote economic expansion. Economic recovery and long-term sustainable growth will, in turn, stimulate intra-regional trade and enhance RI. The Bank's position is made explicit in its 1989 report:

> A realistic structure of exchange rates is critical to intraregional trade. Trade among members of the CEAO (whose currency is the convertible CFA franc) currently represents 10 percent of their total trade. This compares with less than 1 percent of trade for the other members of ECOWAS, for whom currency convertibility has been suspended because of accumulating debts and delayed settlements.[62]

Accentuating the positive by the technique of a ruled box entitled 'How adjustment programs have affected the industrial sector' and by 'before' and 'during' reform comparisons, the Bank waxes confident that growth, sometimes quite substantial, has occurred in manufacturing output, exports and capacity utilization since Côte d'Ivoire, Ghana, Nigeria, and Zambia began implementing adjustment programmes.[63] The message is clear: the correction of macro-economic imbalances and distortions in the form of overvalued exchange rates, protected and inefficient industries, price controls, etc., will create an enabling environment for trade, competition and factor mobility, all of which will enhance rather than hinder regional integration.

Jean-Claude Boidin,[64] who is among the few analysts to tackle directly the issue of the relationship between SAPs and RI, has echoed the above sentiments. He notes that among the core ideas of SAPs is the restoration of economic growth via improvements in the mobility of factors of production. Were that to occur, the prospects for RI will be enhanced. Boidin asserts that:

> This greater mobility will make the national economy more flexible, enabling it to adapt better and faster to the changes that come in the wake of enlargement of the economic area and therefore to benefit from it. Better growth will make the economies less fragile and the operators more dynamic and therefore more willing to face up to competition from the neighbouring countries.[65]

As indicated earlier, SAPs revolve around the twin conditionalities of trade liberalization and privatization of investment and production aimed at facilitating imports while expanding exports. Boidin suggests that an across-the-board liberalization will encourage the development of regional trade by reducing the administrative and tariff barriers (bans, quotas, import licences, duties and taxes, registration and transit formalities, etc.) that are characteristic of Africa.[66] Trade liberalization will stimulate the kinds of new specializations which increase business with neighbouring countries. The removal of these barriers as a result of the implementation of SAPs should ultimately bring the underground economy back into the official circuits. It is assumed that this will, in turn,

> make the genuine complementarity of neighbouring countries – not currently perceived by the operators concerned – visible at last. This redefinition of trade should cut the operators' cost. Official trade can deal with bigger batches. It can use more direct routes and does not need to put up with the danger money of the black market.[67]

The privatization component is designed sharply to curtail the intrusive presence of the state in national economies. It is generally acknowledged that central planning of industrial investments by African governments has led to duplication of industries competing in increasingly restricted regional markets. Boidin argues that this explains the absence of complementarity often observed in neighbouring ACPs.[68] He is confident that transferring investment decisions to the private sector will lead to different industrial choices being made in different countries. In that case, production structures will become more complementary rather than competing, which should spur the development of trade.

Finally, as already indicated, another ubiquitous feature of SAPs is a process of devaluation aimed at streamlining over-valued national currencies and establishing realistic exchange rates and minimum convertibility. In West Africa the non-convertibility of national currencies other than the CFA franc has frequently been cited as a factor in the slow progress towards improved regional trade. This condition has led member states of CEAO, for instance, to reinforce their vertical trade links with France and Europe. Not surprisingly, African leaders have been preaching the need for a monetary union with a common currency or, in the beginning at least, with an effective clearing house for national currencies based on stable exchange rates.[69]

If, indeed, non-convertibility is a barrier to trade between African countries 'then a return to credible parities is a big step towards integration through trade. It will facilitate the working of clearing houses and the development of banking activity (trade financing and cross-border investments) which is a source of regular business'.[70]

A critique of structural adjustment from a regional integration perspective

A key concern of the advocates of RI is that SAPs have been focused too exclusively on individual countries without exploring collective or regional reform responses. Critics find this omission puzzling because of the general recognition that African countries suffer from broadly similar problems. Indeed, one critic has noted that: 'Every country is thinking as an individual, with all its individual adjustment conditionalities. If integration is to be realized, all countries have to streamline their economies and tackle adjustment as a single unit.'[71]

While multi-country adjustment is clearly desirable, it is easier said than done. It is not clear how ultimate responsibility for the loans thus disbursed will be assigned, or whose responsibility it is to bring the countries together for the purpose. Nevertheless, the criticism seems to be striking a responsive chord. Barber B. Conable, president of the World Bank, has conceded that 'there will need to be much greater harmonization of macroeconomic policies – particularly exchange-rate and tariff policies – which can be part of a phased programme of trade liberalization for African products'.[72]

Another criticism based on the West African experience suggests that some parts of the adjustment process militate against RI in the short-term because of the adverse effects they have on next-door neighbours. This has been the case with exchange-rate policies and rapid adjustment of domestic prices. A case in point:

> When Gambia devalued the Dalasi to stimulate its export trade, it saw more than half its groundnut production disappear – the purchase price in Senegal had just gone up and it was paid, of course, in 'revalued' CFAF. This meant a loss of export income for Gambia and an unexpected high cost of collection and intervention for the Senegalese budget. After 10 years of structural over-valuation of the Nigerian currency unit, the Naira (and two years of closed frontiers), the sudden devaluations of 1986–87 overturned the relative prices, destabilising informal trade and production on the frontiers of Benin and Niger and threatening the industries of both countries.[73]

It has been suggested that the more radical the adjustment measures and the more rapidly they are implemented, the stronger the external (cross-border) effects. Such externalities are not surprising, given the permeability of Africa's national boundaries. Regional neighbours, according to Boidin,

> inevitably feel the waves from the shock treatment which countries apply to right their economies and the nearest are the first to be affected. Even if adjustment is along roughly the same lines in all the countries concerned, this regional impact is to a large extent inevitable, since some countries adjust when others do not and the various countries which are adjusting have not coordinated their economic policies and are at different stages in the process of reorganization.[74]

In view of the above consequences, Boidin is even more critical of the manner in which exchange-rate policies have implemented under SAPs. He argues that operating under the new banner of realism and flexible exchange rates, many countries have adopted foreign exchange systems but they have forgotten that stability is also crucial to successful monetary policy.

> Weekly and fairly unpredictable fluctuations in the Cedi, the Naira, the Uganda shilling (between 1983 and 1985) and the Kwacha (until May 1987) are one more source of instability for the economic operators, worsening the exchange risks and possibly acting as a further brake on the development of trade and investments between the States.[75]

Furthermore:

> In a period of macro-economic adjustment, the authorities tend to concentrate on short-term objectives and on the instruments of tax policy. This is understandable and probably unavoidable, but it is not really much encouragement to the development of regional cooperation. Regional integration is an essentially long-term thing and progress towards it primarily

depends on the non-budgetary sides of economic policy – trade policy and liberalization of the flow of finance first and the employment policy and administrative reform afterwards.[76]

Furthermore, it has been argued that the commitment to trade liberalization has led to unwarranted opposition on the part of SAP proponents to price discrimination of any kind, viewing it as a source of distortion and extra cost. However, such a view is inimical to RI in so far as increased regional trade in Africa could benefit from such positive discrimination – i.e., reciprocal preference machinery in the form of preferential tariffs (as in the PTA and the CEAO) and/or the selective raising of non-tariff barriers (as in UDEAC and the PTA projects). In practice, adjustment policies have not been used to sustain intra-African preferences. Instead, they have been used to reduce the size of the existing preferential margins and encouraged the development of trade outside the region.[77] As these are unilateral, individual country decisions, the liberalization measures contained in the SAPs may actually exacerbate the existing asymmetry of access between neighbouring countries. Furthermore, 'By conceding without even negotiating, the countries which adjust pass up the opportunity of obtaining counterparts for their own exports and of leading up to a balanced, ordered process of regional liberalization.'[78]

The central dilemma African countries face is that some parts of the liberalization policies pursued under the SAPs are incompatible with the objective of promoting collective self-reliance through regionalism because they have a tendency to reinforce rather than transcend Africa's historical role in the international division of labour and the extroversion of its political economies. They make a mockery of the exhortations of European leaders and other external officials to intensify regional networks and come at a time when Africa's commodity crunch shows no signs of improvement,[79] and when the rest of the world economy is increasingly preoccupied with its own persistence and expansion. 'The coincidence of externally-oriented reforms with international protectionism is hardly auspicious unless Africa can produce new products which can find new market niches, along the lines of successful manufacturers and commodity exporters from the NICs to Côte d'Ivoire'.[80]

Trade liberalization could choke off any growth prospects as cheaper products from abroad out-compete fragile African industries. Even more importantly, food production might continue to deteriorate under the weight of imported food such as rice, wheat, milk, etc.[81] And yet grain and livestock production, along with petroleum products, are among the few commodities that offer real prospects for complementarity and regional trade.[82] Shaw is even more pessimistic about the future: 'Inter-African trade is unlikely to increase much, other than through smuggling and the black market, until the continent escapes from its colonial heritage of North–South links and produces goods with markets on the continent as well as outside.'[83]

Finally, in what ways do the social consequences of budgetary policies, the hard core of the structural adjustment policies, affect regional cooperation? The dramatic budget cutbacks mandated by SAPs have exacerbated an already difficult situation of falling standards of living for all, and more especially for the poorest segments of society.[84] In an effort to survive these rather difficult circumstances ordinary Africans have taken up a wide variety of informal activities, including smuggling, but an increasing number are also resorting to various antisocial activities, ranging from petty theft to armed robbery. The danger to life and limb is escalating. Meanwhile, some state personnel have been able to become rich amidst the generalized poverty by resorting to all kinds of extortion.[85] Roadblocks have become commonplace on all African roads, even including the streets of Abidjan, the Ivorian capital; once the very symbol of probity, the security forces have turned the streets into a minefield of supplemental income.[86] The net result, as Paxton Idowu has lamented, is that it is much easier to import goods into Nigeria from overseas than from Togo. He adds that: 'If you make the mistake of going by road, apart from the menace of armed robbery, you will be frustrated as a result of impediments created by uniformed men along the border towns.'[87]

To be fair, these roadblocks and other shenanigans preceded the implementation of SAPs. However, they have not disappeared in spite of liberalization. They may have actually increased because of the need to survive the tough economic times of retrenchment and devaluation. As long as this state of affairs continues, it will undermine formal regional trade because the delays created by the ubiquitous roadblocks and the associated 'beer money' make products very expensive. It highlights the two sides of the adjustment coin: liberalization is intended to remove barriers to international and regional trade; yet the austerity imposed by SAPs has placed additional burdens on, as well as created incentives for, state personnel so that they seek to make ends meet by resorting to extra-legal means. The latter have a tendency to compound the risks, frustrations and costs of doing business in national and regional markets. Again, although real, such consequences are clearly unintended, and adjustment may never be able to remove them. However, until they are removed can SAPs make the hoped-for contributions to RI?

Finally, if current trends – budgetary cutbacks, public-sector retrenchment, inflationary pressures and negative growth – continue, there is increased danger that pent-up frustrations will be expressed in xenophobic outbursts directed against citizens from neighbouring countries who will be scapegoated for the soaring unemployment and crime rates in the host country. Unscrupulous leaders may fan these flames by issuing 'quit orders' expelling aliens in order to buy time to prolong their lease on political life.

One potential outcome would add to the nightmare of refugee problems on the continent. In the best-case scenario, the affected countries might respond by temporarily recalling each other's ambassadors or closing their borders. In the worse-case scenario, this could lead to retaliations in kind, border clashes between troops, and prolonged border closures. It could also foster military takeovers in affected countries. Either scenario will not bode well for RI.

If current trends continue, African leaders may well continue to give rhetorical support to formal and comprehensive regional declarations but have increasingly less capacity or even inclination to translate them into concrete action to advance regionalism. A prolonged freeze on public spending will create a strong incentive to reduce the contributions to regional organization budgets more than proportionately, especially if they have to be paid in scarce foreign exchange.

> It is more difficult to maintain investments in general and regional equipment may be particularly hard hit because of the extra problem of sharing out of costs between the various States concerned. The financing of new regional investments is difficult to fit into the tightly controlled priority public investment programmes and has to be left for another day . . . or for foreign aid, the relative weight of which is already excessive in this field.[88]

Or, alternatively, they may redefine regionalism in ways that are more compatible with narrow self- or national interest, even though the wiser course of action for the future seems to lie in the pursuit of the Pan-African ideal of collective self-reliance and balanced regional development. As Shaw argues:

> Regionalism a hundred years after the Berlin Conference is a controversial ideology and policy because of a multiplicity of interpretations, interests, and implications. . . . Regionalism becomes more problematic and antagonistic as growth is elusive and projections are unpromising. Hence the willingness of diverse interests to define it in different ways so as to maximize their prospects of (renewed) growth, if not development.[89]

Curiously, SAPs and RI have something in common: in general, they both promise distant and uncertain benefits while demanding immediate sacrifices. It is best to understand them not only as economic programmes but as political projects as well. Their success and failure must, therefore, be viewed as reflecting either the success or failure of politics. At the level of the primary proponents of SAPs, that political creed seems to be finding fertile ground. There is talk now of 'adjustment with a difference'. In the words of the president of the World Bank:

> First, the process of economic adjustment must be continued and deepened. . . . The experience of the 1980s has shown, however, that it must be 'adjustment with a difference'. Different in the sense that greater account must be taken of the various needs and capabilities of individual countries. Different in that reforms need to be designed not just to overcome the immediate financial difficulties, but to fundamentally transform production structures and build a solid basis for a permanent improvement in peoples' living standards. And different in that additional measures must be taken to protect the poor during the period of transition. The sequencing and funding of adjustment programs must be improved, and there must be clear and strong African ownership of the process.[90]

Conclusions: adjustment and regionalism with a difference

This chapter has supported the view that although adjustment policies are necessarily designed within a national framework, they have consequences that transcend national boundaries and can affect the chances of economic integration in Africa in the long term. More immediately, however, the implementation of the first generation of SAPs have created some adverse conditions for RI partly because they have not paid sufficient attention to the regional dimension of Africa's economic crisis. The evidence points to greater sensitivity towards the regional implications in recent years. However, in the short- to mid-term future at least, neither SAPs nor official declarations alone can be expected to advance very far the cause of regionalism in Africa. A certain reservoir of patience, combined with skilful and mature political leadership, will be necessary to ride out the immediate costs and consequences of the difficult adjustment period. The odds will be against such an outcome without a significant measure of popular involvement and support at a formal level. In the final analysis, regionalism can only triumph over parochialism or petty nationalism with the development of a network of regional private advocacy associations capable of exerting sustained pressure on governments so that they do not falter in their commitments to RI. In their absence, it will take extraordinary leadership and discipline to persuade African states not to subordinate regional commitments and goals to national priorities and programmes, with or without structural adjustment. Unhappily, such leadership is in as much drought as state coffers are empty.

Notes

1. D.S. Copeland, 'Structural Adjustment in Africa', *International Perspectives* 18, no. 2 (March/April 1989): 13–14.
2. World Bank, *Sub-Saharan Africa: From Crisis to Sustainable Growth* (Washington, DC: World Bank, 1989), 149.
3. These include the Onchocerciasis Control Programme (OCP), the West African Rice Development Association, and the International Centre of Insect Physiology and Ecology (ICIPE). Management, consulting, monetary and development finance issues are handled by such organizations as the Eastern and Southern African Management Institute (ESAMI), the Consultative Group on International Agricultural Research (CGIAR), the Union Monetaire Ouest Africaine (UMOA), and the African Development Bank (ADB).
4. Kwame Nkrumah, *Africa Must Unite* (London: Panaf, 1963), 170.
5. Organization of African Unity (OAU), *Lagos Plan of Action for the Economic Development of Africa 1980–2000* (Geneva: International Institute for Labour Studies, 1981), 2.
6. Negussay Ayele, 'Kwame Nkrumah and the Lagos Plan of Action', in Adebayo Adedeji and Timothy M. Shaw (eds), *Economic Crisis in Africa: African Perspectives on Development Problems and Potentials* (Boulder, CO: Lynne Rienner, 1985), 53.
7. Ibid.
8. Ali A. Mazrui, *The African Condition (The Reith Lectures)* (London: Heinemann, 1980).
9. There is a popular belief that Nkrumah's unabashed passion for a continental political union was motivated by a personal ambition to be president of a United States of Africa. This ambition presumably alienated other African leaders. Hence, their antipathy towards a continent-wide integration. This explanation is flawed for two reasons. First, it has yet to be explained just how Nkrumah could have ruled this vast continent without the consent of either these national leaders, legislatures, or of African voters. Second, the gap between rhetoric and commitment remains as wide as ever even though Nkrumah has been a non-(f)actor in African international relations since the praetorian guard in Ghana overthrew him at dawn on 24 February 1966.
10. Carol Lancaster, 'The Lagos Three: Economic Regionalism in Sub-Saharan Africa', in John W. Harbeson and Donald Rothchild (eds), *Africa in World Politics* (Boulder, CO: Westview Press, 1991), 263.

11. Edward V.K. Jaycox, 'Structural Adjustment in Sub-Saharan Africa: The World Bank's Perspective', *ISSUE: A Journal of Opinion* 18, no. 1 (1989): 36–40; *The Challenges of African Development* (Washington, DC: World Bank, 1992).

12. Quoted in Adotey Bing, 'The Bank, the Fund, and the People of Africa', *West Africa* 3658 (21 September 1987): 1832; see also Adotey Bing, 'The Fund, the Bank and the People of Africa – 2', *West Africa* 3659 (28 September 1987): 1889–91.

13. Jaycox, 'Structural Adjustment in Sub-Saharan Africa', 37; see also *The Challenges of African Development*.

14. Jaycox, 'Structural Adjustment in Sub-Saharan Africa', 37.

15. Ernest Harsch, 'After Adjustment', *Africa Report* 31, no. 3 (May–June 1986): 48.

16. Timothy M. Shaw, 'The Revival of Regionalism in Africa: Cure for Crisis or Prescription for Conflict?' *Jerusalem Journal of International Relations* 11, no. 4 (1989): 79–105; Colin Stoneman and Carol B. Thompson, 'Southern Africa After Apartheid: Economic Repercussions of a Free South Africa', *Africa Recovery Briefing Paper*, no. 4 (December 1991): 1–12.

17. Johnson, 'Economic Integration in Africa', 8–10; Bach, 'Francophone Regional Organizations and ECOWAS', 57–59.

18. Bach, 'The Politics of West African Economic Co-operation: CEAO and ECOWAS', *Journal of Modern African Studies* 21, no. 4 (December 1983): 620; 'Francophone Regional Organizations and ECOWAS', 58.

19. Achi Atsain, 'Regional Economic Integration and Foreign Policy', in I. William Zartman and Christopher L. Delgado (eds), *The Political Economy of the Ivory Coast* (New York: Praeger, 1984), 175–218.

20. Julius O. Ihonvbere, 'Toward an African Common Market in AD 2025?', paper presented at the workshop 'Eastern Europe and Africa: Parallels and Lessons', Queen's University, Kingston, Ontario, Canada, 12–13 April 1992.

21. World Bank, *Sub-Saharan Africa*, 158.

22. Phoebe Kornfeld, 'ECOWAS, the First Decade: Towards Collective Self-Reliance, or Maintenance of the Status Quo?' in Julius Emeka Okolo and Stephen Wright (eds), *West African Regional Cooperation and Development* (Boulder, CO: Westview Press, 1990), 92; Eddie Momoh, 'West Africa Responds to Europe 1992', *AED* 11, no. 22 (4–10 June 1990): 4.

23. Atsain, 'Regional Economic Integration and Foreign Policy', 175–218; Kornfeld, 'ECOWAS, the First Decade'; Peter Robson, *Integration, Development and Equity: Economic Integration in West Africa* (London: George Allen and Unwin, 1983).

24. Mary E. Burfisher and Margaret B. Missiaen, 'Intraregional Trade in West Africa', in Okolo and Wright, *West African Regional Cooperation*, 185–214.

25. Timothy M. Shaw, 'Dependent Development in the New International Division of Labour: Prospects for Africa's Political Economy', *Indian Journal of Social Science* 3, no. 2 (1990): 225–54.

26. Cyril Kofie Daddieh, 'Rural–Urban Linkages and Industrialisation in Africa: Some Research Notes on Nzimaland, Southwestern Ghana', World Bank Symposium on African Economic Issues, Nairobi, Kenya, June 1990.

27. Daddieh, 'Rural–Urban Linkages'; World Bank, *Sub-Saharan Africa*, 158.

28. Jean-Claude Boidin, 'Regional Cooperation in the Face of Structural Adjustment', *The Courier* 112 (November–December 1988): 67; Kornfeld, 'ECOWAS, the First Decade'.

29. World Bank, *Sub-Saharan Africa*, 161.

30. Ibid., 153.

31. Oliver S. Knowles, 'ECOWAS: Problems and Potential', in Okolo and Wright, *West African Regional Cooperation*, 150.

32. Ibid., 153.

33. World Bank, *Sub-Saharan Africa*, 153.

34. Ibid., 160–61.

35. Knowles, 'ECOWAS: Problems and Potential', 150.

36. 'UDÉAC solution intégration', *Jeune Afrique Economique* 120 (Juin 1989): 42.

37. Knowles, 'ECOWAS: Problems and Potential', 149–50.

38. Ibid.

39. Ali Mansoor and Andras Inotai, 'Integration Efforts in Sub-Saharan Africa: Failures, Results and Prospects – A Suggested Strategy for Achieving Efficient Integration', in Ajay Chhibber and Stanley Fischer (eds), *Economic Reform in Sub-Saharan Africa* (Washington, DC: World Bank, 1991), 217–32.

40. See *West Africa* 3751, 10 July 1989, 1119.

41. Kornfeld, 'ECOWAS, the First Decade', 90; see also S.K.B. Asante, *African Development: Adebayo Adedeji's Alternative Strategies* (London: Hans Zell, 1991).

42. I am grateful to Dr. Douglas G. Anglin for drawing my attention to these neglected explanations of the failure of RI in Africa.

43. Lancaster, 'The Lagos Three', 261.

44. Ibid., 262.

45. Ibid.

46. Ibid.

47. Cyril Kofie Daddieh and Timothy M. Shaw, 'The Political Economy of Decision Making in African Foreign Policy: The Cases of Recognition of Biafra and the Popular Movement for the Liberation of Angola (MPLA)', in Bahgat Korany (ed.), *How Foreign Policy Decisions Are Made in the Third World: Comparative Analysis* (Boulder, CO: Westview Press, 1986).

48. S.K.B. Asante, 'Africa and Regionalism', *West Africa* 3810 (10–16 September 1990): 2441.

49. Thomas M. Callaghy, 'Africa and the World Economy: Caught Between a Rock and a Hard Place', in John W. Harbeson and Donald Rothchild (eds), *Africa in World Politics* (Boulder, CO: Westview Press, 1991), 64.

50. UN Economic Commission for Africa (ECA), *African Alternative*

    Framework to Structural Adjustment Programmes for Socio-Economic Recovery and Transformation: A Popular Version (Addis Ababa: UNECA, 1991), 5.

51. Ibid., 12.
52. Copeland, 'Structural Adjustment in Africa', 11.
53. Kaye Whiteman, 'The Gallic Paradox', *Africa Report* 36, no. 1 (January–February 1991): 18.
54. Asante, 'Africa and Regionalism', 2441.
55. Christopher Stevens, 'Europe and the South in the 1990s: Disengagement from the South and Integration to the North of the Sahara', paper presented at a workshop on 'Political Economy and Foreign Policy in the Third World in the 1990s', Dalhousie University, Halifax, Nova Scotia, 26–28 September 1991.
56. See 'Africa's Destiny', *West Africa* 3816 (22–28 October 1990): 2690.
57. See 'Great Expectations', *West Africa* 3796 (28 May–3 June 1990): 889.
58. See Salim Lone, 'Africa Moves Towards Radical Restructuring of Political Framework', *Africa Recovery* 5, no. 1 (June 1991): 10.
59. See 'Abuja Summit Reflects New African Priorities', *Africa Recovery* 5, no. 2–3 (September 1991): 7.
60. See 'ECOWAS at 15', *West Africa* (28 May–3 June 1990): 899.
61. Jaycox, *The Challenges of African Development*, 65–7.
62. World Bank, *Sub-Saharan Africa*, 159–60.
63. Ibid., 117, 158–62.
64. Boidin, 'Regional Cooperation', 67.
65. Ibid.
66. Ibid., 67–8.
67. Ibid., 68.
68. Ibid.
69. It is generally believed that it will not be easy for ECOWAS to fashion a common union or at least to establish parities between currencies because CEAO members are unlikely to abandon the CFA, and related central bank and non-CEAO members may find it politically unpalatable to join up and swallow the CFA pill (see Omotunde E.G. Johnson, 'Economic Integration in Africa: Enhancing Prospects for Success', *Journal of Modern African Studies* 29, no. 1 [March 1991]: 12). The situation is currently in a state of flux. Ongoing debates and monetary projects in both France and Africa may trigger such fundamental changes in Franco-African monetary relations as to render this a moot point.
70. Boidin, 'Regional Cooperation', 68.
71. Peter Da Costa, 'A New Role for ECOWAS', *Africa Report* 36, no. 5 (September–October 1991): 38–39.
72. Barber B. Conable, *Reflections on Africa: The Priority of Sub-Saharan Africa in Economic Development* (Washington, DC: World Bank, 1991), 20.
73. Boidin, 'Regional Cooperation', 68.
74. Ibid., 69.

75. Boidin (ibid., 69) prefers the gradual approach to exchange-rate adjustment because it retains an element of stability and predictability during the period of devaluation. He welcomes the periodic, stepped devaluation of Tanzania and Madagascar and the fixing of exchange rates by inter-bank quotations as in the Gambia. With the backing of France, the members of the Franc zone have so far resisted pressures from the World Bank and the IMF to devalue in order to ensure the stability of nominal parities. Failure of the franc zone to devalue facilitates intra-zone trade but makes exports to neighbouring countries outside the zone much more difficult.

76. Ibid., 69.

77. According to Boidin (ibid., 69), 'The reduction of intra-zone preferential margins happens in particular when the country extends to its external partners all or some of the concessions reserved for its partners in the region. Or when it reduces the average level of its MFN customs tariffs, if the regional preference is established as a percentage of the MFN duty (this is the case of the PTA for products on the common list).'

78. Ibid., 69.

79. Kenneth Dadzie, 'Africa's Commodity Crunch', *Africa Report* 31, no. 3 (May–June 1986): 24–28.

80. Shaw, 'Dependent Development', 239.

81. ECA, *African Alternative Framework*, 15.

82. Burfisher and Missiaen, 'Intraregional Trade in West Africa'.

83. Shaw, 'The Revival of Regionalism in Africa', 86.

84. Colleen Lowe Morna, 'Surviving Structural Adjustment', *Africa Report* 34, no. 5 (September–October 1989): 45–48.

85. Ankie Hoogvelt, 'The Crime of Conditionality: Open Letter to the Managing Director of the International Monetary Fund (IMF)', *Review of African Political Economy* 38 (April 1987): 80–85.

86. 'Côte d'Ivoire: Houphouët-Boigny Prepares for the End', *Africa Confidential* 31, no. 5 (9 March 1990): 4.

87. Paxton Idowu, 'Liberalising Trade', *West Africa* 3851 (1–7 July 1991): 1076.

88. Boidin, 'Regional Cooperation', 68.

89. Shaw, 'The Revival of Regionalism in Africa', 91.

90. Conable, *Reflections on Africa*, 17–18.

13

Counter-trade as a Strategy for Regional Economic Cooperation: The Case of the PTA

Berhanu Mengistu

Introduction

Soon after independence, African countries realized the benefits of a large market unfettered by tariff and non-tariff barriers. Several attempts have been made to establish regional groupings for economic integration, which envisions coordination of policies and liberalization of trade. The West African nations established the Economic Community of West African States (ECOWAS) in 1975. A similar economic cooperation arrangement covering the whole of central Africa – the Organization Commune Africaine et Mauricienne (OCAM) – has been in operation since 1981. The Southern African Development Coordination Conference (SADCC) was established in 1980. One of the most active of these regional groupings is the Preferential Trade Area (PTA), established in 1981, for Eastern and Southern Africa. These regional and sub-regional groupings, which have the characteristics of free trade associations, are the initial steps towards the creation of an African Economic Community covering the whole of Africa by the year 2000.[1] This arrangement is expected to abolish tariff and non-tariff barriers, establish common external tariffs, and abolish restrictions on factor mobility among all African countries south of the Sahara.

The PTA, with headquarters in Lusaka, Zambia, has several strategic objectives: the creation of a new economic order, the reduction of dependency, and the promotion of development among the member states. The short-term focus of the PTA, however, is the expansion and promotion of trade among the member states.

273

Currently PTA-member countries have dependent economies which still respond to colonial ties. Foreign exchange reserve is virtually non-existent. Additionally, there is no common currency among these nations, other than the US dollar or some other European hard currency. Given this situation, how is the PTA going to implement its trade expansion? Counter-trade is presented here as a possible means of operationalizing the goals of the organization. Within this context, this chapter will discuss the establishment of the PTA; counter-trade in the context of the Third World in general and the PTA in particular; and finally, identify and analyse potential imports and exports for counter-trade based on production types, levels and comparative advantages. Since this is an initial effort to apply counter-trade as a strategy to implement the objectives of PTA, and, by implication, expand trade at the continental level, no special consideration is given to differences in cultural and political systems among PTA member nations, though these factors have obvious bearings on trade.

The PTA

Leaders of nineteen Eastern and Southern African countries signed a treaty on 21 December 1981 in Lusaka, Zambia establishing a Preferential Trade Area, covering the region. The primary objective of the PTA is to promote cooperation and development in all fields of economic activity particularly in trade, customs, industry, transport, communications, agriculture, natural resources and monetary affairs (Article 3). The Treaty seeks to achieve these objectives by gradually reducing and eventually eliminating tariff and non-tariff barriers such as quotas, as well as quantitative and administrative restrictions on selected imported commodities. The Treaty also aims at erecting a common tariff wall on imports coming from non-member countries (Article 12). Member states have undertaken to simplify and harmonize their trade documents and procedures with the objective of eventually establishing a sub-regional common market and economic community within ten years of Treaty implementation (Article 29). The Treaty requires member states to accord each other the most-favoured-nation status (Article 18), and prohibits dumping (Article 17). To help implement these objectives, the Eastern and Southern African Trade and Development Bank has been established. The Bank's purpose is to provide technical and financial assistance to the member states with a view towards promoting intra-regional trade (Article 33).

The underlying purpose of the PTA, however, is to establish a new economic order and economic self-reliance by avoiding 'inward looking nationalism and vying with each other in efforts to attract foreign investment and aid' and work towards the common good.[2] An added by-product of the PTA may be the increased leverage the African countries will have as a group, in their bargaining with trading partners. Their potential power in this regard was demonstrated during the PTA meeting on 3 and 4 December 1987, at which members urged the European Economic Community (EEC) member countries to extend the period for phasing out the older, noisier African aircraft from European airspace.[3] While the outcome of this has yet to be resolved, the fact that PTA members spoke collectively bodes well for the future of African regionalism.

Since its establishment the PTA has taken some significant steps towards fulfilling its objectives. Included among these are the following:

- Agreement has been reached among member countries to reduce tariffs by 10 per cent every two years and non-tariff barriers. This began in October of 1988 and will continue until October 1996, with the goal of complete tariff elimination.

- Demand and supply survey studies for fertilizers, agricultural tools and implements, pharmaceutical and medicaments have been undertaken.

- The Clearing House, established by the Treaty, has been used with increasing frequency and by more members.

- Harmonization of flight schedules and the establishment of the PTA Aircraft Maintenance and Training Centre is under serious consideration.

- Work has been initiated on a chart for multinational industrial enterprise, harmonization of investment codes, standardization and quality control.

- Negotiations have begun among the concerned PTA members on the establishment of multinational production enterprises.

- A thorough study of supply and demand of the cement industry has been completed.

- An energy plan of action has been elaborated.

- A framework of crop belt systems has been adopted as the basis for specific project development aimed at increasing various crop outputs in the sub-region.[4]

- At the January 1992 PTA summits, members have called for the merger of the Southern African Development Coordination Conference (SADCC) and PTA, to form a single integrated common market.

Given the brief history of the PTA, these are excellent accomplishments. In fact, with the exception of SADCC and ECOWAS, these accomplishments distinguish the PTA from numerous other ongoing and now defunct regional associations in Africa. What is needed, however, is to go beyond negotiations, and implement the PTA objectives in earnest. Counter-trade is one such mechanism for implementing strategy. This chapter advances counter-trade as a stopgap measure towards the desired state where trade will be unencumbered by the absence of common currency or shortage of foreign exchange.

Counter-trade

Counter-trade has been alternately heralded as the saviour of Third World countries, derided as a primitive trade mechanism, or simply ignored as a new fad that will go out of style. What is counter-trade? Counter-trade is an umbrella term used to define international trade transactions in which there is some degree of reciprocity involved. The simplicity of this definition is unavoidable because of the diversity of counter-trade interpretations and transactions.

HISTORICAL PERSPECTIVES

Counter-trade is an ancient practice; the barter of goods and services between societies and individuals predates written history. Prior to the use of cash, societies designed mutually acceptable rates of exchange which met the cultural needs and conformed to the cultural realities of both trading groups. Griffin and Rouse point out that these early trading relationships were based upon personal ties of mutual trust, benefits and balance.[5] The original forms of counter-trade were quite probably bilateral clearing arrangements, which, when completed, left neither side in a chronic position of deficit or surplus. Any such chronic imbalances would destabilize the relationship and imply a breakdown of mutually shared benefits, respect and status.[6]

Initially, the trade resulting from these mutually beneficial relationships was to the benefit of the entire community and involved goods for the mass consumption of the trading groups. With the rise of the centralized state, trade not only began to be orchestrated by dominant élites, but also took on decidedly vertical aspects. These emerging relationships, while still conducted on the basis of barter, were maintained by superiority and enforced by coercion.[7]

By the eighteenth century, the practice of barter declined significantly. With the monetization of the global economies and the sudden growth of industrial technologies, gold, pound sterling and the US dollar increasingly became the medium for exchange in a dramatic rise in general, with increasingly vertical aspects when the theories of Adam Smith and contemporaries began to gain credence.

While simple barter significantly declined in world usage, it has never entirely disappeared from the realm of world trade. Witness, for example, the long history of barter among socialist countries. In such systems, counter-trade facilitates the planning within the group and increases the important intra-/inter-regional ties as well as encouraging regional autarky. An example of barter of this nature is the exchange of Soviet oil and other products for Cuban sugar. Counter-trade in this respect also serves to conserve hard currency for dealings with the West and to dispose of both excess production and difficult-to-sell goods. Counter-trade also promotes the development of new export markets and increases the use of excess capacity for Soviet-bloc nations.[8]

Barter has also existed throughout history at the local level of most Third World countries, as well as many small farming communities worldwide. In the United States, the Amish would currently typify this type of trade. In such instances, mutual exchanges of products for labour, such as fresh milk for cloth-weaving, are simply part of everyday life.

Recently counter-trade has not been limited to communist countries or small farming communities, however. Many developing nations have seized upon the concept and are implementing it with startling rapidity. Korth believes that in times of economic turmoil, such as evidenced since the 1960s, many changes in the economies of the world are produced.[9] He heralds the recent growth in counter-trade as one such development.[10] In fact, the growth rate of counter-trade as a trade practice is phenomenal. The annual growth rate of counter-trade from 1980 to 1981 was 50 per cent, 64 per cent from 1981 to 1982, and a 117 per cent increase occurred between 1982 and 1983.[11] In 1985, the US Department of Commerce estimated that counter-trade entailed 20 per cent of all world trade. In support of this, Griffin and Rouse have stated that barter arrangements are resurrected whenever global liquidity problems imply limited capacities to maintain vital imports or service existing debts.[12]

COUNTER-TRADE AS A DOUBLE-EDGED STRATEGY

The question currently facing us is whether or not counter-trade can be adapted in today's world as a mechanism for both debt relief and the promotion of economic development. To examine this question, a brief look at how counter-trade is practised and perceived in the world today is necessary.

COUNTER-TRADE PRACTICES

Counter-trade is currently enjoying a renewed vitality as a trade mechanism, while simultaneously being derided as primitive. These trade practices encompass not only the Soviet-bloc agreements, but also the OPEC nations who routinely link the sale of oil to developed nations with the reciprocal, Western purchase of manufactured commodities.[13] To expand our understanding of counter-trade, we must first broaden our definition. Beyond our general definition, there are also identifiable trade practices clustered under the rubric of counter-trade.

Barter is the direct exchange of goods or services without the involvement of currency, and is the historical practice most are familiar with. In current practice, however, pure barter is rarely used. When barter is used it is generally referred to as *bilateral clearing arrangements*. These transactions are barter, with the difference at the end of the transaction being settled by cash payments. One example of this is New Zealand's annual exchange of frozen lambs for Iranian crude oil.

Compensation arrangements or *buybacks* are the repayment in goods or products which are the direct result of the goods or services provided by the seller. Two separate contracts are involved, dealing with the two separate aspects of the agreement. In this type of situation, an industrialized country will supply the plant, equipment and technologies necessary for the production of a desired product. In return, the 'host' country agrees to return a percentage of the plant's output for a predetermined number of years. An example of this type of transaction is Occidental's agreement to build chemical plants in the Soviet Union, while agreeing to buy the chemicals produced for sale to the West.

Counter-purchase is the buyback of goods or services for cash. The buyback items are not necessarily related to those provided by the seller. Again this involves two separate contracts, based on cash payments for each separate contract. In such a transaction, a country is typically approached about the purchase of a product. They condition their import of the product on the seller's agreement to buy one of their exports. An example of counter-purchase is Colombia's coffee for buses from Spain.

Switch trade is a change in the exported product's destination or in the currency used for settlement, and can come into play with any type of counter-trade transaction. These types of transactions are typically handled by switch-traders who offer the necessary technical advice and assistance.

Offset practices are long-term transactions that are military in nature, or of primary importance to the importing country's government. As such, they will not be discussed in great detail in this chapter.

The definitions, explanations and examples of counter-trade practices only serve narrowly to define counter-trade; they do not give the full picture of its diversity. Not only are all the variant practices subject to interpretation, but they are also constantly being improvised and tailor-made to match the specifics of each deal. Each specific counter-trade practice described above exists in many different forms, with a variety of players. Transactions through counter-trade, however, are construed by the organization of General Agreement on Tariffs and Trade (GATT), and by most of the industrialized world, as encouraging bilateralism. However, counter-trade is not limited to bilateral trade, as shown below.

The theoretical transactions depicted above could involve a minimum of three contracts, but more likely six would be used. Each transaction would be separate, and involve contingency clauses relying upon the counter-traded products. For example, country A would sell coffee beans to Country B, contingent upon the receipt of semi-finished goods from Country C. Money or credits in local currency would be used to pay for either all the goods, or perhaps just the excess amounts of goods. Country B would then ship industrial parts to County C, to be used in the manufacture of some product. Country C would use those parts to begin the manufacture of some semi-finished good, to be shipped back to Country B and to Country A. All three countries could finish the goods, in slightly different manners, and export them for hard currency. Such a series of transactions would use no hard currency (preserving it for debt repayment), would actually increase the amount of hard currency coming into the countries, and would stimulate and enhance the economic development of both the region and the individual countries.

Where multiple bilateral counter-trade occurs, especially in a region, the cumulative effect is that of multilateral trade. For example, Country A, with surplus foreign exchange, may import more of commodity X than it needs from Country B, then exchange that surplus of X for commodity

Y from Country C. Country C may not have ever been able to buy commodity X from Country B, lacking the necessary foreign exchange. Country A gets more of commodity Y than would have been possible with just a straight buy, and Country B sells more of commodity X than would have been possible. All involved countries benefit from the transaction.

Various views of counter-trade

With the rise in counter-trade, major world economic players must address the practice and re-evaluate their opinions of it. Reactions to counter-trade as a trade mechanism are varied, and appear to divide along North–South lines as well as East–West.

THIRD WORLD

The debt crises of the developing nations have been a major cause of the re-emergence of counter-trade. The lack of hard currency available to developing nations has fostered a need to be creative in maintaining required imports and promoting exports. Additional socio-economic pressures resulting from population growth only add to the pressures already keenly felt by Third World governments.[14]

As previously alluded to, some in the Third World see counter-trade as a mechanism allowing a country facing severe problems of liquidity to maintain existing economic strategies for growth and to avoid extreme deflationary measures.[15] Others see it as an alternative to the domestically intolerable austerity programmes of the IMF.

Counter-trade appears to fulfil varying objectives of the underdeveloped nations. These range from the long-term Group of 77 objective of a New International Economic Order, to an entire gamut of short-term goals. By most accounts, the objectives of counter-trade include:

1. the conservation of hard currency;

2. the maintenance of necessary and required imports;

3. the promotion of traditional and new exports;

4. the disposal of excess production or the use of excess capacity; and

5. the stimulation/maintenance of growth in the export sector as well as import substitution in the industrial sector.

As can be seen, these objectives neatly fit into the needs mentioned earlier: promotion of economic development, trade and debt relief. It would appear, based on these objectives and criteria, that counter-trade may be one mechanism able to satisfy both the lending institutions and the debtor countries and at the same time allow PTA member countries to expand their activities and merge with SADCC, thereby creating an integrated and expanded common market.

Counter-trade also rounds out some of the medium-range objectives of the Third World. It can be used as a means of balancing and stabilizing trade between countries, further promoting economic development and adding to the ability of debtor nations to pay their debts. For Third World nations, counter-trade also represents a method of acquiring technology, international licences and increased domestic employment.[16]

INDUSTRIALIZED WORLD

Most of the major Western financial and trade organizations, including the United States government, are opposed to counter-trade. The IMF, for example, is concerned that it could potentially place restrictions on payments and transfers for international transactions.[17]

The GATT members are opposed to bilateralism. Their fundamental objection to all bilateral arrangements, including counter-trade, is that such arrangements, by their nature, may undermine the principle of non-discrimination, as well as place quantitative restrictions on international commerce. GATT not only labels counter-trade as a bilateral mechanism, but further claims that it encourages the spread of bilateralism. In general, the US government opposes counter-trade as both uneconomical and trade distorting. The essence of the US opposition, however, is the degree to which it is government mandated. Despite this basic opposition to counter-trade, US policy is not designed to intervene or to prohibit companies from engaging in the practice. This posture results from the belief that companies engage in counter-trade practices at their own risk and are capable of making independent judgements regarding risks and potential problems.[18]

The problem with all these analyses, however, lies in the fact that counter-trade is being compared with a system of free international trade within the context of an internationally agreed-upon monetary system. Counter-trade is best understood when it is compared with the no-trade option facing many Third World nations in general and PTA members in particular. The goods acquired in counter-trade are acquired for the purpose of immediate consumption or sale to a third party for cash or another good for immediate consumption. Counter-trade goods are not used for currency. Counter-trade fundamentally remains a means to increase world trade, and not simply a means for alternative financing.[19] Furthermore, as discussed earlier, counter-trade is not limited to bilateral trade. Even when it is conducted bilaterally, the effects are still that of multilateral trade.

Discussion and analysis

Some have viewed counter-trade as the culmination of a lengthy process whereby the 'forces of political and economic liberation/sovereignty in the Third World have come of age'.[20] To view any single mode of trade, including counter-trade, as the only game in town is to fall into the same trap that the industrialized nations have built for themselves. They see the use of the US dollar or other foreign currency exchange as the 'one right way' of conducting trade. Yet this approach does not appear to be sustainable in the light of the evidence presented above. However, the US and other industrial powers insist on maintaining the present course without regard for the costs to the greater world community or the long-range consequences to their own economies. Counter-trade does appear to fill in many gaps in the present inequitable situation.

The need for change in the world economic system is becoming apparent. It is also becoming evident, even to the IMF and most Western powers, that current austerity programmes are not acceptable, nor will they be successful. The Third World has fallen deeper and deeper into debt, and export prices have declined while populations, interest payments and energy and technological import prices have steadily risen. In this decade alone, net transfers of funds between the IMF and sub-Saharan Africa have reversed themselves. Capital now flows overwhelmingly from Africa to international creditors as Africa scrambles to pay back interest on ill-advanced loans.[21]

As Griffin and Rouse point out,[22] historically, barter was based upon mutual trust, benefits and balance. This parity between trading partners does not exist in today's world economic system. Unless counter-trade is based upon parity, determined by levels of development and the nature of needs, it will not be helpful to the Third World in the long run. When trade partners have widely disparate resources and needs, coupled with different levels of development, there is a tendency for domination to occur.

Counter-trade may be used to its best advantage as a strategy for trade among members of the PTA. Among the PTA members as a whole or even the Third World, parity may exist leading to a solid base for counter-trade. Such *lateral counter-trade*, among relative equals, would benefit those of similar developmental needs and conditions. Implicit in *vertical counter-trade*, among the industrialized nations and the Third World, is the risk of domination. It would seem appropriate that the Third World should discontinue vertical counter-trade altogether, for in the final analysis, need must dictate the method and manner that one nation will connect with another.

The implementation of counter-trade, how it can actually be realized in the Third World, or even among PTA members, is a topic that needs to be carefully addressed on a case-by-case basis. As each counter-trade transaction is unique, a study of implementation techniques is beyond the scope of this study. However, in a previous work Mengistu and Haile-Mariam did an empirical analysis of production data from the nations participating in the PTA.[23] The production figures of twenty-four products, ranging from cattle to soap to lumber to grains, were compared and then graphed to illustrate comparative production advantages among PTA members. Where two nations had a 1:1 ratio of production, there was no comparative advantage, and similarly, no apparent basis for counter-trade involving that product. Where there was a 1:2 or greater ratio, however, the figures suggested the possibility of specialization by one country for counter-trade to the other, with the stipulation that a similar product for counter-trade specialization could be identified in the second country. There is no need to reproduce here the study by Mengistu and Haile-Mariam cited above.[24] It is important to note, however, that without taking into account social, political, ethnic or religious factors that may affect such analysis, their study has demonstrated that there is a demand as well as a supply side to lateral counter-trade. It is also important to note that this study suggests that the claim that the Third World in general and sub-Saharan African countries in particular are not natural trade partners is not justified.

Counter-trade is not being advanced as the only or the best game in town. Under the best of circumstances, common currency should be used to facilitate trade and the integration of PTA with SADCC. In the absence of trade, and in the current system where nations are limited by the amount of foreign currency they earn, counter-trade is a welcome substitute. What is produced and traded under counter-trade is not meant to supply the world market, but to supply local needs. Some PTA members either produce more or have the capacity to produce more of a product than other members, and that lends support to the notion of lateral counter-trading based on the comparative advantages.

Counter-trade must be understood not only within the current context of the no-trade situation that exists among African countries, but also as an issue of freedom. It presents the PTA members with the opportunity to determine for themselves what and when to produce. Currently, production for export has two fundamental problems. First, it is based on Western demands which may change without sufficient warning for Third World adjustment. This is primarily the result of different levels of development. A classic example of unequal development resulting in Third World market changes is the substitution of synthetic materials for copper. Zambia, one of the funding members of the PTA, was unable to forecast such technological changes beyond its level of development and plan accordingly.

Second, there is no relationship between production for export and production for consumption. As a result, export production has been emphasized more than consumption production. In counter-trade, the product is consistent with production and the market forces are closer not only in location but in use. Also, counter-trade expands counter-traders' options for trade. No longer is the market dependent upon the industrialized nations' whims. If the United States is not interested in a counter-trade product or transaction, the odds are that current PTA members or any number of other Third World nations are likely to be interested in the product.

At stake also in this question of whether to counter-trade or not, is a larger issue of freedom. The Third World should have the freedom to trade with those whom they choose. Currently, GATT, the IMF and the US government, among others, are passing negative judgement not only on who may trade with whom, but on a trade mechanism that has served them well in the past. Political ideologies and economic realities are being ignored by such institutions, whose sole concern remains debt repayment. The larger issue of development is ignored. Development and debt repayment are not separate issues, however. The severity of the debt problem and the increasing inability of the African countries to pay the debt have irrevocably intertwined the two issues. Counter-trade appears as a viable option for the Third World in general and PTA members in particular, both as a development and a debt-relief strategy. Currently, few alternatives presented to the Third World address both issues of development and debt relief. This fact alone would call for further analysis of counter-trade as a strategy, by both the Third World and the international financial institutions.

Counter-trade as a regional economic cooperation strategy appears to be viable. The objections voiced by the industrialized countries are for the most part based upon ideology or interest to maintain the status quo rather than trade feasibility. Counter-trade, used in conjunction with alternative avenues, may in fact lead the Third World in general and the PTA in particular into a situation of integrated common markets and a relative economic development.

Summary

This chapter has attempted to point out the possibility for the expansion of trade through counter-trade among the PTA member countries. It does not pinpoint which countries should import or export which products to which PTA member countries. Such a proposition is beyond the scope of this chapter and requires an in-depth study of all the forces affecting African trade. The costs associated with trade, cultural values or relative standards of living need careful analysis. For instance, the initial transportation costs may be prohibitively expensive, making the transactions uneconomical. In addition, there are many taboos and biases in Africa regarding the consumption of certain kinds of food, which may further constrain trade. Furthermore, the differences in the member countries' standards of living may hinder exchange of goods for goods. A PTA nation may produce an item well in excess of the per capita for that product, but because of its higher standard of living, the country may choose to consume the excess over the conceptually established norm in this analysis rather than export it. Therefore, to determine exactly which products can be counter-traded within the PTA requires taking into account the cultural, political, sociological and economic forces that may affect trade.

The factors cited above notwithstanding, counter-trade has been shown to be a viable option for the PTA member countries. The PTA itself has conducted several studies on inter-country specialization in the production of major basic food crops, livestock, fisheries and forestry development.[25] A system of counter-trade, such as outlined here, would utilize those studies and others and could pave the way for increased production, assuming that other constraints on production are mitigated. In addition, the ultimate pay-off may be an increased measure of self-reliance at the regional level, leading to a reduction in tension among the quarrelling African nations and to a greater prosperity for the region as a whole.

Notes

1. Adebayo Adedeji, speech given at the Head of States Meeting, United Nations Economic Commission for Africa, *Preferential Trade Area* (Lusaka, Zambia: Government Printer, 1981), 35.

2. Adebayo Adedeji, 'A Preliminary Assessment of the Performance of the African Economy in 1987 and Prospects for 1988', *Ethiopian Herald*, 5 January 1988.

3. *Preferential Trade Area, Reports of Council of Ministers Meetings*, 28–30 November 1987, Annex 4 (Lusaka, Zambia: Government Printer).

4. Preferential Trade Area for Eastern and Southern African States, *Reports of Council of Ministers Meetings*, 1985, 1986 and 1987.

5. John C. Griffin and William Rouse, 'Countertrade as a Third World Model of Development', presented at the Third World Studies Conference, Omaha, Nebraska, 1984.

6. John C. Griffin and William Rouse, 'Countertrade as a Third World Strategy of Development', *Third World Quarterly* 8, no. 1 (1986): 179.

7. Griffin and Rouse, 'Countertrade as a Third World Model of Development', 4.

8. Christopher Korth, 'An Overview of Countertrade', in Christopher Korth (ed.), *International Countertrade* (London: Quorum, 1987).

9. Ibid.

10. Ibid., 9.

11. Willis Bussard, 'An Overview of Countertrade Practices and Individual Nations', in Korth, *International Countertrade*, 17.

12. Griffin and Rouse, 'Countertrade as a Third World Strategy of Development'.

13. Ibid., 184.

14. Pompiliu Verzariu, *Countertrade, Barter, and Off-Sets: New Strategies for Profit in International Trade* (New York: McGraw-Hill, 1985), 21.

15. Griffin and Rouse, 'Countertrade as a Third World Model of Development', 24.

16. A. Dearden, 'Setting the Scene: The Role of an International Bank in Barter and Countertrade', paper presented at the International Barter/Countertrade Conference, Zimbabwe, 1987, 2.

17. Verzariu, *Countertrade, Barter, and Off-Sets*, 16.

18. Frederick E. Howell, 'Countertrade: A View from the US Department of Commerce', in Korth, *International Countertrade*, 158.

19. Sarkis Khoury, 'Countertrade: Forms, Motives, Pitfalls, and Negotiation Requisites', *Journal of Business Research* 12 (1984): 268.

20. Griffin and Rouse, 'Countertrade as a Third World Strategy of Development', 204.

21. United Nations Secretary General's Advisory Group, *Report on Financial Flows to Africa* (Lusaka, Zambia: Government Printer, 1988).

22. Griffin and Rouse, 'Countertrade as a Third World Model of Development',

and 'Countertrade as a Third World Strategy of Development'.

23. Berhanu Mengistu and Yacob Haile-Mariam, 'Countertrade as a Strategy for Implementing the Preferential Trade Area's Objectives', paper presented at the Academy of International Business Conference, Atlanta, Georgia, 1988.

24. Ibid.

25. Preferential Trade Area, *Reports of Council of Ministers Meetings*, 12–15 December 1985.

14

Conclusion

Kidane Mengisteab
B. Ikubolajeh Logan

Shortcomings of SAPs

Many of the chapters of this book suggest that recent experiences with SAPs in sub-Saharan Africa lead to the inescapable conclusion that, as presently conceived and applied, the programmes have only limited potential for actually 'adjusting' the region's economies. So far, SAPs have not demonstrated the ability to redress a number of thorny issues, including balance of payment difficulties, the terms of trade, social resource distribution and mass participation. All of these elements are critical for economic development. There is little doubt that unless problems like these are resolved effectively, sub-Saharan Africa's political economies cannot become transformed into self-sustained, effectively competing entities in the global economy of the twenty-first century. We revisit and summarize below some of the central issues discussed in the book: the need for a broad-based approach to development, the call for a social agenda and emphases on human rights, the role of the public and private sector, and the key shortcomings of SAPs.

At the most fundamental level, SAPs are purely and completely economic strategies that are designed to address specific macro financial aspects of the development agenda. Admittedly, proponents of the programmes make no claims to their political or social competencies. However, in this implicit disclaimer lies a fundamentally serious flaw because the targeted agenda of the programmes is rooted deeply in the economic, political, and social dilemmas of sub-Saharan Africa.

Albeit grudgingly, the World Bank and IMF now concede partially to the chorus of protestations concerning the narrow world view embedded in SAPs and are trying to implement programmes with a more 'human face'. There is also an emerging consensus, among theorists and practitioners alike, that a holistic, multifaceted approach is the best guide for policy and praxis towards alleviating poverty in sub-Saharan Africa. Part of this emerging consensus is that the tunnel vision of SAPs must be broadened to accommodate a more panoramic appreciation of the complex regional, national and sectoral interconnectedness that underpins the socio-economic crises. Unfortunately, even the programmes that ostensibly originate from this new philosophy seem to pay homage to the same old macro-economic gods. For example, the sectoral adjustment programmes in which the World Bank collaborates with the African Development Bank (ADB) are still keyed to trade liberalization and the privatization of parastatals.

While economic parameters (especially quantifiable ones) have always been centre stage in development planning, there is also increasing call for a wider view, including poverty-alleviation strategies. Poverty alleviation requires hybrid programmes that tackle economic and social welfare concerns simultaneously – as an integral package in which one does not supersede the other. Several chapters in the early section of this book express a concern, already voiced by many, that adjustment, even with a 'human face', forces governments to retrench in critical social services like health and education. The SAP agenda also does not pay any attention to human rights and mass participation, which represent a crucial requirement for development. Simple economic growth under a tyranny does not transform the economy, create the socio-cultural environment for research and development, alleviate poverty and set the framework for sustained social and economic output.

Some attention is now being paid to mass participation in Africa, especially with the current excitement over pro-democracy movements around the world. Even so, this kind of political reform has yet to be linked to economic reform in an integrated package by the World Bank, IMF, or any other major international agency. The current line of approach is rather *ad hoc*. It is as if democratization and economic reform are remote complements, if at all, and many of the sub-Saharan African leaderships with whom the World Bank and IMF conduct routine business do not represent the interests of their people.

Another serious limitation of SAPs is their conceptual polarization of the actual and potential roles and abilities of the private and public sectors. In the general wisdom of market liberalization proponents, state operated/owned enterprises (SOEs) have been inefficient at distributing critical resources, and at managing leading productive sectors. Unfortunately, the message of unbridled marketization that comes with this criticism is fraught with some empirical difficulties, two of which merit some attention here. First, no system in the world has a completely *laissez faire* market. As a result, it is difficult to grasp the empirical foundation upon which neo-liberal thinking advocates this policy for sub-Saharan Africa. Second, there is no doubt that a *laissez faire* market will transform sub-Saharan African economies (in what direction is less obvious); but it is equally clear that the market, itself, will be seriously transformed in the interaction with African institutions and circumstances. Any statements of prescience regarding how this marriage will work should be treated with circumspection. It is, therefore, problematic that SAP thinking reflects such unmitigated confidence in the role of the market in structural transformation.

The argument that market control has been made incumbent by the failure of SOEs might be true from a purely economic perspective. However, a realistic assessment of the effectiveness of SOEs must also consider the roles they have been expected to perform. Much of the evidence indicates that, in addition to economic objectives, SOEs have been used to accomplish political and social goals that involve state patronage and kinship obligations. SOEs must, therefore, be assessed from both standpoints. From an economic perspective, the circular argument can be made that the enterprises failed precisely because they have not operated in terms of strict economic optimization. On the other hand, they failed also at social welfare distribution because resource allocation was based on ethnic and class hegemonies rather than on poverty criteria. Thus SOEs can be regarded as failures from both the economic and social standpoints. The important questions at this stage of adjustment in sub-Saharan Africa are: 1) whether governments can afford to relegate all responsibility for resource allocation to the market; and, 2) whether the market can be more effective than SOEs at making economic and social welfare decisions.

The report card on adjustment in several countries has already shown that social unrest is a short-term outcome of complete market control of all sectors of the economy. Any alternative strategy or package of strategies must be capable of maintaining an equilibrium between social, political and economic objectives. SOEs were biased towards the first two at the expense of the last. There is no evidence either in the developed or developing world to indicate that the market can accomplish the task of establishing a more feasible equilibrium between all three. Consequently, the main objective of adjustment in the twenty-first century will be to find the best attributes of the market and the state that can move sub-Saharan Africa's economies towards such an equilibrium. As such, advocacy for marketization should not necessarily preclude government participation in resource distributions. As argued in Chapter 8, a strategy needs to be designed to wed the market and the state into a new and complementary partnership.

Another criticism of SAPs, brought out in the Introduction of this book and also in Chapters 4 and 6, is that SAPs are wholly domestic in their nature and orientation, even though the tasks that they are designed to accomplish, and even some of their strategies, have significant international implications. Yet there has been no attempt to forge connections between SAPs and GATT trade negotiations. Clearly, the success of devaluation and export promotion, for example, are contingent upon the international economic climate which is underpinned by the policies of other governments and trading blocs. SAPs, or any other strategy for economic development in sub-Saharan Africa, cannot afford to treat domestic aspects of structural transformation to the exclusion of important external controls on economic development.

Although SAPs are directed primarily at the domestic economy, they have a restricted agenda which has limited them to the capitalist sector while ignoring the so-called informal and traditional sectors. If adjustment is to be more successful, it must be based upon a strategy that accommodates the activities of the wider sub-Saharan African economy. Essentially, structural adjustment cannot succeed if it strives to 'adjust' one segment of the economy while ignoring the others. This problem is linked to the fact that SAPs do not address the processes underlying structural transformation. Unfortunately, adjustment cannot succeed unless it is relevant for the processes that direct structural change. Market operation is only one of those processes. To assume otherwise, and ignore traditional and informal processes (and the institutions that direct them) is to miss impacts on the market that should be central to adjustment and to the quest for economic development.

Perhaps it is unfair to criticize SAPs for all of these shortcomings when, in reality, there is no alternative that can address all of the issues discussed above. That is why we have argued in this book that the development agenda of the twenty-first century must be multi-pronged. No single programme or strategy can accomplish the tasks facing sub-Saharan African economies. On the other hand, an *ad hoc* approach with a variety of individual, unconnected approaches is bound to be just as counterproductive. What is necessary is a package that integrates concern for domestic welfare, political change, structural transformation and international trade into one comprehensive programme of action. It is towards this rather complex end that we advocate regionalisation, mass participation, environmental responsibility, democratization and government/market partnership as fundamental complements in domestic adjustment strategies. Clearly, this list is not exhaustive, but it should provide serious food for thought.

Towards a broad-based alternative approach

The alternative approach advocated in the book does not reject SAPs in their entirety. Rather it is a call to make SAPs more compatible with the elements already listed above, thereby moving towards the continent's sustainable development.

Resource allocation by the self-serving state is clearly incompatible with socio-economic development. However, the market's trickle-down process, by itself, is also insufficient to redistribute resources in a manner that would alleviate poverty, transform the large subsistence sector, and promote an environment-friendly system of production. Hence a democratic state that would be more likely to allocate resources in response to social needs becomes imperative. The book has not aspired to provide a blueprint for the type of democracy that is appropriate for Africa. The specific forms of democracy are likely to differ from country to country depending on the different conditions, including ethnic relations and regional inequalities that exist in individual countries. However, several chapters, including those by Mamdani, Saine and Mengisteab, stress that in addition to allowing political rights which would enable citizens to influence decisions, democracy must also facilitate access to resources for those that are largely deprived. In other words, unlike liberal democracy, democracy in Africa needs to expand the domain of public decisions to the sphere of economics in order to become relevant. If it fails in this regard, its potential for improving human conditions, fostering socio-economic development and resolving the multitude of chronic conflicts that have plagued the continent will be severely undermined.

The type of democracy advocated in this book might be incompatible, at least in the short run, with the dictum of SAPs, namely, that the state should refrain from active participation in economic activity. In the longer run, however, the two are likely to be increasingly complementary to each other. Through favourable allocation of resources, including political power, democracy can help bring about the transformation of the subsistence sector into a surplus-producing exchange economy and, thereby, bridge the duality of African economies. Such a transformation of the predominant sector of African economies can, in turn, be expected to promote a more properly functioning market system. At that point in time, it may be possible to reduce the state's redistributive role.

The present democratization process on the continent is an extremely useful first step in the right direction. However, the transition from authoritarian rule to democracy is only at its infancy and it has yet to evolve into the type of democracy envisioned in this book. Furthermore, as Krugmann's chapter suggests, the fragile transition now underway faces the risk of being eroded by a number of factors, including unbridled market forces and powerful corporate interests.

Another element in the broad approach to development advocated in this book is regionalism. Proponents of SAPs tend to view regional economic integration in developing countries as a barrier to free international trade and a hindrance to their full integration into the global economic system. De Melo and Panagariya, for example, argue that regional integration in developing countries would lead to regional protectionism instead of promoting a growth-stimulating environment.[1]

This book has attempted to refute such arguments. It contends that, due to their colonial heritage, African economies are already highly extroverted and the export sector continues to engross a lion's share of available resources.[2] African countries have also opened up their economies considerably since the early 1980s.[3] Yet their marginalization from the global economy has remained unabated, suggesting that openness, while perhaps necessary, is clearly insufficient to integrate African economies properly into the global production system. Without implementing structural changes in their production systems and diversifying their export mix, they are unlikely to succeed with export promotion. African countries already rely excessively on external sources of dynamism to the near exclusion of domestic and regional stimuli for growth and change. It is estimated that about 80 per cent of the variations in Africa's growth rates between 1960 and 1980 are attributable to growth rates in OECD imports and Africa's barter terms of trade.[4]

African countries cannot afford to continue along the same lines. It is highly doubtful that the global economy is open enough to enable them to diversify their products by relying on export promotion. They have to strengthen their collective self-reliance and reduce their external dependency. It is simply unwise and too risky for them to continue to depend for their future development almost entirely on global economic conditions over which they have little influence.

SAPs do not encourage a fresh approach in this regard. Rather they produce reliance on external sources of growth and, thereby, exacerbate the malintegration of African economies with the global economy. Their advocacy for devaluation as an export-promotion strategy is, for example, of limited relevance to African countries. As Mengisteab in his chapter on devaluation argues, these countries simply lack the necessary level of economic diversification to benefit from devaluation. Diversification-promoting measures need to be promoted at least simultaneously.

Collective self-reliance through regionalism can provide African states with relatively larger markets and a wider resource base on which they can build infant industries in selected products. As de Melo and Panagariya point out, regionalism may not improve considerably the market access of developing countries, since their market sizes are limited.[5] Nevertheless, their market access under regionalism would be greater than without regionalism. African countries would also have a better chance of expanding their markets under regionalism. When accompanied by democratization that transforms the peasant sector and improves its purchasing power, regionalism has the potential to promote economic diversification by benefiting from both import-substitution and agriculture-led industrialization strategies simultaneously.

If accompanied by democratization, regionalism, which appears to have a trade-off with global integration in the short run, would in the long run integrate more dynamic African economies with the global production system by promoting internal integration and economic diversification. It also has the potential to propel a market system that improves the coordination of available resources with social need and engenders efficiency in resource allocation in the continent. In the short run, however, the approach that is proposed here is more compatible with a mixed economic system than with the *laissez-faire* type of marketization that SAPs advocate.

Again, the book has not attempted to provide a general blueprint for the proper mix of the roles of the state and the market for the entire continent. The desirable mix would depend on the level of diversification of the economy, on the degree of transformation of the peasantry, and on the level of development of the private sector of each country. We envisage that the more the economy develops the less the role of the state in economic activity may become. In the meantime, the more holistic strategy proposed here seems to be better suited than economic liberalization to bring about adjustment with transformation in Africa.

Notes

1. Jaime de Melo and A. Panagariya, *The New Regionalism in Trade Policy: An Interpretive Summary of a Conference* (Washington, DC: World Bank, 1992).
2. Kidane Mengisteab and B.I. Logan, 'Implications of Liberalization.Policies for Agricultural Development in Sub-Saharan Africa', *Comparative Political Studies* 22, no. 4 (January 1990): 437–57.
3. Ali Manscor and Andras Inotai, 'Integration Efforts in Sub-Saharan Africa: Failures, Results and Prospects – A Suggested Strategy for Achieving Efficient Integration', in Ajai Chhibber and Stanley Fischer (eds), *Economic Reform in Sub-Saharan Africa* (Washington, DC: World Bank Symposium, World Bank, 1991), 217–32.
4. Stephen R. Lewis, 'Africa's Trade and the World Economy', in Robert J. Berg and Jennifer S. Whitaker (eds), *Strategies for African Development* (Berkeley, CA: University of California Press, 1986), 476–504.
5. De Melo and Panagariya, *The New Regionalism in Trade Policy*.

Index